Traditionalism, Conservatism
and British Political Culture

WHO CARES WHAT HAPPENS TO THE BLOODY COUNTRY!

Traditionalism Conservatism and British Political Culture

BOB JESSOP
Downing College, Cambridge

LONDON GEORGE ALLEN & UNWIN LTD
Ruskin House   Museum Street

Printed in Great Britain
in 10pt Times Roman type
by Cox & Wyman Ltd,
London, Fakenham and Reading

Preface

This book presents a critical review of some recent studies in British political culture and develops an alternative theoretical approach to the questions they seek to answer. It is particularly concerned with voting behaviour and political stability and focuses on two themes relevant to these concerns. One theme, that of deference, seeks to explain working-class Conservatism; the other, that of civility, seeks to explain political stability. Both themes are criticised on theoretical and empirical grounds and are reformulated in such a way that they can be articulated with class theory. The bulk of this work then attempts to validate these criticisms and the reformulated approach with reference to published data and original research. It concludes with a consideration of the implications for comparative political research and future studies of British political culture.

In writing a book such as this one cannot avoid incurring debts to many institutions and people. I would like to record my thanks to those who have helped me in this task. Financial assistance was received from the Social Science Research Council, from the Faculty of Economics and Politics at Cambridge University, and from the Governing Bodies of St John's College, Cambridge, and Downing College, Cambridge. The Master and Fellows of Downing have been particularly kind and helpful in supporting me while this book was written. In addition, three opinion poll organisations kindly allowed me to examine their files and reproduce copyright material. These were Opinion Research Centre, National Opinion Polls, and the Gallup organisation. I am very grateful to these firms and especially to Nick Spencer, James Spence, and Bob Wybrow, respectively, for the encouragement and advice they offered. Jay Blumler also very kindly provided me with unpublished data from his study of attitudes to the monarchy. I should also like to extend thanks to those who have helped in other ways. Howard Williams and Peter Hearn helped to administer the second survey. Gavin MacKenzie, Tony Giddens, and Frank Parkin provided much valuable criticism and advice. Philip Abrams acted as supervisor of the doctoral dissertation upon which the book is based. Any errors of omission or commission must naturally be blamed on me. Finally, I would like to acknowledge once again the help and support of my wife, Lesley.

Bob Jessop

Contents

Figures and Tables

Chapter 1

Political Culture and Political Explanation

In the recent past two themes have been emphasised in the study of British politics. One theme traces the stability of our political system to the happy combination in a large majority of the people of such traditional British traits as the habit of obedience or submission to authority, a sturdy independence and willingness to stand up for one's rights, the spirit of compromise, patriotic pride, and distrust of the state. The development of these civic virtues is linked in turn to the slow and peaceful evolution of the British democratic system and to the moderation and political acumen of her governing class.[1] The other theme explained the continuing support (at least among the manual working class) for the Conservative Party in terms of deference to the successors of this governing class and/or a pragmatic evaluation of that party's abilities to safeguard the economic and social welfare of the nation. The persistence and combination of deference with a more instrumental or materialistic political outlook has also been traced to the history, traditions, and character of the body politic.[2] In both cases, therefore, the explanation of significant features of the British political system has referred to the nature and development of British political culture.

We read and hear less of these interpretations today. This is doubtless due in part to the rise of alternative explanations and competing approaches and, more directly, to the launching of several critical assaults on the two themes themselves. It is also due, and probably more significantly so, to secular trends in the political system itself. After a long run of success in the 1950s and early 1960s not only did the Conservative Party lose two elections in a row but also, and more importantly, its image as the 'natural' party of government. And, in Northern Ireland, the stability of the political system has been called violently into question once again. Things have come to the point where a political commentator can now write of the 'death of deference' and a senior Cabinet minister can wonder whether the country is becoming ungovernable.[3] As times change, so do political theories.

None the less, neither theme has been subjected to a full critical examination nor has its relevance to contemporary circumstances been adequately assessed. In particular, although alternative explanations do exist, little attention has been paid to the validity of the first of these themes. Similarly, the relevance of the second theme to the past and present behaviour of the middle classes has been largely ignored. Even for the working classes, little genuinely critical attention has been focused on the validity of the deference interpretation. And, although they share features and protagonists in common, there has been a neglect of the relations between the two themes. Yet, as will be argued below, there are sound theoretical and empirical reasons for questioning their relevance, their validity, and their interrelations. But there are better reasons still against rejecting them completely and for their reformulation in such a way that they have a continuing relevance to the understanding both of British politics and the politics of other nations. In the following pages, therefore, we shall review various types of evidence for and against both themes and try to relate these two interpretative traditions. We shall also consider the major alternatives to them. Finally, to aid us in this task, we shall present new survey data to throw further light on these problems.

Political culture provides a conceptual framework common to both themes—particularly as they have been developed by academic commentators. Each interpretation refers, more or less explicitly, to the central values of English society in its explanations of political behaviour. The deference studies link a diffuse value system that has a traditional and elitist content to electoral support for the party most closely identified with it in terms of activists, leaders, and outlook. McKenzie and Silver, for example, argue that 'British political and social culture has acted directly upon both the Conservative elite and large parts of the working class, disposing the one to promulgate and the other to accept doctrines and policies which have continued to nourish working class Conservativism.'[4] The civility studies are concerned even more explicitly with political culture and, in particular, with the 'civic culture.' Their model of democratic political culture is premised on an elitist view of democracy that complements nicely the outlook expressed in the traditional, elitist value system examined in the deference studies. It emphasises that mass involvement in politics should be intermittent rather than continuous, mediated through secondary associations such as parties and pressure groups rather than direct, and constrained by 'parochial' and 'subject' or deferential orientations.[5] Because the majority of British people accept this limited political role, it is argued, the government can get on with its job and govern effectively so as to ensure general prosperity and political stability. Furthermore, as McKenzie and Silver point out, this modest formal political role of the general population provides a context which has facilitated the survival of deference long into the age of the universal franchise.[6] Since both themes concern the impact of cultural factors—orientations and their distribution—on political behaviour, it seems appropriate to begin our own investigations with a brief examination of the validity and utility of political culture concepts and explanations. In our first chapter, therefore, we shall provide a framework within which to assess the significance of two particular themes in 'political culturology' and also to present alternative explanations. In the next four chapters we shall then discuss these themes and alternatives before proceeding, in later chapters, to present our own data.

1.1 Political culture and political causation

Political structure is typically defined in terms of patterned relations between interacting individuals, groups, and/or institutions. In contrast, political culture is typically defined in terms of orientations to political action situations.[7] The absence of any such orientations provides the limiting case of a 'parochial political culture' (Almond and Verba) or a low level of political culture (Nettl).[8] Definitions aside, however, most political scientists employ 'political culture' as a mere catchword or residual category for all sorts of influences that are neither legal or institutional and that include both structural and orientational factors. Moreover, as with most residual categories, little real attention is paid to the nature of this 'political culture' and its explanatory power is correspondingly weak. Dennis Kavanagh even cites the 'deference' theme in this context—arguing that it is a stereotype and non-explanatory.[9] It will be interesting to examine the theme from this viewpoint. However, not all political scientists have treated the 'political culture' concept in so arbitrary a fashion and it is with more positive treatments of the concept that we are concerned in these pages.

Even where political culture is the main focus of analysis and is defined in a positive, *sui generis* manner, however, it is still

B

too often resistant to meaningful theoretical and empirical analysis. The basically tautological nature of the typical definition —that political culture is the pattern of orientations to political action situations—seems to be the main cause of this recalcitrance. For, as Hughes and Pinney declare, this definition is such that 'the only apparent possible line of further investigation lies in refining the analytic statement rather than in operationalising the original concept'.[10] The result is that political scientists have tended to analyse political culture through such categories as cognitive, evaluative, and expressive orientations or orientations to community, regime, or government. Alternatively, they have chosen, somewhat arbitrarily, a number of topics such as attitudes to other people, problem-solving, co-operation and individuality, and the political system.[11] Not only are the possibilities of meaningful theoretical analysis vitiated in these formal and/or arbitrary ways, but the utility of the culture concept in empirical analysis is also weakened. It is thus all too common to find that the cultural approach leads to a mere redescription of the behaviour in question and not to a causal explanation.[12] While some philosophers would argue that causal explanation of action in terms of the orientations it embodies is logically impossible, the poverty of the culture concept is almost certainly due to less profound reasons. For, not only are the philosophical objections unsound, but there are also more fruitful conceptions of political culture.

The philosophical problems involved in cultural explanations of political action are rooted in the simple fact that statements about political culture and political structure are abstracted from the same data, namely, verbal and non-verbal behaviour. It is only natural to ask, therefore, whether culture and structure can, in any meaningful sense, be causally related or whether they are simply different ways of looking at the same phenomenon. Some social scientists have ignored this problem through the subtle incorporation of culture into their definitions of structure and/or of structure into their definitions of culture.[13] Others, while distinguishing between the two concepts, have assumed that they are more or less homologous in structure and content.[14] Yet others have resolved the problem through, on the one hand, the behaviouristic denial of mental states or, on the other hand, the insistence on a pure *verstehende* technique which treats action as the logical concomitant of the actor's ideas, motives, reasons, and beliefs.[15] It is the latter school of thought which is most closely identified with the argument that causal explanations of action are logically inadmissible.[16] Rejection of their views does not, of course, imply an acceptance of one or more of the other approaches mentioned above. Nor, on the other hand, does it necessarily imply that *all* explanations of action must be causal. It does, however, open the way to a more fruitful analysis of the relations between culture and action.

We can best consider these views through an examination of one protagonist. Peter Winch, in *The Idea of a Social Science*, argues that social relations between men and the ideas which men's actions embody are really the same thing considered from different points of view. Actions are intelligible only as the outcome of motives, reasons, decisions, and concepts held by the actors in question and these in turn are intelligible only as part of a patterned, coherent cultural system. The relationship between ideas and actions is thus an internal, logical or conceptual one and not an external, contingent, and causal relationship. If we try to explain the causes of, say, Conservative voting in terms of the deferential ideas of the voter, we shall merely redescribe the action and not explain it. Even accepting these views, however, it is obvious that no account of political action can ignore the specific meaning and the complex cultural context in which such actions occur. Political culture could not be invoked in causal explanation but it would still remain an important sensitising concept. Equally, the way would still remain open to causal explanations through accounts of how the actor came to possess the orientations in question. In the current political culture literature this is a field of inquiry well covered as 'political socialisation'.

Winch's basic argument seems to be that things that stand in an internal relationship cannot also stand in a causal relationship. Although this is still philosophically contentious, this writer at least agrees with those philosophers who reject Winch's arguments. For it is not necessary that two things be separately experienced in order to stand in an external relationship to each other—they need only have different referents.[17] In this respect we may note that there are predicates applicable to values and beliefs that are inapplicable to actions and vice versa. Thus we may say that a belief is true or false, an action effective or ineffective, but not vice versa. Furthermore, the possession of beliefs and values is a state of affairs identifiable independently of the actions in which they are typically expressed. It is possible, for example, to obtain indicators of a deferential orientation other than from a deferential action. And, as Kavanagh points out, some beliefs are less actionable than others—he cites the case of beliefs about the possibility of influencing the government which may never be put to the test.[18] On both these grounds, therefore, we may argue that orientations to action are suitable candidates for inclusion in causal explanation of that action.

The causal model appropriate to such explanations is that of contingent necessity rather than Humean constant conjunction. It is certainly true that the latter is inapplicable to cultural analysis because of the variations in the actionability of beliefs; but this does not mean that an alternative causal model is ruled out as well. Orientations need not be expressed directly in action and, even when so expressed, they can result—especially when there is uncertainty in the situation or ambiguity in the orientations—in different actions. Conversely, apparently similar 'actions' can be associated with different orientations or combinations of orientations. Thus social deference is not invariably associated with Conservative voting, nor Conservative voting with social deference. It is precisely because there is not, as Winch suggests there is, a one-to-one correspondence between orientation and action, that causal analysis of the relationship between the two is appropriate and perhaps necessary.[19] It is with such analyses that we shall be concerned below.

There would seem to be two main classes of causal explanation in the cultural approach to political analysis. The first of these involves a more or less straightforward connection between individual orientations and political behaviour. The deference studies fall into this class—they connect deferential orientations to a socially ascribed elite with voting for the party most closely identified with that elite. The second class of causal explanations relates emergent or 'group' properties of culture to political behaviour and system performance. The civility studies, for example, relate the distribution of acquiescent and directive attitudes in a society to the relative stability of its political institutions. Other studies have emphasised the importance of consensus on dominant values for the stability of political systems. What is important here is, not the attitude of any given individual, but the relation between the attitudes of different individuals in the system. The direction of causality examined in cultural analysis can also flow from action system to orientations; and this, too, shows the same two classes of explanation. Thus parental behaviour can be linked to children's political beliefs; or the distribution of power to the incidence of alienative orientations. Much political culture analysis has been concerned only with the link from attitudes to behaviour and has not considered the effects of political structures on people's attitudes. This tends to result in acceptance of the inevitability of current attitudes and neglect of possible changes resulting from alterations in political power.[20] We shall be concerned with both classes of explanation and both directions of causal connection.

1.2 Analysing political culture

Given the logical possibility of establishing causal relations between political culture and political action, it is still necessary to provide a meaningful conceptual framework within which to analyse these relations. There are three major obstacles in the path of such an analysis. Firstly, there is the temptation to talk of *the* political culture and its effects in any given society. Instead we must specify exactly what orientations (or characteristics of such orientations) are related to which actions among which sections of society. Secondly, in attempting such a specification, we must go beyond the simple analytic or subject-matter categories and develop concepts that have both a theoretical and empirical relevance. Lastly, we must not ignore the dialectical nature of the relationship between self and society, between actor and culture, and overemphasise constraints imposed by given orientations and cultural patterns. These orientations and patterns are themselves the product of interaction and individual innovation. They provide not only constraints on action but also opportunities and resources for action. Individuals continually construct and reconstruct meanings and values. They seek to communicate new ideas as well as to manipulate established ones. In short, the constraints imposed by culture are not incompatible with free will and creativity. While it is not easy to overcome these obstacles, a concern with the values and beliefs of sociologically meaningful groups and individuals is an essential first step in avoiding both metaphorical notions of 'the' political culture and overemphasis on cultural constraint.

On both theoretical and empirical grounds the distinction between centre and periphery is particularly significant in this context. Thus Pye has reviewed several studies of political culture and reports that 'in no society is there a single uniform political culture, and in all polities there is a *fundamental distinction* between the culture of the rulers or power holders and that of the masses, whether they are merely parochial subjects or participating citizens.'[21] This finding reinforces the theoretical arguments in favour of such a distinction—arguments based on the significance of power and exchange relations for the dynamics of all political, social, economic, and cultural systems. Thus it will be useful to distinguish between the central or dominant value system and value systems of less powerful groups, strata, classes, or individuals. The *central value system* comprises those beliefs, values, symbols, ideas, and meanings, that are espoused by those with the 'most' power in a given society.[22] Less powerful groups will also have more or less distinct value systems which will demand examination in their own right. In complex societies, of course, there will often be several competing dominant value systems associated with different power elites. For example, the political centre may espouse a meaning system somewhat different in content and emphasis from those propounded by the economic, social, or cultural centres. Similarly, in periods of rapid social change and situations beset by fundamental contradictions, conflicting value systems may be propounded by elites (and non-elites) whose symbolic and material interests are differently affected thereby. But there must be limits to the diversity and incompatibility of these different value systems, especially the more central value systems, if the society in question is to be stable.

The type and degree of consensus required for stability varies from social structure to social structure in determinate ways. In societies where power is distributed more or less equally stability and the content of the central value system will both depend on the consensus of all members of society. Where power is unequal in distribution, however, the overall level of consensus will be relatively unimportant for stability provided there is a reasonable degree of consensus, or institutional integration, between the different power centres. For it is they that have the power to disrupt the system and it is they that define the core institutional order of that system. In short, the ruling ideas of any society are those of its ruling class or power centres.

In such inegalitarian societies there are important discontinuities between the central value system and peripheral value systems owing to the differential location and interests of centre and periphery. In situations of minimal discontinuity we find an attachment to the dominant value system but an attachment that interprets these values in deferential or aspirational contexts rather than from the original central or ruling viewpoint. A greater degree of discontinuity is found among peripheral groups whose primary orientation to the dominant value system is accommodative or pragmatically acquiescent. This is the type of value system Parkin has labelled the 'subordinate' value system[23] and defines as neither fully endorsing nor fully rejecting the *status quo*. Finally, at the extremes of discontinuity we find two distinct types of value system—the fully developed contraculture and the completely parochial subculture that can be interpreted without reference to the dominant order. Whereas the radical oppositional contraculture is directly and forcefully related to the dominant order and cannot be understood without some reference to it, the parochial subculture comprises a purely local culture, or 'little tradition,' that exists almost totally outside the mainstream of national life and is related only minimally, if at all, to the dominant institutional and cultural order.[24] The latter type of culture is eroded as societies develop and become both more complex and more integrated; in its place develop the deferential or aspirational, the subordinate or accommodative, and the oppositional or countercultures. All four types of non-dominant culture can be combined with elements from the others and this will result in ambiguities, inconsistencies, contradictions, and so on, in the meaning systems of peripheral groups. We shall be particularly concerned in later pages with the consequences of such incoherence in peripheral value systems.

An adequate delineation of political culture will consider not only the extent and incidence of commitment to various values but will also examine the nature and content of these values. Pattern variable analysis of one kind or another is often used to outline the content of value systems and to assess their relative coherence. In addition to the well-known Parsonian pattern-variables, there are others developed specifically for political analysis and relevant to the problems in hand. Thus Lipset employs an egalitarianism *v* elitism variable and argues that British political culture is weighted more towards elitism whereas American political culture is weighted more towards egalitarianism. Likewise, Nettl employs a constitutionalist *v* elitism variable and also sees the British political culture as leaning more in the elitist direction than the American political value system. Other pattern variables have been used by these as well as other writers.[25] An alternative method of content analysis, already mentioned, is the use of somewhat arbitrary subject classifications that focus on predefined and supposedly significant political phenomena. Neither type of approach has contributed much to our political understanding and it may well be more useful to present each political culture in terms of its more or less unique configuration of values, meanings, symbols, beliefs, and so on. The latter approach at least has the merit of placing each element in its appropriate context.

Two variables useful in this third kind of cultural analysis are those of secularisation and radicalism. The sacred–secular distinction has a long history and is related to the concept of structural differentiation. Most of its proponents argue that, the greater the degree of such differentiation, the greater the level of secularisation in the societal value system. While there is considerable support for this hypothesis, especially when societal value system is understood as central value system, we are not primarily concerned with this aspect of secularisation. For our purposes, it is sufficient to state that *secularisation* refers to the relative rigidity of the specification or interpretation of values. Secular cultures are those in which central specification is loose and there is a corresponding freedom of interpretation for individual members of that society. The latter will interpret these values in the light of situational constraints as well as personal preferences. Thus it is always possible for the centre(s) to affect their interpretations by altering the context in which such decisions must be made.[26] In many cases, therefore, secularisation merely provides the illusion of individual autonomy and liberalisation rather than the substantive benefits of these institutions. A 'sacred' culture, on the other hand, is one characterised by moral absolutism—its values are precisely specified by the relevant authorities, action is imbued with heavy moral significance, and deviance is severely sanctioned. Whereas secularisation tends to legitimate any dissent or innovation that can be represented as an extension or respecification of dominant values, sacred cultures tend to be associated with the proscription even of innovations intended to strengthen traditional institutions and power structures. In the former case we have a situation of 'repressive tolerance,' in the latter one of 'repressive intolerance.' Most students of English political culture treat it as relatively secular in character and, as we shall argue below, there is much support for this interpretation.

While the concept of secularisation is particularly applicable to dominant value systems, that of radicalism is particularly suited to the analysis of peripheral cultures. These vary in their degree of radicalism from the parochial subculture, with its minimal level of concern with the dominant order, to the outright opposition to the total structure of power and rewards that is characteristic of an hegemonic counterculture. Between total unconcern and total hostility we find the deferential, aspirational, and accommodative orientations of most members of the periphery. Whereas the deferential and aspirational members seek to improve their individual position within the structure of rewards and even, in extreme cases of aspiration, to enter the ruling elites themselves, the accommodative response is more concerned with defending and, if possible, improving the position of peripheral groups within the overall social structure. Accommodation thus displays characteristics of both the aspirational and the oppositional responses—it is concerned with mobility *within* a system accepted as legitimate or, at least, inevitable, but it is also a collective, and thus potentially disruptive, response to existing inequalities. The 'trade-union consciousness' characteristic of accommodative responses represents an uneasy compromise with the *status quo* that could develop into a much more radical, political class consciousness.[27] The crucial difference between the two lies in the orientation of the former towards the redistribution of secondary or symbolic resources and rewards, in contrast to the concern with the redistribution of control over the primary bases of power —the means of production, coercion, status attribution, and value creation—that is characteristic of radical class consciousness.

'Trade union consciousness' need not be confined to economism, that is, to a concern with the distribution and supply of material goods and services. It can also be concerned with the availability and allocation of policy benefits in the political system and that of prestige and influence in the stratification system. More significantly, in the present context, it can also be concerned with cultural commitments themselves. In this sense, 'trade union consciousness' manifests itself in the need for *symbolic reassurance*. It involves a concern that certain values, beliefs, understandings, and symbols, are still valid and that their moral custodians are fully committed to their realisation and implementation. Within the political system, for example, voters may seek reassurance that the government is still committed to 'full employment,' 'maintaining Britain's standing overseas,' etc, and will demand not simply—or indeed not even—political action but political words reaffirming the validity of these commitments and the integrity of the government's support for them. Provided these voters receive such symbolic satisfactions, they will remain politically passive. It is the mark of a skilled politician that he can distinguish between those situations and constituencies demanding rhetoric and those demanding substantive political action.[28]

Finally, in addition to these two basic variables for studying the nature and content of political cultures, we shall mention two important variables for the study of emergent properties of cultural systems. These are the degree of institutional integration and the level of consensus. *Institutional integration* refers to the consistency of the different dominant value systems, the compatibility that exists between the dominant economic, political, social, and cultural values. *Consensus* refers to the average level and intensity of commitment to different values and beliefs and applies not just to the various central elites but to the whole population of a society.[29] A stable social order requires the commitment of all those with power to disrupt the system and is thus dependent on both consensus and institutional integration. But, as we pointed out above, the greater the degree of power hierarchisation in a society, the less the need for consensus and the more the need for institutional integration. In studies of advanced industrial societies, therefore, we should pay particular attention to the degree of institutional integration and not concern ourselves solely with the overall level of consensus.

1.3 Concluding remarks

We have now presented both the context and the concepts for our study of British political culture. We shall be concerned with the validity of two themes in the study of British politics—those of deference and civility—and their relevance to the changes that have occurred in the British political system in the last few years or so. These themes will be compared with others drawn from alternative traditions of political analysis and especially from 'class' analysis. In examining these questions we shall be particularly interested in the nature and content of the dominant political value system and with its subcultural and contracultural variations. Thus it will also be necessary to consider the structure of power and the role of political parties in creating and sustaining commitment to political values. Finally, although both of the major themes under consideration emphasise the continuity and stability of the political system, we shall also be concerned with possible sources of discontinuity and instability. We begin these tasks in our next chapter with a critical review of the deference studies.

1.4 Notes and references

1 See, for example, G Almond and S Verba, *The Civic Culture* (Princeton, New Jersey: Princeton University Press, 1963) pp455–6 and 473–505; H Eckstein, 'A theory of stable democracy,' in *idem, Division and Cohesion in Democracy* (Princeton, NJ: Princeton University Press, 1966), pp225–88; and E A Nordlinger, *The Working Class Tories* (London: MacGibbon and Kee, 1967), pp210–52.
2 See, for example, R T McKenzie and A Silver, *Angels in Marble*

(London: Heinemann, 1968); Nordlinger, *Tories*; F Parkin, 'Working class conservativism: a theory of political deviance,' in *Br. J. Sociol.* (1967), xviii, pp280–90; R Samuel, 'The deference voter,' in *New Left Review* (1960), i, pp9–13; P Anderson, 'Problems of socialist strategy,' in *idem* and R Blackburn, Editors, *Towards Socialism* (London: Fontana, 1965), esp. pp263–4; and S M Lipset, 'Must Tories always triumph?,' in *Socialist Commentary* (November 1960), pp10–14. The extent to which deference accounts for middle-class voting is nowhere examined empirically. Parkin's analysis strongly implies that it is applicable for this class; and Rose writes that deference influences middle-class people as well. Butler and Stokes suggest that deference is indeed *more* relevant to middle-class voting behaviour. See—Parkin, *loc. cit.*; M Abrams and R Rose, with R Hinden, *Must Labour Lose?* (Harmondsworth: Penguin, 1960), esp. p80; and D E Butler and D E Stokes, *Political Change in Britain* (London: Macmillan, 1969), pp113–15.

3 See: A Watkins, 'The death of deference,' *New Statesman* (9 January 1970); and P Cosgrave, quoting an anonymous minister, in *The Spectator* (21 July 1972).

4 McKenzie and Silver, *Angels*, p252.

5 See the references cited in note 1 above and also R A Dahl *Who Governs?* (New Haven: Yale University Press, 1961), esp. pp223–6; W Kornhauser, *The Politics of Mass Society* (London: Routledge, 1959); and E A Shils, *The Torment of Secrecy* (London: Heinemann, 1956).

6 McKenzie and Silver, *Angels*, p251.

7 A review of definitions of political culture up to 1962 is to be found in Y C Kim, 'The concept of culture in comparative politics,' *J. Pol.* (1964), xxvi, pp313–35. See also L W Pye, 'Political culture,' in *Internat. Encycl. So. Sci.* (1968), xii, pp218–25, and D Kavanagh, *Political Culture* (London: Macmillan, 1972). On political structure, see particularly G Almond and B Powell, *Comparative Politics* (Boston: Little-Brown, 1966).

8 Almond and Verba, *Civic Culture*, pp17–19; J P Nettl, *Political Mobilisation* (London: Faber, 1967), pp67–8.

9 Kavanagh, *Political Culture*, pp55–6; and *idem*, 'The deferential English: a comparative critique,' *Government and Opposition* (1971), vi, pp333–60.

10 D D Hughes and E P Pinney, 'Political culture and the idioms of political development,' in Pinney, Editor, *Comparative Politics and Political Theory* (Chapel Hill: University of North Carolina Press, 1966), pp67–96 at p70. Hughes and Pinney themselves argue that the definition is in fact tautological—a view we contest below.

11 See, for example, Almond and Verba, *Civic Culture*, pp15–26; R A Dah, Editor, *Political Oppositions in Western Democracies* (New Haven: Yale University Press, 1968), pp352–6; Y C Kim, 'The functions of political orientations,' *World Pol.* (1964), xvi, pp205–221; and R Rose, *Politics in England* (London: Faber, 1965), pp28–30.

12 *cf* Kim, *J. Pol.* (1964), pp313–35.

13 See, for example, T Parsons, *The Social System* (London: Routledge, 1951), pp5–6 and *passim*; and, for a phenomenological structuralist, C Levi-Strauss, 'Social structure,' in A L Kroeber, Editor, *Anthropology Today* (London: University of Chicago Press, 1953), p257.

14 Parsons seems to take this view in his later writings.

15 There are few Skinnerian behaviourists in political science; for the *verstehende* approach, see P. Winch, *The Idea of a Social Science* (London: Routledge, 1958).

16 Behaviorism, on the other hand, does provide a causal analysis, in terms of operant conditioning to particular responses or modes of behaviour under given external stimuli.

17 W G Runciman, *A Critique of Max Weber's Philosophy of Social Science* (London: Cambridge University Press, 1972), p26.

18 Kavanagh, *Political Culture*, p14.

19 The arguments in the preceding three paragraphs have been influenced by, *inter alios*, the following books and articles: Runciman, *Critique*; A J Ayer, 'Man as a subject for science,' in *Philosophy, Politics, and Society, III*, edited by P Laslett and W G Runciman (Oxford: Blackwell, 1967), pp6–24; D Davidson, 'Actions, reasons, and causes,' *J. Phil.* (1963), lx, pp685–700; A C McIntyre, 'A mistake about causality in social science,' in *Philosophy, Politics, and Society, II* (Oxford: Blackwell, 1962), edited by P Laslett and W G Runciman, pp48–70; and *idem*, 'The idea of a social science,' *Proc. Arist. Soc.* (1967), pp95–114.

20 *cf* C Pateman, 'Political culture, political structure, and political change,' *Br. J. Pol. Sc.* (1971), i, pp297–311.

21 L W Pye, 'Introduction,' in *Political Culture and Political Development*, edited by *idem* and S Verba (Princeton, NJ: Princeton University Press, 1965), p15.

22 For an analysis of the meaning of power and for a fuller discussion of the central and peripheral value systems, see R D Jessop, *Social Order, Reform, and Revolution* (London: Macmillan, 1972), pp54–80 and *passim*.

23 F Parkin, *Class Inequality and Political Order* (London: MacGibbon and Kee, 1971), p88. The present discussion draws quite fully on Parkin's analysis of meaning systems.

24 See: J M Yinger, 'Contraculture and subculture,' *Am. Sociol. Rev.* (1960), xxv, pp625–35. Almond and Verba hint at these distinctions in their discussion of parochial, alienative, and allegiant political cultures: see *Civic Culture*, p22.

52 See, for example, S M Lipset, *The First New Nation* (London: Heinemann, 1964), pp209–13; Nettl, *Political Mobilisation*, pp83–91; D Apter, 'The role of traditionalism in the political modernisation of Ghana and Uganda,' *World Pol.* (1960), xiii, pp45–68; and M Czudnowski, 'A salience dimension of politics for the study of political culture,' *Am. Pol. Sc. Rev.* (1968), lxii, pp878–88.

26 *cf* B F Skinner, *Beyond Freedom and Dignity* (London: Methuen 1972) for a behaviourist attack on the ideas of freedom and dignity; and H Marcuse, 'Repressive tolerance,' in R P Weiff *et al*, *A Critique of Pure Tolerance* (London: Cape, 1969), pp93–137, for a new left attack on the notion of tolerance.

27 The distinction between 'trade-union consciousness' and 'political class consciousness' was first employed by V I Lenin, *What Is To Be Done?* (London: Panther, 1970); parallel distinctions are to be found in Gramsci ('corporate' or 'bloc' consciousness *v* 'hegemonic consciousness'), Lukacs ('contingent' *v* 'necessary' consciousness), and other left-wing writers.

28 The best discussion of this phenomenon can be found in M Edelman, *The Symbolic Uses of Politics* (Urbana: University of Illinois Press, 1967); see also T Arnold, *The Symbols of Government* (New Haven: Yale University Press, 1935).

29 These definitions are borrowed from A Stinchcombe, *Constructing Social Theories* (New York: Harcourt, Brace, and World, 1968), pp181–8; Stinchcombe also provides an excellent discussion of the relationship between institutionalisation and power.

Chapter 2

Deference, Class and Political Behaviour

Perhaps the most influential approach in the long history of voting studies has been that of class theory. This argues that the major determinant of political behaviour is 'class position'. Many other approaches start, moreover, from this theory and attempt to explain supposed deviations or exceptions. The deference studies, for example, are premised on this approach and seek to explain, in terms of certain deviant psychological and cultural orientations, why a stable proportion of working-class voters do not vote in accord with their supposed class interests. In so doing they imply not only that deferential voting is incompatible with class *voting* but also that an explanation of voting in terms of deference (or, indeed, of its alternative—secularism) is incompatible with class *theory*. Thus, an adequate assessment of the deference studies must not only consider the consistency and validity of the deference thesis itself but also the validity of class theories of political behaviour and their compatibility with deferential voting. A start on this task is made in the present chapter.

2.1 Deference and secularism

The deference studies are concerned more or less explicitly with an apparent difficulty in class theories of politics. Their problem is that of explaining the electoral success of the Conservative Party in the most heavily—and longest—industrialised and urbanised society among Western liberal bourgeois societies. Since 1886 there have been fifteen British general elections in which a single party has won a safe majority of seats. On twelve of these occasions that party has been the Conservatives.[1] This success has been achieved only by virtue of the continuing support of a large section of the manual working-class for the Tory Party. Yet the 'class interests' of workers are supposed to lie with the

Labour Party. It is this apparently deviant political behaviour that the deference thesis is particularly concerned to explain.

The studies focus on the social and, more especially, the ideological bases of voting rather than on the socio-psychological mechanisms of particular voting choices or the impact of electoral campaigns. Nor are they concerned in the main with the floating vote but rather with the stable core of support for each major political party. Within this context they distinguish two kinds of working-class Conservatism: deferential and secular or pragmatic. Deferentials are mainly characterised by their preference for ascribed, socially superior political leadership, whereas seculars are oriented more towards the economic and welfare capabilities of the different political parties.[2]

Deference is related not only to the elitist background of the Conservative Party leadership but also to the party's attempts to identify itself with traditional values and institutions and with the nation as a whole. For, not only would deference seem to involve preference for a socially ascribed elite as uniquely qualified for high political office, but also, and especially so for McKenzie and Silver, encompasses an affirmation of the traditional social and moral order. Parkin also emphasises this aspect in his discussion of working-class Conservatism but he treats it as a concomitant of deference rather than as one of its major features.[3] Conservative party propaganda, aimed so assiduously at the working class, has found such an identification fairly easy to achieve due to the basic similarities between Conservative values and those of the dominant elites. Indeed, the prominence of elite individuals in the Tory Party and the comparatively successful institutionalisation of dominant values among the population at large have combined to encourage the party to foster, the lower orders to accept, such an image. As Parkin argues in his reformulation of the deference thesis, 'political deviance, examined from a national or societal level, is manifested not in working-class Conservatism, but rather in electoral support for Socialism on the part of *any* social stratum.'[4]

There has always been a second basis of Conservative support, however, in the party's paternalist concern for the worker's well-being and its more general claims to political acumen. To the extent that this basis of support is independent of deference, any decline in the latter could be compensated by an increase in the proportion of non-deferentials voting Conservative for secular or pragmatic reasons. And, indeed, McKenzie and Silver claim to have found some evidence for this in their surveys. They write of a fall in the proportion of younger deferentials voting Conservative compared with the proportion among older deferentials and of an increase in the proportion of younger seculars voting Tory compared with older secular voters.[5]

The deference studies, then, related Conservative voting to the existence of deferential orientations among certain working-class voters and also to the more pragmatic support of an electorally less stable section of that class. Seculars and deferentials—to the extent that they are distinct types—are equally deviant in their voting behaviour but they deviate from the supposed class 'norm' for different reasons. Deferentials are comparatively unconcerned with the material interests of their class and see politics as a way of displaying and receiving esteem in an hierarchical society. Secular voters are concerned with their material welfare but fail to see this as linked *unconditionally* to the Labour Party. Hindess argues that the distinctive attribute of secular voters is an absence of solidaristic class consciousness rather than commitment to deferential norms.[6] Even so, it is possible for seculars to support either of the major parties, whereas deference is supposedly linked insolubly to support for the Conservative Party. In the absence of any attempt in the deference studies to explain why some secular voters should support Labour rather than the Conservatives, their major contribution must lie in their documentation and explanation of the deferential vote. Unfortunately, it is precisely at this point that we encounter serious difficulties in their analysis. For, as both Jessop and Kavanagh have pointed out, the notion of deference is decidedly ambiguous. It is a concept with many meanings and it is invoked to explain many disparate political facts.[7]

2.2   Nature of deference

Studies of deference typically invoke the work of Bagehot in their discussion of the deferential voter. They do not pay careful attention, however, to the distinctions he has drawn nor to the various objects of deference he cites in the *English Constitution*. For Bagehot at any rate, it is possible to defer not only to an hereditary, aristocratic elite but also to the middle class, to the £10 borough renters and the £50 county renters. He also distinguished between social deference and political deference and, indeed, remarked upon the *lack* of political deference among the population.[8] More recent work on English political culture fails not only to provide a general definition of deference but also neglects to make even these distinctions explicit. Yet the theoretical and substantive significance of 'deference' clearly varies with the exact meaning given to this highly ambiguous term. It will be worth prefacing our remarks, therefore, on the political significance of deference with a brief comment on its general character.

Deference refers to the appreciation or derogation of one or more persons by others with whom they are involved in direct or indirect social relations.[9] In return for this appreciation the recipients of deference typically bestow some sort of recognition upon the deferential other—recognition not necessarily as an equal but at least as someone who knows his place in society and the behaviour appropriate to it. Entitlements to deference and their appropriate responses vary by society, situation, and period. Appreciation or derogation can provide the essence of some interactions, such as greetings or courtly behaviour, and can constitute a secondary aspect of other interactions. In its more usual, hence more attenuated, forms, deference typically involves the acquiescence of someone in the actual or imputed wishes of another person in return for acceptance, again actual or imputed. Where compliance is with actual rather than imputed wishes, the medium of influence over the deferential person is advice, information, encouragement, or simply acceptance, and is based on his recognition and appreciation of the more or less diffuse status of the person to whom he defers. In the case of symbolic deference, or of deference to imputed wishes, the deferential acts in accord with his own beliefs as to how the recipient would wish him to act and he is rewarded by his own feelings of moral worth and self-esteem. The imputation of such wishes is often based on understandings about the recipient's own values, interests, standards, or preferences—understandings gleaned through such ways as direct observation, opinion leadership, the mass media, or simple intuition. Just as deference can be based on many and varied entitlements, so, too, can it result in compliance in many spheres of behaviour. Voting on the basis of advice from the socially prestigious or the social standing of party elites is just one manifestation of deferential behaviour.

Not all deference is rooted firmly in face-to-face interaction with the recipients of deference—some deference is mediated, symbolic, and putative in character. Commitment to the relevant value systems and interaction with appropriate local opinion leaders play an important mediating role where, for example, voters do not come into direct contact with national party leaders or MPs. Clearly, this must be the case with 'deferential' voting in urban areas not only for working-class electors but also

c

for many middle-class voters—few of whom, if any, can actually interact directly or often with members of the dominant elites. In rural areas in the past, however, there was probably a firmer structural basis for such deferential behaviour in social relations between workers and the aristocracy or landed gentry. It seems plausible to argue that where there is not such a structural base rooted in regular interaction, then 'deference' will be less likely. Perhaps this is part of the explanation for the decline in 'deference' and in the proportion of 'deferentials' who actually vote Conservative. However, it seems equally plausible to argue that deferential voting need not mean deference to candidates and party leaders but simply deference to those who support them in higher strata—a deference more likely to exist today even in urban areas. Whatever the merits of this interpretation, however, it is not the sort of deference implied by the deference studies themselves. To this we now turn.

Even a cursory examination of recent studies reveals at least four different usages in their discussion of deference and it is hardly surprising that the implications of deference vary accordingly. The following four types of deference can be discerned:

1   *Ascriptive socio-political deference.* Deference towards a socially ascribed elite as uniquely qualified for high political office. This is the operationally significant type for empirical studies of voting behaviour. Thus both Nordlinger and also McKenzie and Silver employ operational definitions or indicators that involve the expression of a preference for a prime minister of exclusive social background rather than one who has been upwardly mobile from the working class. Ralph Samuel employs a similar indicator in assessing working-class deference. In other contexts, however, all four have treated deference as involving something more than this.[10]

2   *Ascriptive social deference.* Deference towards the high-born and/or wealthy. This type is slightly more ambiguous. It seems to involve deference towards the high-born and/or those who have inherited wealth (often combined with a public school education). Mere possession of wealth is not apparently a qualification for this type of deference although it may be the basis for some form of meritocratic or achievement-oriented deference. In addition to its ambiguities, this type would seem less relevant to voting or other political behaviour. None the less, it is *potentially* relevant in so far as the Conservative Party is actually led, or at least

believed to be led, by such men to a greater extent than the Labour or Liberal parties. Much of the evidence for the deferential character of English political culture is drawn from this type of deference as it is manifested in attitudes towards class and status. Thus attitudes towards the monarchy and aristocracy figure in McKenzie and Silver's operational definition of deference and these authors also cite the Tory appeal to monarchy, aristocracy, and property as a deferential appeal. Nordlinger invokes the congruence of class, status, and authority relations in his discussion of deferential culture. Butler and Stokes define deference, in operational terms at least, as favourability to the Royal Family. A similar approach is found in other writers.[11]

3 *Socio-cultural deference.* Deference towards a traditional social and moral order. This sort of deference seems to involve far more than simple interpersonal relations and is best characterised as 'traditionalism' in order to distinguish it from preceding types. It is the most inclusive type of orientation invoked in the discussion of deference and involves simply the 'receptive affirmation'[12] of the legitimacy of established institutions, traditions, and values, and the rejection of innovations threatening the order they embody. Traditionalism figures most strongly in Parkin's reformulation of the deference thesis and in political analyses of new left writers. It can also be found in the analyses of the main deference studies.[13]

4 *Political deference.* This is of an entirely different kind and refers to deference towards the government *whatever its social or partisan composition*. This type of deference is most relevant to the analysis of civic orientations but it is included as an aspect of the Tory deferential's value system by McKenzie and Silver and by Samuel. Deferentials, according to the former authors, believe the ordinary voter should confine himself to voting and supporting the government and see policies benefiting ordinary people as the consequences of the generosity and benevolence of politicians with elite backgrounds. They believe, according to Samuel, that 'matters of state and economy are no proper concern for the working classes.'[14] It is surely more fruitful, however, to treat political deference and social deference as analytically independent phenomena—especially as there is a wide measure of agreement between Labour and Conservative working-class voters on the nature of society and the role of their class within it[15] and, secondly, because the civility models postulate a more or less equal

distribution of political deference either side of the major party cleavages in a stable democracy. Nordlinger's study does maintain the analytical distinction, as Bagehot did a century before, and thus is able to examine the inter-relations between ascriptive socio-political deference and aspects of political deference. More generally, recognition of this distinction is not incompatible with explanations of widespread political deference in terms of the traditional domination of political life by the high-born and the wealthy and a consequential generalisation of social deference to the political institutions which they controlled.

This list is by no means exhaustive. Rose, for example, has written that deference will be paid increasingly to an intellectual rather than ascribed elite although, in an earlier work, he gave his support to the importance of ascriptive socio-political deference.[16] Similarly, Grainger, although he refers to the uncritical use of the deference concept and an overemphasis on social deference— which he describes as hardly 'the prime or perennial element in English political life,' suggests that deference to moral and intellectual authority has been important.[17] Other writers have also used the concept.

In the narrower context of the four types distinguished above, however, we may point out that 'ascriptive socio-political defer- ence' is clearly both politically relevant and potentially advantag- eous to the Conservative Party on account of its historically strongly ascriptive social elite leadership. Ascriptive social defer- ence on grounds of high birth and inherited wealth and, secondly, socio-cultural deference or traditionalism have political relevance only when some mechanism exists for translating non-political into political commitments. Party propaganda oriented to non- political beliefs and values is one such mechanism and has been widely used for this purpose in the past. Another such mechanism can be posited on the twin assumptions that political action, e.g. voting, is an expression of life-style and social values as well as purely political considerations and that the Conservative Party is peculiarly identified with the ruling class and the traditional social and moral order. This mechanism will only operate where non-political considerations are salient and where the Conservative Party is indeed seen as the sole, or at least one, legitimate custodian of the traditional order and/or as the creature of the ruling class. To the extent that ascriptive social deferentials and traditionals are motivated by a politically oriented 'trade union consciousness' and see their interests as linked to the electoral success of another party whose policies and actions are not incompatible with the established order—to that extent are they likely to vote other than Conservative. Conversely, non-deferentials may vote for this party on purely instrumental rather than ideological grounds— these are the seculars or pragmatists found in the deference studies. Again, the primary element in these instrumental orientations is likely to be 'trade-union consciousness' although it is possible for even those with a radical, oppositional political outlook to vote on narrowly instrumental grounds for a party not identified in its basic values and assumptions with the hegemonic counter-culture.

In short, too little consideration has been given by earlier students of deference to the precise nature of this 'deference' and to the adequacy of various indicators in relation to the type of deference being considered. There has also been too little consideration of the mechanisms which connect more inclusive types of deference to political behaviour and especially to Conservative support. What is required, therefore, is a series of indicators that correspond to the several sorts of deference involved in these studies and an effort to uncover the mechanisms whereby deference is related to political behaviour. Before we proceed to examine the empirical evidence for and against the deference thesis, however, there are several further theoretical points to be made.

2.3 Further comments on deference and traditionalism

Although the deference studies present it as such, it is by no means clear that deference is a *cause* of Conservative voting. Thus not all deferentials vote Conservative—only half of those in the major studies do so—and few voters cite deferential reasons when explaining their political allegiance (see Chapter 5). Moreover Conservative support has remained more or less stable over a period when the Party has had three very different prime ministerial party leaders—Macmillan, Sir Alec Douglas Home, and Heath; and, despite Heath's petit bourgeois background and electoral unpopularity, the Tory Party was none the less able to win the 1970 general election.[18] Nordlinger suggests—but does not consider further—that deference may be a *result* of Conservative partisanship. And Parkin has argued that deference and Conservatism are correlates that are both determined by a third factor—exposure to the dominant value system.[19] Although deference cannot be purely the result of Tory partisanship (otherwise there would be no Labour deferentials), it is possible that the greater commitment of Conservative workers to such deference is a product of partisanship combined with the more elite leadership of their party. Conversely, the expression of deference among supporters of both parties is compatible with the idea that deference is a dominant value relatively well institutionalised in all classes and party groups. Whatever the correct interpretation, the question certainly needs further inquiry.

Secondly, much of the deference literature concentrates solely on the working class but fails to give any explanation for this. Is it meant to imply that deference is a peculiarly working-class phenomenon or is it meant to imply that the middle classes are so obviously deferential that special investigation is quite redundant? Alternatively, is it meant to imply that the extent of middle-class deference is irrelevant because it is normal for the middle classes to vote Conservative and no special mechanisms need to be invoked in explanation. If the first reason is the correct one, then what are we to make of the arguments of Butler and Stokes, of Parkin, or of Rose, all of whom imply or explicitly state that deference also operates in the middle class? If the last reason is the correct one, then the deference studies obviously accept a class theory of politics for the middle class but not for the working class—yet a fifth of the middle-class two-party vote usually goes to Labour. If class theory is so inapplicable to the working class, why is it assumed that it works for the middle class? Whatever the explanation for this neglect, the middle-class vote does deserve some examination in terms of class and deference theories.

In this connection, for example, it is important to note that many other countries also have large working-class conservative or clerical party votes but have not been considered 'deferential' in the same way.[20] Is deference to be seen as a peculiarly British phenomenon, therefore, or can it be generalised to other countries? Or is it, perhaps, that deference explains working class conservatism neither abroad nor in Britain? Conversely, other countries which have had social democratic governments have been successful despite sizeable working-class conservatism because there is also considerable middle-class support for socialist parties.[21] And in Britain, too, the few electoral successes of the Labour Party have been critically dependent likewise on a favourable swing among the middle classes.[22] It is just as important, therefore, to consider why the middle classes vote left as why the Tory worker is still alive and well.

The arguments propounded by Parkin are particularly relevant here. Although concerned explicitly with working-class Conservatism, the thesis he puts forward also has implications for middle-class Labour voting. This thesis argues that it is not working-class Conservatism that is deviant, but voting by *any* class for the Labour Party. Only those in isolated structural positions who are thereby insulated against appeals to traditional values and who are able to sustain a countercultural tradition favourable to the Labour movement will, in fact, be found to support that party. In contrast to other deference studies, therefore, the Parkin thesis is concerned not just with the ideological bases of Conservatism but also with its structural roots. Since insulation is most closely linked with strong working-class occupational and residential communities, this theory implies that deferential voting is by no means incompatible with a class theory of politics. In his focus on dominant and contractural value systems, Parkin also employs a conceptual approach that coincides with the general perspective outlined in Chapter 1.

There are certainly problems with this thesis as with other deference studies. It does not, for example, consider bases of support for the Conservative Party other than deferential commitment to the dominant social and economic order. Thus it ignores secular or pragmatic support for that party. Nor does it consider the problem of those sufficiently insensitive to the dominant order that they overlook its connections with the Conservatives. Thirdly, the model seems to imply that Labour voters have a really radical, socialist counterculture that is totally opposed to the traditional order. It neglects the possibility, therefore, that they might simply be 'trade union conscious'—that is, half-committed to the dominant order and trying to promote their group interests within it. Lastly, this particular model does not provide a convincing explanation of the middle-class Labour vote in terms of structural insulation from dominant institutions and values. It is no more true that all middle-class Labour voters live and work in proletarian surroundings than it is that all working-class Tories live and work alongside the middle classes. Another explanation must exist, therefore, for their alienation from the dominant order and/or for a corporate consciousness that leads them to support the Labour Party.[23] Lastly, Parkin treats the dominant value system as essentially unchanging—the institutions and values that he mentions could easily have been included in the list of dominant institutions in the nineteenth or earlier centuries.[24] It is true that such continuity is a major characteristic of British political culture but recognition of this fact should not be allowed to blind us to the way in which new elements are continually added and the whole is thereby changed. The increasingly dominant emphasis on economic growth, technical efficiency, technological advance, and intellectual merit, for example, are ignored and so, too, is their possible impact on the image and votes of political parties.

Finally, deference has been related not only to voting behaviour but also to many other political phenomena, especially strong and effective government and also political stability. Whatever the actual relations between deference, however defined and measured, and voting behaviour, therefore, we must still consider these other questions on their own particular merits. This requires us to examine the relations between the first and second themes mentioned above, i.e. the relations between the civic culture and deferential behaviour. This we shall do in our next chapter. But, before proceeding to such an examination, we shall need to consider the major alternative to deference theory.

2.4   Class and political behaviour

In their criticisms of the class thesis the deference studies imply that it makes the following six assumptions about voting behaviour. Firstly, class is determined by the present occupation of the household head. Second, the major determinant of voting behaviour is class position. Third, the major division between classes is that between manual and non-manual occupational classes. Next, that political parties 'represent' class interests. Fifthly, the Labour Party 'represents' the interests of the manual working class and the Conservative Party those of non-manual workers, their families, and other dependents. Therefore, sixthly, the working class votes Labour and the middle class votes Conservative. This model does not, as we have already indicated, provide a very good fit for the two-party vote in Britain. Indeed, it provides rather a poor fit, since about one-third of the working class fail to vote for their supposed 'class party' and one-fifth of the middle class does likewise. It also ignores the existence of the Liberal Party, nationalist parties, the unionist and Protestant unionist parties in Northern Ireland, and immigrant parties. There are various reasons for this lack of fit, at least some of which are theoretical rather than purely empirical.

We can improve the fit of the 'class model' of political behaviour if we reformulate the assumptions on which it is premised in a more realistic manner. Even fairly crude attempts can prove successful. For example, Rose defined the ideal typical working-class voter as a trade union member, a council tenant, with limited education, and subjectively working class. He found great variation in Conservative voting according to class position defined in these terms. Thus three-quarters of ideal typical workers voted Labour, whereas only two-fifths of those lacking two or more of these characteristics did so. Moreover, there were more of the latter working-class persons than there were ideal typical workers.[25] It is certainly worth considering, therefore, more sophisticated models of class voting. In particular, unless we intend to assert some metaphysical link between class position and voting behaviour, it is obvious that subjective factors must be included as intervening variables in the analysis of voting behaviour. Otherwise, we shall be guilty of an elementary mistake— failure to distinguish between 'class-in-itself' and 'class-for-itself.' But even before examining the nature and origins of class consciousness, several useful points can be made about the analysis of objective class position.

Even if we confine the concept of class to economic factors, it is by no means clear that present occupation is a perfect indicator of objective class position. It is really necessary to view both the economic power position and the economic exchange or market position of any person in order to determine his overall class position. Capital resources, managerial skills, labour power, the nature of the market, union strength, employer paternalism, and many other factors, are relevant to an assessment of economic class position. Occupational position provides only limited information about these various factors. And, if occupation is an inadequate general indicator, it is even more true that the distinction between manual and non-manual occupations is open to objection. The power and exchange position of routine non-manual workers is less advantageous in many senses than that of skilled manual workers. Certainly, there is some argument for including the former within the working class on purely theoretical grounds. And recent work has shown that their life-style and class self-identities suggest greater affinities with manual workers than higher strata.[26] The effects of such a classification do not, however, reduce the level of cross-class voting but rather increase it and thus the apparent problem with which class theories are faced.[27]

All these factors affect the development of class consciousness, the emergence of 'classes-for-themselves.' It is important to view this process as *process*, that is, dynamically rather than statically. For, at any given point in time, the absence of a strong correlation between class-in-itself and class-for-itself could well be due to the

effect of particular dynamic relations between power and exchange positions rather than to any inaccuracy in class theories.
We must examine the changing market and power positions of
any class, therefore, and also their relation to the dynamics of
other power systems.[28] This requires macrostructural analysis
as well as survey analysis and both must be oriented to changes
over time. A marginal class, for example, is more likely to become
class-conscious than one that is relatively secure and unexploited.
Marginality in turn can be due to adverse market conditions, to
technological change, to political action, to bad luck, or some
other factor. More generally, the emergence of structural contradictions that produce depression, unemployment, or rapid
inflation, will encourage the development of class consciousness
and class struggle. Conversely, the progressive development of
forces of production and the growth of output due to technological
innovation, expansion of new markets, etc, will encourage the
acceptance of the class structure and dominant order. In either
case, it is important not to extrapolate what may be purely
temporary trends into predictions about long-term relations
between class and party in a given society.

Secondly, it must not be forgotten that classes grow from a
number of other social groups and classes and that there is a
continual influx and outflow, on a wider or narrower scale, in any
particular class-in-itself. The greater the mobility between different
classes, the less likely is there to develop a distinctive class
consciousness in any class. On a similar level it is necessary to
examine the microsocial pressures on the formation of class
consciousness. There is always a set of such pressures on individual members of an economic class deriving from their interaction
with others. Close contacts with employers, class heterogamy,
differential social mobility within the nuclear family, heter-
ophilous class contacts in work and leisure activities, etc, will
all tend to inhibit the development of class consciousness.

Thirdly, if we examine class in the context of the total social
structure and the institutionalisation of values, norms, and
beliefs about social reality, then yet more pressures militating
against this development can be found. We have argued that there
is a strong link between power and institutionalisation in all
societies and that the ruling ideas are those of the dominant elites.
If one now assumes that radical class consciousness is a derogated
phenomenon, several pressures can be identified. Schools, the
mass media, dominant institutions, and other agencies of socialisation, will transmit and reinforce values inimical to radicalism.

The agencies of social control will tend to punish or dissuade the dissemination of radical ideas. Moreover, the acceptance of dominant values encourages people to adopt higher strata as reference groups so that commitment to them is reinforced through the exchange of deference for advice, information, encouragement, recognition, etc. The greater commitment of higher strata, dominant classes, political elites, and so on, to the central value system means that their political environment is more homogeneous and that their values are likely to be further reinforced. Conversely, there is likely to be greater heterogeneity and ambiguity among lower strata, etc, so that support for deviant values will be weakened. Allied to this is the well-known difficulty of getting people to change values to which they are already committed, as opposed to reinforcing values they already have. Thus the whole structure of society encourages the attenuation of class consciousness. Hegemony is embedded in social structure and it is difficult to dissolve its influence without dissolving the total system.[29]

Finally, it should be noted that class struggle is itself an important factor in the development of class consciousness. The more organised and less spontaneous the class struggle, then the more likely it is to develop a radical consciousness and to perpetuate this beyond the immediate local conflict. The trade union and the political party are important agencies in the institutionalisation of deviant values in this respect and their continuity helps to sustain deviant commitments over time.

With these constraints in mind, it is obvious that a radical class consciousness will develop only under certain highly specific conditions. Firstly, there must be adverse market conditions that affect the class as a whole and this must lead to class struggle. Secondly, the class must preferably be locally concentrated—both residentially and occupationally—and more or less hereditary in composition. This reduces the microsocial pressures towards conformity to the dominant value system and helps sustain solidarity. Thirdly, there must be some organisation capable of formulating and advocating a class-conscious ideology and of mobilising class support in the economic and political spheres.

These exacting conditions are rarely met in contemporary British society and it is correspondingly reasonable to expect that class voting will be limited. But the absence of class voting is *not* incompatible with class theory. On the contrary, we should in fact expect to find widespread cross-class voting, especially among the subordinate classes, in most class-stratified societies. *The appropriate test for a class theory is not the extent of cross-class voting but its incidence.* If cross-class voting is minimal where a class theory would predict strongly developed class consciousness and highest where class theory would predict weakly developed class consciousness, then the theory will have received considerable *prima facie* support.

However, there is a further problem in the analysis of class theories of voting behaviour. This concerns the role of political parties in the model. Parties are crucial agents in the electoral process—without their direction and shaping of behaviour few, if any, members of the periphery would bother to vote. The deference studies' version of the class model assumes that political parties 'represent' class interests and thereby mobilise the support of particular classes. But the notion of 'representation' is exceedingly complex. At its most simple it means only that particular parties enjoy the historical loyalties of different classes and are able to mobilise these loyalties at elections. It can also refer to symbolic representation through, for example, the recruitment of members and leaders predominantly or exclusively from one class or through a strong rhetorical stress on class interests in the party policy or programme. And it can refer to material representation of class interests through, say, the passage of legislation beneficial to one class rather than another. Thus it is quite possible for a party to appeal to class interests but not to reflect them in its legislation, and vice versa. Sartori argues, for example, that the class appeal of parties may be played down to the point of invisibility because class loyalties are firm and the party is appealing to cross-class voters. Conversely, class appeal may be emphasised because class support is low or dwindling. Indeed, it is essential even where class politics is an important feature of a party system for the party representing a minority class to stress non-class factors if it is to win a majority. The Conservative Party belongs to this type and is well-known for appealing to national and individual interests rather than solidaristic class interests. If this fact is combined with the macrostructural and microsocial pressures on acceptance of the dominant value system, it is apparent that class appeal and class voting will not be as important in British politics as might at first be thought. In short, another of the assumptions underlying crude class theories of voting behaviour is either wrong or vague to the point of being misleading. If at least one of the parties in a class-stratified society, disregarding for the moment the important question whether it 'reflects' class interests, does not appeal to them, then part of the explanation for cross-class voting has been found.

But let us also examine more closely what the appeal to class interests actually involves. If class appeal means only an appeal to trade-union-conscious interests, then all parties can appeal to any given class. Moreover, on this level it is quite possible for the interests of different classes to coincide rather than conflict—if the distribution of economic power is accepted as given, then co-operation to increase productivity can be in everyone's material interests.[31] But it is more difficult for all parties convincingly to appeal to the same class and promise to redistribute, not the marginal product, but ultimate power, in its favour. Yet, where the two major parties appeal to the economistic interests of voters, their choice of party is more difficult than where only one party promises to advance his interests. In such circumstances, we have to explain, not class splitting or class deviance, but the reasons underlying any political choice or none. Historical party loyalties, microsocial pressures, the past performance of political parties, the 'nature of the times,' general life-style, commitments to dominant or countercultural values, these and other factors can be expected to influence the choice. It goes without saying that these are the circumstances in Britain.

In short, a sophisticated class theory must consider the political influence of class in relation to the total structure of class-stratified societies and the effects of this on the voters' class consciousness and the class appeal of parties. This in turn involves a concern with the relative institutionalisation of the dominant value system and the emergence of subordinate and counter-cultural values and movements. To the extent that the central value system is successfully institutionalised and voters are deferential or aspirational in outlook, then they will not support any radical or merely corporately conscious political party. With the emergence of 'trade union consciousness' the prospects for class politics begin to improve. Even so, one should not expect too great an association between objective class position and voting for 'class parties.' For this requires extraordinary historical and structural conditions rarely encountered in contemporary Western industrial societies. None the less, class theory is still useful in the study of 'normal politics' and we shall attempt to test it in later chapters.

2.5 Summary and conclusions
In this chapter we have critically reviewed the theoretical arguments and assumptions of the deference theme and its major alternative, class theory. Although the two are often presented as

incompatible, there are good grounds for subsuming deferential voting under class theory. For deference to social and political elites is one aspect of commitment to the dominant value system of class-stratified societies. A deferential vote can therefore be treated as a non-class-conscious vote. Furthermore, by subsuming deference under class theory we overcome the problem of its apparent specificity to Britain although all industrial countries have working-class conservative voters. The content of the dominant value system, including the appropriate recipients of deference, can be treated as irrelevant in a comparative analysis of its institutionalisation and so we can generalise our results to other countries. Thirdly, deference by itself explains only a limited amount of cross-class voting (see below) and must therefore be supplemented by other factors for a complete account of electoral behaviour. Class theory can provide some of these other factors. Lastly, class theory has been far more concerned with the structural location of class-conscious people and, in contrast to the deference studies proper, is able to provide an explanation not only for the link between deference and Conservatism but also for the social location of deferentials.

More generally, we have seen that deference is a problematic concept that requires careful treatment and analysis. The relations between deference and voting behaviour are by no means easy to follow and more attention must be paid to the mechanisms which relate it to political choice. The same stricture applies to the class approach to political behaviour. Here, too, most analyses have ignored the complex relations between objective class position and electoral choice. In both cases, therefore, future work must be more subtle and more sensitive to the complexities of social structure and individual action.

2.6   Notes and references

1   As McKenzie and Silver point out, 1886 marks the start of modern electoral history in Britain since the Third Reform Act of 1884, and the redistribution in 1885 carried the country most of the way to 'one *man*, one vote, one value.' The figures are an updated analysis based on their discussion: see *idem*, 'Conservativism, industrialism and the working-class Tory in England,' in *Studies in British Politics*, edited by R Rose (London: Macmillan, 1967), pp21–33.
2   *Ibid*, p28; Nordlinger, *Tories*, p64.
3   Parkin, 'Working class Conservatives,' *BJS* (1967).
4   *Ibid*, p282.
5   McKenzie and Silver, *Angels*, pp183–90.
6   B Hindess, *The Decline of Working Class Politics* (London: MacGibbon and Kee, 1970), pp21–2.

7 See: B Jessop, 'Civility and traditionalism in English political culture,' *Br. J. Pol. Sci.* (1971), pp1–24; and also Kavanagh, in *Government and Opposition* (1970), pp233–60.

8 W Bagehot, *The English Constitution* (London: Fontana, 1965), Chapters 8 and 9, cited in Kavanagh, in *Government and Opposition* (1970), p334.

9 *cf* E A Shils, 'Deference,' in *Social Stratification*, edited by J A Jackson (London: Cambridge University Press, 1968), pp104–32; and Jessop, *Social Order*, pp65–8.

10 The McKenzie and Silver item involves stating a preference between two men as prime minister: one is an MP's son who went to Eton and Oxford and was an officer in the Guards; the other is son of a lorry driver, ex-grammar school and Bristol University, who entered the army as a private and was promoted to captain; both are party leaders. Nordlinger employs two similar questions relating to choices between a peer's son and a clerk's son and between a grammar school man and an old Etonian; these are then combined to produce a dichotomous classification into deferential and pragmatist. Samuel's operational definition involves stating a preference for political leaders drawn from families used to running the country; his theoretical definition is the acceptance of privilege and profit as legitimate bases of political power.

11 McKenzie and Silver, *Angels*, pp250 and 252; Nordlinger, *Tories*, pp34–5; Butler and Stokes, *Political Change*, pp113–15; and H Eckstein, 'The British political system,' in *Patterns of Government*, edited by S H Beer and A Ulam (New York: Random, 1962), pp70–269.

12 The phrase is Shils': see his paper, 'Tradition and liberty: antinomy and interdependence,' *Ethics* (1958), lxviii, pp153–65 and esp. pp154–6.

13 See, for example, Parkin, in *Br. J. Sociol.* (1967); Anderson, in *Towards Socialism*, esp. pp31–2; McKenzie and Silver, *Angels*, pp166–7 and *passim*.

14 McKenzie and Silver, *Angels*, p166; Samuel, in *New Left Rev.*, p11.

15 McKenzie and Silver, *Angels*, pp244–7.

16 Rose, *Politics in England*, p41; and Abrams and Rose, *Must Labour Lose?*, pp87–8.

17 J H Grainger, *Character and Style in English Politics* (London: Cambridge University Press, 1969), p254.

18 *cf* R Rose, 'Materialism that moves the voter,' *The Times* (5 June 1970).

19 Nordlinger, *Tories*, pp64–5n; Parkin, in *Br. J. Sociol.* (1967).

20 See, for example, M Dogan, 'Le vote ouvrier en Europe occidentale,' *Revue Francaise de Sociologie* (1960), i, pp25–44; S M Lipset, *Political Man* (London: Heinemann, 1960), pp220–63; and S M Lipset and S Rokkan, Editors, *Party Systems and Voter Allignemnts* (New York: Free Press, 1967), *passim*. Dogan's results show that the proportion of the non-agricultural manual working class vote going to socialist and communist parties ranges from four-fifths in Finland to half in Germany; Lipset reports that a half of manual workers in the United States voted Republican in 1950 (*op cit*, p286).

21 *cf* Kavanagh, in *Government and Opposition* (1970), pp348–9; and J Gyford and S Haseler, *Social Democracy: Beyond Revisionism* (London: Fabian Society, 1971), pp2–5.

22 See, for example, Henry Durant's presentation of Gallup Poll data on elections from 1945 to 1966 in *Studies in British Politics*, edited by R Rose (London: Macmillan, 1969, second edition).

23   In other work, Parkin has presented an analysis of some other factors that facilitate middle class radicalism: see *Middle Class Radicalism* (Manchester: Manchester University Press, 1968).

24   Indeed, Thompson includes most of them in his description of the dominant centres in the nineteenth century, excluding only the mass media and adding both Empire and the Whig and Tory Parties: see E P Thompson, 'The peculiarities of the English,' in *Socialist Register 1965*, edited by J Saville and R Miliband (London: Merlin Press, 1965), p327.

25   R Rose, 'Class and party divisions: Britain as a test case', *Sociology* (1968), ii, pp129–62.

26   *cf* M J Kahan, D E Butler, and D E Stokes, 'On the analytical division of social class,' *Br. J. Sociol.*, (1966), xvii, pp122–32.

27   *cf* Butler and Stokes, *Political Change*, pp73–6.

28   *cf* Jessop, *Social Order*, *passim*.

29   Lipset provides an analysis very similar to the present one in his discussion of class voting: see S M Lipset, *Revolution and Counterrevolution* (London: Heinemann, 1969), pp156–69.

30   *cf* G Sartori, 'From the sociology of politics to political sociology,' in *Politics and the Social Sciences*, edited by S M Lipset (London: Oxford University Press, 1969), pp65–100.

31   *cf* N I Bukharin, *Historical Materialism* (Ann Arbor: University of Michigan Press, 1969), pp294–7.

Chapter 3

Civility, Hegemony and Stability

Social and political philosophers have long been interested in the explanation of societal stability. Class theories have also figured prominently in this context and they have provided equally useful insights into the causes of stability. Indeed, one of the earliest explanations, that provided by Aristotle in his *Politics*, sought to account for political stability in terms of the size of the middle class. The civility studies do not attempt to refute class interpretations nor do they take the implied falsity of such views as their starting point. Rather, they treat Western politics as the 'democratic translation of the class struggle' and seek to explain why Western political systems remain stable and effective. But class struggle is taken as given and not the focus of analysis. Instead of examining the varying nature of the class struggle or asking why subordinate classes adopt democratic means in pursuit of their goals, the civility studies seek an explanation at another level—that of national culture rather than class culture and of general political orientations rather than class consciousness. Class tends to be an irrelevant datum rather than the crucial variable in these studies. In contrast, however, we shall argue that class theory can be reformulated to incorporate concerns with civility and stability and can be shown to provide an adequate explanation of social and political stability—or at least an account more adequate than that provided by the civility studies and similar interpretations.

3.1 The civic culture and political stability

The civility studies ask the question whether there is 'a democratic political culture—a pattern of political attitudes that fosters democratic stability, that in some way "fits" the democratic political system.'[1] In this context, a 'democratic' political system is one in which elites compete regularly for the control of the government and in which such control depends on the electoral decision of the people.[2] Given this definition, it is hardly surprising that these studies are particularly concerned with political deference and popular participation and with the appropriate balance between them. Some sort of balance is clearly necessary if the political system is to remain both democratic and effective. Insufficient political deference would result in the immobilisation of governments as their scope for independent action and room for manœuvre were destroyed by 'demand stress.' On the other hand, insufficient participation would encourage the government to ignore popular opinion and destroy its credibility as a democratic institution. Confronted with this dilemma the civility studies emphasise the need for political deference and popular allegiance rather more than they emphasise the need for the duties of voters to participate actively in the political process. The basic ideas underlying this approach would seem to be quite commonsensical but the manner in which they are developed and the evidence upon which they rely are far less easily acceptable. Before criticising them, however, we shall summarise its proponents' arguments more fully.

Nordlinger provides a more coherent exposition of the civic culture than do Almond and Verba. We shall therefore follow his analysis and point out similarities and differences between these two accounts. Nordlinger argues that democratic stability requires a dualistic political orientation among the electorate—they must be allegiant and acquiescent, on the one hand, vocal and active, on the other hand. He criticises Almond and Verba for talking loosely of a need for passivity and activity on the grounds that passivity could indicate an underlying disaffection from the political system rather than attachment to the *status quo*. These latter authors do argue, however, that stability requires allegiant orientations in any political system and they describe the civic culture as 'an allegiant participant culture.'[3] Nordlinger also points out that a straightforward balance between passivity and activity is in fact compatible with a fragmented political culture in which one section of the population was permanently passive and another section normally active—with potentially disastrous results for political stability. These considerations are not entirely lost on Almond and Verba, however, for they discuss elsewhere the possibility of mixed 'subject-participant' and mixed 'parochial-participant' political cultures and argue that these can lead to cycles of authoritarian and democratic government rather than to stability.[4]

Nordlinger therefore concludes that what is required is a mixture of acquiescent and directive attitudes on both (or all) sides of the main cleavage(s) about which political competition occurs. This can be realised in one of two ways. The majority of the adult population might each maintain a balance between acquiescence and directiveness in their orientations to the political system. Alternatively, while particular individuals maintain mainly deferential or participant orientations, there might be a mixture of different individuals within the major political conflict groups. The same ideas can be found in Almond and Verba's discussion. They mention two sorts of mixture found in the civic culture—a fusion of parochial, subject, and participant orientations within individual 'citizens' and, secondly, a mixture within the political culture as a whole of such 'citizens' with those who have parochial and/or subject orientations only. They also note that the tension between governmental power and responsiveness can be partly resolved by cycles of involvement and inactivity among individual voters and by a general shortfall between subjective competence and sense of civic duty, on the one hand, and actual rates of participation, on the other. As long as the government suspects that citizens might become politically active, then, whether or not they actually do so, it will not step beyond the bounds of responsible democratic governmental action.[5]

Almond and Verba also discuss a further three prerequisites of stable democracy. There must be a balance between emotional and instrumental orientations towards political activity and also between consensual and conflictual orientations. Thirdly, there must be diffuse social trustfulness. But Nordlinger argues that the 'dualistic political orientation' encompasses both types of balance. For acquiescence is typically based on emotional attachments to the wider political system and on agreement as to the rules governing political behaviour; while directiveness is usually calculative and self-interested. He also argues that acquiescence is normally rooted in diffuse social trustfulness and that the other functions ascribed to it by Almond and Verba are irrelevant to the stability of democratic polities.[6]

The civility studies also examine the sources of the civic culture or 'dualistic political orientation.' These are found in 'a complex process that includes training in many social institutions—family, peer group, school, workplace, as well as the political sytem itself.'[7] The wide variety of political experiences—direct and indirect, equalitarian and inequalitarian, past and present—involved in the acquisition of civic orientations is most conductive to maintaining the complexities, tensions, and inconsistencies of the civic culture. For, in so far as training is implicit, then inconsistencies can be passed on without recognition. And, in so far as many types of training occur simultaneously, different aspects of the civic culture will be learnt from different sources.[8] While this argument might seem a trifle fanciful, it does, in fact, provide a good description of how political socialisation works in an hegemonic society.

Such are the basic arguments of the civility studies. Several other theorists share their elitist assumptions and mention similar factors in explanation of political stability. In one of the earliest 'empirical democratic theories,' for example, Berelson argues that there must be a balance between involvement and indifference, between consensus and cleavage, between individualism and collectivism, between progress and conservatism, between stability and flexibility, if the democratic political system is to prove both stable and effective. Similar traits characterise '*homo civicus*' as lovingly described by Dahl and also Crick's somewhat apolitical 'political man.' Even in theories concerned more with structural than cultural prerequisites of stability we none the less find these same emphases. Thus, in his discussion of the authority structure most conducive to democratic stability, Eckstein argues that there must be a balance between authoritarian, democratic, and constitutional elements within the political system itself as well as in the other societal subsystems.[9] It should not seem too arbitrary, therefore, if we go on to criticise empirical democratic theories as represented by the 'civic culture' and 'dualistic political orientation.'

3.2   Problems with the civility theme

The civility studies outlined above differ both in focus and in level of explanation from the deference studies. Whereas the deference studies focus on party support within the political system and simply relate individual orientations to individual voting choices, the civility studies stress the role of emergent cultural properties and display an overriding concern with the stability of the political system as a whole. It is this latter concern that creates most of the difficulties with their analysis. For it encourages the proponents of the civility theme, as it does the other elitist theorists of democracy, to treat general political inactivity as inevitable rather than as an artefact of particular socio-political systems.[10] The correlates and consequences of such an assumption are the concern of the present section.

Throughout the discussion of the civic culture there is little recognition of the important differences between the dominant value system and peripheral values. Indeed, Nordlinger believes that the orientations of political elites are unimportant provided the electorate is appropriately acquiescent and directive. If only these conditions are met, he argues, the elite will necessarily act in such a way as to produce a stable political democracy owing to the imperatives of electoral competition. Almond and Verba simply say that the elite and mass political cultures must be complementary and that the decision-makers must believe in the democratic myths as much as the non-elite if the system is to be stable and democratic.[11] Thus neither study recognises the implications of inequalities in the distribution of power for the relevance of consensus in producing political stability. Both studies neglect the extent to which the relative emphasis on deference and participation is determined by the particular version of the democratic myths promulgated by the elite and by the elite's own political performance. By virtue of their emphasis on mass political culture, they necessarily neglect the extent to which elites also share in the democratic myths. And, because of their acceptance of the elitist model of democracy, they ignore the extent to which the balance between allegiance and alienation among the non-elite is determined by the actual availability of opportunities for participation and political influence.[12]

Furthermore, the nature of the 'culture-mix' required for stable democracy is nowhere precisely stated in the civility studies. It may well be true, as Rose points out, that this 'avoids giving a false sense of precision.'[13] But, if we are to test any hypothesis relating culture-mix to stable democracy, some more or less precise specification of the range of variation in deference and participation is quite essential. This requirement is underlined by consideration of the explanation provided by Evans-Pritchard and Fortes for the stability of African political systems. These anthropologists argue that the stability of primitive political systems is due to 'a balance between power and authority on the one side and obligation and responsibility on the other.' Indeed, '(t)he structure of an African state implies that kings and chiefs rule by consent. A ruler's subjects are as fully aware of the duties he owes to them as they are of the duties they owe to him, and are able to exert pressure to make him discharge these duties.'[14] But if the stability of African kingdoms as well as of Western democracies is explicable in terms of a balance between acquiescence and participation, then something more than the general principle of 'balance' is required to explain particular instances of stability. In effect, this balance must be specified so as to allow for the institutional structure and distribution of power in the societies concerned. The precise nature of the balance will clearly vary from society to society and it is a recognition of this important and obvious fact that is missing in the civility studies.

The civility studies further complicate matters by arguing that this balance (however struck) may be achieved either through a balance between different orientations within each individual or through a balance across individuals who have different patterns or orientation. Yet we also need some stipulation of the relative efficacy of the two distributions if the hypothesis is to be tested. There is also the difficult problem of ranking cultures in terms of a dualistic political orientation—can one usefully discuss variation in deferential and participatory attitudes in terms of a *single* ranking criterion or must one make do with a partial ordering and its attendant problems?

A first requirement of an adequate explanation is that the variables under investigation be carefully defined. But the civility studies do not discuss the nature of democracy in any great detail and seem, as do most elitist theorists, to equate it with the Anglo-American system of government. This failure is related to another —the basic circularity of the arguments involved. This becomes apparent in Verba's discussion of the methodology of the civic culture study. He writes that the civic culture model 'derives from an examination of democratic institutions as well as analysis of the experience of two relatively stable democracies, the United States and the United Kingdom.'[15] That is, the model was developed from an examination of the polities of the two countries whose stability it is supposed to explain and whose culture is found to correspond most closely to that required by the civic culture model! When Verba goes on to point out that '(t)hough the civic culture is conducive to the maintenance of democracy where it is found (*sc.* in the United States and Great Britain), there have been just too few studies to allow one to assume that it is the only feasible pattern for democratic politics,'[16] it becomes just a little unclear as to exactly what the civic culture model is meant to explain and how comparative an approach it permits.

Similar criticisms apply to the treatment of the major dependent variable—stability. Almond and Verba leave it undefined and Nordlinger treats it simply as the persistence of constitutions and governments through time. Even given adequate definitions of the democratic system and the major independent and dependent variables one would require that the civic culture be related to stability by virtue of some specific causal laws. Yet Almond and Verba merely talk of a 'fit' between the civic culture and stability and Verba admits that there may be other cultures that fit as well. Nordlinger, however, argues that the dualistic political orientation is a necessary condition of stability in a democratic polity and that, given the technological and institutional infrastructure, it is also a sufficient condition.[17]

But even the dualistic political orientation appears to be absent in at least one class of stable liberal bourgeois democracy —those with subcultural cleavages and with tendencies towards immobilism and instability which are deliberately turned into more stable systems by the leaders of the major subcultural groups. In these systems it is elite rather than non-elite political cultures that (*pace* Nordlinger) are the key independent variable. More-over, one of the favourable conditions for stability in such 'con-sociational democracies'[18] is the existence (*pace* Almond and Verba) of very distinct lines of cleavage between different racial, ethnic, linguistic, or other subcultures, rather than a balance between consensus and cleavage. In this way little opportunity is provided for face-to-face conflict and there is a strong possi-bility that the self-defeating nature of conflict will be recognised Two other conditions are a widespread approval of government by 'grand coalition' and a moderate degree of nationalism.[19] Even if it is argued that these conditions suggest the existence of acquiescent and consensual orientations, it must still be admitted that the manner in which the appropriate culture-mix is achieved is rather different from that implied in the civility studies. In short, the existence of stable 'consociational democracies' under-lines the importance of specifying the balance required in a political culture in the light of the particular institutional and power conditions of different societies.

Finally, it may be noted that Almond and Verba and Nord-linger do not satisfactorily consider the problem of the direction of the causal relationship, if any, between political culture and political stability. It is possible that effective and authentic democracy results in a civic culture rather than that the civic culture produces stability in such a system. The pattern of responses to items tapping subjective competence strongly suggests that the direction of causality is from political performance to civility rather than vice versa. For those nations are subjectively most competent that have most cause to be so and, within each nation, those in higher socio-economic strata express more competence than those of lower status.[20] Furthermore, Verba's discussion of Germany provides no data which would enable one to demonstrate that the political culture changed between the downfall of the Third Reich and the stabilisation of the Bonn Republic—yet just such data would be required to test the direction of causality in this case study. The limited evidence available—both in Verba's own discussion and in Edinger's analysis of the Federal Republic's political culture—suggests that the effectiveness and stability of the Bonn governments is producing acquiescence and participant orientations rather than vice versa.[21]

The main problem with the deference studies was the ambiguity of the 'deference' concept and the resulting failure to discuss the mechanisms whereby deferential orientations are translated into political action. The civility studies display the same problem on another level. They are very unclear as to the nature of the balance required for stability and consequently fail to relate in any meaningful or causally adequate manner the pattern of civic orientations to political stability. In short, both themes are vitiated on the theoretical level—whatever their empirical contributions —by a failure to specify their independent variables and relate them to the topics they are meant to explain.

3.3 Class theory and stability

The persistent attachment among some writers to the civic culture or citizenship approach to political stability cannot be based on its adequacy as a theoretical model. Nor can it be due to lack of satisfactory alternatives. For these abound in no mean measure. Almost all of them, it is true, also emphasise the importance of consensus, of one kind or another, in securing stability. Indeed, recent Marxist writings are particularly prone to emphasise the importance of consensus—even if a 'false' consensus—in the stability of capitalist societies. The problem thereby posed is that of the compatibility of consensus with persistent, socially structured inequalities. Just as class theory is often taken to imply that workers cannot (or should not) vote for a conservative party so it may seem odd that subordinate classes accept the institutional structure and values that create and define their lowly position in society. Why is it that individuals who so obviously differ in their command over power and rewards none the less share certain common values and manage to co-operate in the maintenance of society so that these inequalities are continually reproduced and often intensified? Is the explanation to be found in theories that deny the importance of class or is this problem also capable of resolution within a class theoretical framework?

Several writers, both Marxist and non-Marxist, are confident of their abilities to handle this problem. For, just as a class theory of voting requires us to look at more than class-in-itself at a given point in time, so, too, a class theory of stability involves more than Aristotelian digressions on the size of the middle class or the extent of inequality. They argue that a large part of the explanation is to be found in basic structural characteristics of a class society that operate to produce attachments not only to conservative parties but also to liberal bourgeois institutions as a whole. We have already discussed the microsocial pressures and macrostructural factors that inhibit the emergence of radical class consciousness and encourage the acceptance of dominant values (see Chapter 2). Before proceeding to an appraisal of this approach, however, it is necessary to mention several other features of class stratified societies that are alleged to facilitate the stability of the political system as a whole.

Firstly, unequal control over the means of production is generally accompanied by unequal control over the 'means of mental production' so that values favourable to stability are propounded and reinforced more effectively than potentially destabilising or dissensual values. In the light of our earlier discussion, this factor requires no further comment. Secondly, social relations in a capitalist society are mystificatory and disguise the 'true' extent of exploitation and oppression. The formal equalities of the economic and political markets, for example, although combined with substantial real inequalities, none the less tend to legitimate the *status quo*. Related to this is the institutionalisation of the class struggle which has been effected through the incorporation of unions and labour parties into the key structures and day-to-day running of state and economy. Technology has also contributed increasingly to the mystification of power and exchange relations. Not only has it greatly facilitated a continuous expansion in economic production and political policy benefits, it has also encouraged accommodative and deferential attitudes through its elevation of the technical expert and through its apparently autonomous and impersonal constraints on individual action in a secular society.[22]

Thirdly, while it would be wrong to treat ideological hegemony purely as something that just happens, merely as a superstructural derivative of economic and social domination, it is also misleading to treat it entirely as something deliberately created by a ruling class through indoctrination and manipulation. For a stable system is, in many respects, self-sustaining. Subordinate involvement in institutions is often sufficient to lead to their acceptance without further effort on the part of dominant elites. People come to accept that which exists as legitimate—not consciously as a result of moral reflection but unthinkingly as a result of their continuous involvement in its ongoing operations. If institutions are once reified in this way, it becomes difficult to challenge them as long as they continue to work reasonably well. And even then the challenge will often take the form of a reassertion of the basic values overarching the institution and an effort to respecify them in changed circumstances.[23] Finally, even when these three sets of factors do not produce consensus, it is occasionally argued that consensus is not all that important in any case. If institutional integration is assured, then the attitudes of less powerful members of society are irrelevant provided they can be induced or coerced into compliance. In the absence of a dominant consensus, the presence of mere muddle and inconsistency in the attitudes and values of the non-elite will be sufficient to ensure stability.[24]

These factors and processes have a cumulative effect on social consciousness to produce a more or less willing compliance among the subordinate classes in the operation and reproduction of the total system. In this respect, moreover, we must not ignore the virtuous circle that connects such hegemonic stability and its material base. For, on the one hand, legitimacy and stability permit the continuing expansion of production in different power systems and a continuing increase in the absolute levels of reward going to the periphery; and, on the other hand, this ability of the system to 'deliver the goods' expected by subordinate classes encourages the legitimation of the system. In the absence of emergent contradictions that destabilise the system, redistribute power, or shatter the reified values of those involved, the system is largely self-sustaining.[25] Thus, the combined result of institutional inertia, increasing production, and conscious indoctrination, is political, economic, and social stability.

This sort of theorising is not totally unproblematic. Indeed, so inclusive and all-encompassing is it, that any empirical test is extremely difficult. Particularly problematic in this respect are the manifold ramifications and interrelations among the basic concepts of the theory. The notion of ruling class or dominant elite, for example, cannot be considered independently from the related concepts of 'ruling ideas' or dominant values and consensus, since part of the explanation of class rule hinges on its ability to secure consensus on its ideas. If a given class cannot establish such agreement, then its domination is correspondingly reduced. Yet the circle must be broken if class theories of political stability are to be tested. This requires an independent specification of the dominant elites so that we can then compare the commitment of other classes, strata, and political groupings, to the dominant values thereby indicated. We shall indeed attempt such a specification and comparison in our next chapter, when we come finally to examine the nature, content, and distribution of British political culture.

If it is true, however, that, as inequalities of power increase, the extent of consensus required for stability decreases, we may even find that dissensus on the values of the dominant elites is compatible with stability. This problem is less relevant to an analysis of class theories of voting behaviour because the electoral situation is one of institutionalised formal equality and every vote has more or less the same value. Outside the realm of formal equalities the relation between consensus and power becomes especially important. Thus, while a conservative party must actually win a majority of individual votes to secure governmental power, it is usually sufficient for stability that the powerful minority can reach an understanding among themselves. The crucial factor in the latter context is not consensus, therefore, but institutional integration at the centre. This has been recognised not only by class theorists but also by the elitist theorists of democracy. Indeed, in the face of overwhelming empirical evidence that most citizens are politically apathetic and misunderstand or even reject democratic principles, the elitist theorists have almost been forced into a 'realistic,' 'empirical' acceptance of the critical importance of specifically elite consensus.[26] Class analysis goes beyond elitist empirical democratic theories, however, in attempting to explain this non-elite outlook as the product of particular societal structures and in questioning the validity of western democracy.

3.4 An alternative approach

In discussing the deference studies and the class theory of political behaviour, we argued that it was possible to link these interpretations via the distinction between dominant and contracultural values and their basis in social structure. A similar line is possible in the case of civility and hegemony. For a reading of the civic culture studies themselves and an examination of British political culture both suggest that civility is a major element in the dominant political value system. Accordingly, we should not treat it as a mere theoretical model constructed by political scientists to specify the necessary and/or sufficient conditions of stability; rather, we should treat it as an attempt to describe the dominant political values of Great Britain and the United States. Indeed, as Verba himself points out, these values are the original source of ideas for the model. Once this is recognised, it becomes a simple matter to relate civility to stability by assuming that a commitment to the dominant value system is a precondition of stability in any society. In his respect, it is even possible to support the general elitist assumption that such commitment needs to be greatest among elites and can be relatively limited and ambivalent among the non-elite. For the weight to be attached to any individual's opinion, as we have argued several times before, is mainly determined by the power he can wield.

To adopt such an approach is to deny the validity neither of civility theories nor of class theories. On the contrary, it only specifies their relevance to political stability in Britain. The importance of civility is recognised in treating it as a key element in the dominant political value system and its elitist implications are thereby rendered understandable. Likewise, class theory is used to analyse the incidence of civic orientations as well as the non-normative sources of political passivity. For, in addition to those who believe it is proper to defer to the government, there are others who are simply indifferent, fatalistic, or alienated. The sorts of factors mentioned above, and central to class theories, would seem to explain this pasivity rather well. Thus, in the case of the civility theme as well as that of deference, we find that, while there are good reasons for questioning their utility and/or validity, there are also good reasons for retaining them in reformulated versions that are then articulated with class analysis. It is with the merits of such reformulated versions that we shall be concerned in the remaining chapters.

3.5 Notes and references

1 Almond and Verba, *Civic Culture*, p473.
2 *Ibid*, p477; and Nordlinger, *Tories*, p211. This sort of definition generally derives from the well-known reformulation of democratic theory provided by J A Schumpeter in his *Capitalism, Socialism, and Democracy* (London: Allen and Unwin, 1950), pp269–96.
3 Nordlinger, *Tories*, pp210–26 and esp. 218; Almond and Verba, *Civic Culture*, pp22 and 31.
4 Nordlinger, *Tories*, p218; Almond and Verba, *Civic Culture*, pp23–6.
5 Nordlinger, *Tories*, pp214–15; Almond and Verba, *Civic Culture*, pp21–2 and 479–87.

6 These other functions are: the facilitation of civic co-operation among citizens, the moderation of emotional attachments to sub-national groups, and the distantiation of the individual from the elite. See Almond and Verba, *Civic Culture*, pp487–92; and Nordlinger, *Tories*, pp218–24.

7 Almond and Verba, *Civic Culture*, p498.

8 *Ibid*, p499; Nordlinger, *Tories*, pp123–36.

9 See, for example, B Berelson *et al*, *Voting* (Chicago: University of Chicago Press, 1954), pp305–23; B Crick, *In Defense of Politics* (Harmondsworth: Penguin, 1964); R A Dahl, *Who Governs?* (New Haven: Yale University Press, 1961), pp223–8; Eckstein, in *Division and Cohesion*, pp225–88; W A Gamson, *Power and Discontent* (Homewood: Dorsey, 1968), pp2–21; M B Levin, *The Alienated Voter* (New York: Holt, Reinhart, and Winston, 1960), pp61–75; W Lippmann, *The Public Philosophy* (London: Mentor, 1964), pp30–70 and 123–38; T Parsons, '"Voting" and the equilibrium of the American political system,' in *American Voting Behaviour*, edited by E Burdick and M Brodbeck (New York: Free Press, 1959) esp. pp91–3; E A Shils, 'Ideology and civility,' *Sewanee Review* (1958), lxvi, pp450–80; and *idem*, 'The prospects for Lebanese civility,' in *Politics in Lebanon*, edited by L Binder (New York: Wiley, 1966), pp1–13.

10 See J Walker, 'A reply to "Further reflections on the elitist theory of democracy",' *Am. Pol. Sc. Rev.* (1966), lx, pp391–2. Other criticisms of the civility studies are to be found in: B M Barry, *Sociologists, Economists, and Democracy* (London: Collier-Macmillan, 1970); P Bachrach, *The Theory of Democratic Elitism* (London: University of London Press, 1969); C Pateman, *Participation and Democratic Theory* (London: Cambridge University Press, 1970); W G Runciman, 'Some recent contributions to the theory of democracy,' *Eur. J. Socio.* (1965), vi, pp174–85; and D Thompson, *The Democratic Citizen* (London: Cambridge University Press, 1970).

11 Nordlinger, *Tories*, p213; Almond and Verba, *Civic Culture*, p486 and 486n.

12 *cf* Barry, *Sociologists*, pp51–2; and Pateman, in *Br. J. Pol. Sc.* (1970),

13 *cf* R Rose, *People in Politics* (London: Faber, 1970), p50.

14 *cf* E E Evans-Pritchard and M Fortes, Editors, *African Political Systems* (London: Oxford University Press, 1940), p12.

15 *cf* S Verba, 'Germany: the remaking of a political culture,' in *Political Culture and Political Development*, edited by L W Pye (Princeton: Princeton University Press, 1965), pp130–70 at p133.

16 *Ibid*, p134.

17 Almond and Verba, *Civic Culture*, p473; Nordlinger, *Tories*, pp250–2.

18 *cf* A Lijphart, 'Typologies of democratic systems,' *Comparative Pol. Stud.* (1968), i, pp3–44; and *idem*, 'Consociational Democracy,' *World Pol.*, xxi, 1969, pp207–26. The consociational democracies reviewed by Lijphart are: Austria, Switzerland, Lebanon, Holland, Belgium, and Luxembourg.

19 Lijphart, in *Comp. Pol. Stud.* (1968), p25.

20 Almond and Verba, *Civic Culture*, *passim*.

21 Verba, in *Political Culture and Political Development*; L Edinger, *Politics in Germany* (Boston: Little-Brown, 1968), pp81–122.

22 The factors cited in this paragraph are discussed in more detail in one or more of the following: Parkin, *Class Inequality*, pp48–102; H Marcuse, *One-Dimensional Man* (London: Sphere, 1968) and *idem* in *Critique of Pure Tolerance*; J. Habermas, *Toward a Rational Society* (London: Heinemann, 1971), esp. pp62–122; R Glasser, *The New High Priesthood* (London:

Macmillan, 1967), esp. pp122–65; N Young, 'Prometheans or troglodytes: the English working class and the dialectics of incorporation,' *Berkeley J. Sociol.* (1967), xii, pp1–27; R Miliband, *The State in Capitalist Society* (London: Weidenfeld and Nicolson, 1968), pp146–229 and *passim*; and Anderson and Blackburn, *Towards Socialism, passim*.

23 *cf* Arnold, *Symbols*, p106; and N J Smelser, *Theory of Collective Behaviour* (London: Routledge, 1962).

24 See especially M J Mann, 'The social cohesion of liberal democracy,' in *Am. Sociol. Rev.* (1970), xxx, pp423–39.

25 For a fuller discussion, see Jessop, *Social Order*, pp127–31.

26 See, for example, H J McCloskey, 'Consensus and ideology in American politics,' *Am. Pol. Sc. Rev.* (1964), lviii, pp361–82.

Chapter 4

Political Parties and Political Culture

We have now presented theoretical critiques of the civility and deference themes and have suggested their reformulation in terms of class theory. If we are to assess the validity of these reinterpretations, three main problems must be considered. Firstly, a model of the power structure must be constructed so that we can determine the nature and content of the dominant value system. Secondly, the attitudes and images of the main political parties must be considered in relation to the dominant values. Finally, some attention must be paid to the general character of popular beliefs in a class-based hegemonic society so that we can assess the available British data against an appropriate model. Only then will it be possible to state some preliminary conclusions concerning the validity of the deference and class theories of voting behaviour and the civility and hegemony interpretations of stability. We discuss the first two of these issues in this chapter and the third issue in the next chapter.

4.1 The structure of power in Britain

In the ensuing pages we shall be concerned primarily with the extent to which different classes and party groups are committed to dominant and deviant values and institutions. Any study of dominant values must be premised on a model of the power structure. However, there are many competing models for Britain— ranging from exoteric constitutional history, where power resides with the people in parliament, to esoteric neo-Marxist models, for which power resides in reified structures.[1] Rather than conduct an exhaustive inquiry into the structure of power, we shall take as given the relatively pluralistic model implied by some neo-Marxist writers and use it as the basis for our investigations.

This model sees power as exercised and held by various groups and institutions rather than by a single, monolithic ruling class.

Even if power is ultimately rooted in control over the means of production, it is none the less mediated through many agencies and institutions. Moreover, notwithstanding this basic plurality in the exercise and holding of power, there are distinct, structured inequalities in the distribution of control and rewards so that competition between different classes and strata is far from perfect. Most important and powerful are the various capitalist organisations and institutions together with the traditional upper social and economic classes. In alliance with these forces, the state is also playing an increasingly important role in the maintenance and reproduction of inequalities. The bureaucratic and military elites play a supporting role rather than an autonomous, independently influential one. The whole structure is characterised by institutional integration and is able to maintain itself in control through a combination of hegemony, institutional inertia, and the skilful exercise of social, economic, and political power. In comparison institutions and groups such as the unions, co-operatives, nationalised industries, consumer groups, the labour movement, and all non-elites are seen as having little fundamental power however greatly they can momentarily tilt the balance that exists between the dominant elites and the rest of society.[2] Such is the model that we shall use to construct the dominant cultural system. We are not concerned to demonstrate its ultimate validity but simply wish to see whether it is a useful interpretive tool in the present context. That is, does the dominant ideology implied by such a model enable us better to understand British politics?

This model involves several immediate implications for the nature and content of the dominant value system. It will clearly be concerned with the legitimation of these dominant institutions and their power and rewards. Private enterprise will be identified with the national interest, the benefits of *noblesse oblige* in a hierarchically structured society will be emphasised, the functional necessity of economic inequalities will be stressed, and so on. Conversely, attempts to undermine or overthrow these institutions and to challenge the structure of power will be derogated in the strongest terms. Secondly, in so far as the structure of power does change, the dominant value system will also change correspondingly. While many of today's dominant institutions could also be included in a list for the nineteenth or earlier centuries, the actual constellation of power and the exact composition of the elites that command them has changed constantly. Because the processes of change have been so gradual and gentle, however, the immediate impression is one of cultural and political continuity.

In three hundred years Britain has changed from a pre-dominantly agricultural and rural society via an entrepreneurial industrial society into a managerial, bureaucratic, industrialised and urbanised society. The landed aristocracy, monarchy, and the church have lost power and the Cabinet, the civil service, and, to some extent, organised labour, have each gained in power. The Empire has come and almost gone; the Commonwealth that replaced it is now in decline. However, the changes that have occurred have been slow—the result of an emphasis on adaptation, assimilation, compromise, and consensus within the changing plurality of elites. In no institution is this more clear than the Conservative Party. It has always sought to unify the political opinions of different groups in the ruling class and to enable new elites to enter the governing circle at the same time as it quietly drops the political interests of declining classes and elites.[3] Moreover, those elites and institutions that have declined have not been dismissed totally from the political or economic stage—they retain much of their symbolic significance even when they have not, as with the monarchy, actually increased it. They also retain important vestiges of actual power and continue to have mystificatory effects. The overall result is a certain inconsistency, obscurity, and muddle in the dominant ideology at any given time and a general impression of stability in the midst of change. It is for this reason that 'traditionalism' is a particularly appropriate term for the dominant value system.

Thirdly, with particular reference to ascriptive social deference rather than traditionalism as a whole, the pattern of recruitment to the dominant elites indicated in this model has quite clear implications for appreciation and derogation. It is a sociological commonplace that recruitment into these elites is strongly influenced by traditional, ascriptive criteria. The upper middle class is not only the most successful in terms of self-recruitment overall, it also provides a vastly disproportionate number of recruits into the centre. Much of this recruitment is channelled via the public and direct grant schools and/or the ancient universities (see Table 4.1). It is also clear that some elites are socially more exclusive than others. The dominant economic elites, especially the City elite, together with Conservative Cabinets and the top professions, have the strongest representation of traditional upper middle class recruits. The civil service, the Labour Party, the trade unions (not included in Table 4.1), and the academic profession are less exclusive in this respect. This is also apparent if one examines the type of public school attended—

E

Clarendon schools being more strongly represented in the former elites than the latter. It is also universally true that the higher one proceeds in each elite, the more exclusive the backgrounds of its members become. We can see this pattern in a comparison of managers with directors, academics in general and the Oxbridge elite, bishops and archbishops, judges and Law Lords, administrative officers in the civil service and the topmost administrators, MPs and Cabinet Ministers, and even unsuccessful candidates. in parliamentary elections and local government compared with successful candidates.[4] Of particular interest is the fact that those elites cited as most dominant in the model are also the most exclusive.

Table 4.1 RECRUITMENT TO DOMINATE ELITES IN BRITAIN

Elite group	Public school %	Direct grant %	Oxon Cantab %	Upper middle %	Working class %	Source
Economic						
Bank of England	77	6				Newsom
Top directors	77	11				Newsom
1000 directors	58		20	54+		Copeman
10 000 directors	48	13				Frankel
Top professions	69					Bishop
Political						
1963 Con Cabinet	91					Newsom
1970 Con Cabinet	67					Original
1967 Lab Cabinet	42					Newsom
1970 Con MPs	50		53			Times
1970 Lab MPs	10		31			Times
Local councils				11	46	Sharpe
CLP leaders				32		Janosik
Quasi-political						
Generals 1870–59	90+			90		Otley
1968 Law List	81		76			Goldstein
Top Military 1967	55	15				Newsom
1966 Top Admin	54					Chapman
1966 Admin C/Serv	55					Chapman
Admin entrants	34	29		50		Chapman
Committee men	46		48		6	Guttsman
Hospital boards				80		Stewart
Cultural						
Bishops 1960–8	85	6	89	72		Morgan
BBC Governors	50+		56	40	12	Guttsman
Oxbridge heads	49	11				Newsom
Redbrick heads	33	13				Newsom
All academics	21	10	30	20	38	Halsey
Chancellors 1967			84			Collison

For sources, see footnote 4 below.

Whether or not one wishes to dignify this bias with the accolade of a 'central value' does not affect the significant demonstration effects that such bias must have for the subordinate classes. Moreover, so obvious is this pattern of recruitment, that it has attracted its own set of legitimations that seek to justify it to the classes left out in the cold. To the extent that such legitimations and demonstration effects are operative among subordinate classes, it is reasonable to expect that they will employ the same criteria when they themselves have the chance of selecting the members of an elite—in elections to parliament, local government, voluntary association committees, and so on. This argument stands whether or not such bias in selection implies anything at all about the actual values and policy preferences of individual members of powerful and prestigious elites.[5]

In addition to this particular effect, however, these recruitment data also have several other implications. There is some evidence, for example, that achievement-oriented criteria apply in the recruitment to elite positions that require little or no capital or few family connections for successful performance. The civil service, academic life, local government administration, the lower professions, and union organisation, are five examples. While none of these exactly qualify as dominant elites it is also true that upper middle-class background is not absolutely necessary for recruitment into the latter even if it is a considerable help. The demonstration effect will be qualified to the extent that this is known among the periphery. Moreover, it means that some members of all elites, and certain elites as a whole, will not share the predominant background of the centre. Whether or not this affects the attitudes of individual members will depend on the extent to which participation and promotion within the relevant elite turns on values as well as, or instead of, background. If advancement depends on accepting or affirming certain dominant values, then background is neither here nor there. However, it is quite likely that those whose position and life-chances depend on intellectual attainments and professional qualifications are less likely to be committed to traditionalism than those whose position depends on having the 'right' background and education and on the ownership of property and inherited capital.[6] This applies not only to individual members of any elite but also to those elites as a whole that depend more on intellectual than material resources.

There also seems to be some evidence from these recruitment data to suggest the emergence of new values and institutions associated with the technological and economic systems and also the increasing integration of the Labour Party into the centre. This is suggested in any case by the changing constellation of power within the economy and the increasing emphasis on technological progress and economic growth in the dominant ideology.[7] Within the Conservative Party, for example, landowners and company directors seem to be in decline compared with the increasing numbers of economic technocrats who have entered Parliament under Heath's leadership.[8] This reflects one aspect of the integration of new elites and institutions into the centre. Rapidly growing fields, such as property speculation, investment trust management, the science- and technology-based industries, will always push new men into positions of power and influence. But, as these institutions become established, a complex integrative process occurs. On the one hand, the ascendant institutions are incorporated into the centre and linked with already established organisations and elites through various techniques such as mutual accommodation, mergers, interlocking directorates, intermarriage, political penetration, and social interaction. On the other hand, new entrants into these institutions become increasingly exclusive in background. Just as the Conservative Party is able to absorb ascendant classes and strata, so, too, the public schools not only absorb their offspring but also send many of their other alumni into fields that have acquired a position of some dominance. Technology and science, the mass media, advertising, and public relations, are coming to take their place alongside business, trade, and the Labour Party in this respect.[9] This last aspect is reflected in the increasing social and economic *embourgeoisement* of the Labour Party which is slowly losing such working-class MPs as it has.[10] Even if the values and criteria of dominant elites change, it would seem that the class that meets them remains the same.

Finally, and with particular reference to civility rather than traditionalism, the present model has obvious implications for the general patterns of authority and participation that will be preferred by the dominant elites. One does not have to accept the precise formulation of Eckstein's congruency theory of political stability to see that, in an institutionally integrated centre, nonpolitical power and authority structures will influence expectations as to the appropriate role of the periphery within the political system. Eckstein shows that there is a remarkable similarity between the authority patterns of government and administration in Britain and those of parties and pressure groups Moreover, other institutions, such as big business corporations, public schools, trade unions, professional associations, and the Whitehall clubs, are also structured in this way. The basic pattern is one of strong leadership tempered by constitutionalism—that is, one of a relatively autonomous and secure leadership restrained by a broad and explicit framework of procedural and substantive rules. Democratic participation has only a small part in the overall pattern.[11] The same elitist pattern characterises the relations between dominant institutions as well as their internal organisation. Even where there are severe disagreements on specific issues and policies, for example, the different elites agree to confine bargaining and consultation to the centre and not to include outsiders who might 'rock the boat.'[12] The collectivist, corporate state is certainly pluralistic but it only recognises a plurality of elites and dominant institutions.[13]

It is hardly surprising, therefore, that the dominant version of the civic culture is also elitist and authoritarian rather than egalitarian and participatory in content. The starting point and mainspring of political action, as so many writers have argued, has always been the government.[14] While the idea of the 'balanced constitution' dates at least from the eighteenth century, when it was the basis of the Old Whig view of representation, the balance between authority and popular participation has always been weighted more heavily in favour of the former than the latter. This can be seen not only in the various political theories but also in the practice of institutions. The role of the voter, for example, is confined to making a highly structured and intermittent choice between two alternatives put to him by party 'selectorates' and then to allowing the government to get on with its task of government. The political parties are correspondingly authoritarian and hierarchical in structure, Parliament is composed of MPs who are party members first and delegates second, and the Cabinet is relatively independent of the legislative assembly.[15] It is not accidental that the whole system has so often been described as being monarchical in character.[16]

Although our choice of model may seem arbitrary, certain conclusions about the dominant value system none the less follow quite firmly. It remains to see, therefore, whether or not these implications prove useful in understanding political attitudes and behaviour. In terms of the present model we would expect commitments to the dominant value system to be shown in a receptive affirmation of such traditional and symbolic institutions as the Church, religion, the Royal Family, Empire, and aristocracy; and also of such powerful institutions and elites as the public schools, the ancient universities, the parliamentary system, the military and bureaucratic elites, the mass media, and, above all else, private productive property and capitalist enterprise.[17] Furthermore, it would also be apparent in deferential behaviour towards dominant elites and institutions and, particularly in the present context, electoral support for parties identified with these elites and institutions together with a more general acceptance of an extremely limited political role. Finally, if it is true that an increasing emphasis is being placed on scientific and technical industries, on the importance of economic growth, and on the co-operation of the state and industry in the pursuit of these aims, then people committed to dominant institutions and values should also support these goals and practices.

4.2   Political parties and dominant values

Parkin has argued that Labour voting in any class must be seen (or can usefully be seen) as deviant in terms of the dominant value system and that identification with this value system leads to Tory voting. However, he presents no direct evidence on the relation between voting behaviour and dominant value commitments, relying instead on correlations between social location and voting to support his case. But in what ways may the dominant value system be said to prescribe, approve, or encourage Conservative voting and to prohibit, derogate, or discourage Labour sympathies? Moreover, Nordlinger has argued, although in a different context, that, if a political system is to be stable, then supporters of all major parties must be committed to the (dominant) civic culture.[18] He, too, presents little direct evidence for this argument. But, if the Labour Party is committed to the civic culture as Nordlinger implies, then how or why does it avoid commitment to other dominant values? Or is it the case that the Labour Party is neither traditional nor civil, or, perhaps, neither radical nor incivil? It is these problems we shall consider in this section— beginning with a discussion of the ways in which dominant values could be linked with political parties and voting behaviour.

Conservative voting could be a dominant value in its own right —prescribed by those with most power not only for themselves but also for the rest of society. The economic, political, social, and cultural elites may publicly endorse Conservatism and derogate Labour sympathies in addition to their advocacy of other values and beliefs. Alternatively, without being actively encouraged by these elites as a civic virtue, Conservative sympathies could none the less follow from attachment to dominant institutions. If voters come to see—or are encouraged to see—the Conservative Party as symbolically identified with the dominant order and/or defending its material interests, then it is possible that they will also come to support that party at the polls. Thirdly, this party could itself create such an identification through its own propaganda efforts. If it emphasised its affinities with dominant elites, publicly identified itself with the central values, and sought to defend dominant institutions against attack, then it could generate the necessary votes for political victory.

Conversely, the Labour Party could be negatively identified with these values, institutions, and elites, as a result of its own attacks on them. Those who support the dominant order could well be led to vote Conservative simply because of Labour policies on nationalisation, public schools, decolonisation, or hereditary peerages. Fifthly, other deviant or subordinate movements, such as trade unions, cooperatives, tenants' associations, pacifist movements, or fringe leftwing political groups, could attack the dominant order and the Conservative Party and perhaps endorse the Labour movement. This might have the effect of strengthening traditionalist support for the Tories and increasing countercultural allegiance to the Labour Party. Lastly, Labour voting could emerge simply from individual reflection on the demerits of dominant institutions and elites and on their symbolic or material identification with the Conservative Party or similar, but negative, association with the Labour Party.

There is some evidence for the operation of all six mechanisms in British politics. Whether or not this means that they are major determinants of voting behaviour is an entirely different question. Thus dominant institutions and elites do tend publicly to endorse and sustain the Conservatives. This is particularly apparent in the contributions and proclamations of private enterprise and in the party's leadership by the traditional upper middle classes. It is true that this support is neither unanimous nor uncritical but, even within the centre, those elites and institutions that are formally neutral or prone to support Labour are less dominant than those that favour the Tory Party. Moreover, even without such explicit endorsement, voters could be led to identify the Conservative Party with the dominant order by virtue of the style and background of its local and national leaders and also the type of legislation and governmental role it favours. Moreover, the Party itself has encouraged such an identification in popular party literature and platform rhetoric. Indeed, McKenzie and Silver conclude their review of Tory propaganda since 1867 as follows:

The central argument which emerges in the popular party literature is that the Conservatives are uniquely qualified to govern Britain and that the institutions of the country are safe in their hands alone. ... Since the Liberals, Radicals, and Socialists have no real concern for the greatness of their country, they are disposed to betray its interests to her enemies, and they are therefore wholly to be distrusted in the handling of defence and imperial and colonial affairs. And in their domestic policies, the parties of the left, by their attacks on British institutions—the monarchy, the House of Lords, religion, and the established economic order, including above all the institution of private property—and by their attempts to foment jealousy between classes, represent a fatal threat to the unity and well-being of the national community ... Furthermore, the standard of living of the workers is best guaranteed by a party which understands and is competent to manage the economy ... (Elections are therefore) moments of considerable national peril when the electorate, if they are sufficiently misguided, may respond to the siren call of the 'general uprooters of all that is national and good.'[19]

From this review and that of Harris on postwar economic thought in the Conservative Party, it is abundantly obvious that it has sought not only to defend but also to identify itself positively and exclusively with the dominant order.[20] The attempt is not likely to have been hindered by elite endorsement and the party's obvious affinities with the dominant order.

The attitude of the Labour Party to these central values and institutions is far less clearcut and unambiguous. It did not become a socialist party even in theory until 1918 and from the start it embraced not only gradualist parliamentarism but also many Liberal policies and much of the social conservatism of the union leaders. The Labour Party has continued to show a fundamental ambivalence towards socialist values and policies ever since and has generally resolved the resulting tensions in favour of those on the centre or the right. There are few members even in the constituency parties who are totally opposed to the dominant order and the increasing proportion of middle- and upper-middle-class members will probably further dampen their influence.[21] A populist strain in party rhetoric has certainly produced attacks on monarchy, aristocracy, militarism, public schools, inherited privilege, empire, and capitalism. But it has rarely been articulated with radical, politically class-conscious proposals and the same brand of populism has been associated with the defence of a national nuclear policy, xenophobic reactions to immigration, anti-intellectualism, suspicion of the Soviet Union, and other views more often associated with the Conservative Party's image.[22] While the more liberal and progressive party members have opposed these latter views, they have not exactly adopted class warfare as the appropriate basis of Labour policies and programmes. On the contrary, their primary orientation is towards personal or individual rights rather than the total reorganisation of society or even the simple redress of class or group inequalities.[23] While the Labour Party is at best a 'trade union-conscious' party in rhetoric, therefore, in many respects it is practically indistinguishable from the left and centre of the Tory Party.

Moreover, when we turn from party rhetoric to look at Labour's actual performance, it appears even less radical and opposed to the dominant order. Labour politicians and trade unionists legitimate the aristocracy and monarchy through their acceptance of peerages. They support the established church and religion in general. Labour has done very little to undermine the public schools even though it has introduced comprehensive schooling in the state sector. It is a parliamentarist party *par excellence* with a firm commitment to the liberal bourgeois institutions of our political system. Above all, it is committed to a strengthening of the capitalist order rather than to its abolition. Even before the last war its economic policies were almost identical with those of the Tory Party and there has been little real divergence since.[24] With the possible exception of steel nationalisation (described significantly enough as a hostage to its left wing) and its experiment with nationalised road haulage, the Labour Party has sought to increase the international competitiveness and efficiency of British industry. It adopted even before the Conservative Party the new techno-economistic outlook and tried to rationalise and modernise industry, to encourage the scientific and technical industries, and to pay for increased welfare benefits through economic growth rather than redistribution. If it has encouraged the development of the 'permissive society,' it has certainly not presided over any great redistribution of wealth, power, prestige, or income.[25]

To find left-wing movements critical of the dominant institutional order one must turn outside the Labour Party. It is in such fringe groups as the Communists, the new left, the anarchists, the Trotskyists, and similar movements, that opposition and radicalism are crystallised. The trade union movement is simply 'trade union' conscious and has been incorporated into the political and economic system. Likewise, the co-operative movement, originally offering a radical alternative to capitalism, is now established as one more bureaucratic, managerial, trading-stamp empire among others and has entered into partnership with many private concerns. While some of these radical fringe groups do endorse the Labour Party they are much more likely to attack it or to exploit it.[26] In any case they have a limited impact except possibly to reinforce the commitment to the *status quo* among the vast majority of citizens.

Overall, therefore, we must look for an explanation of any relationship between traditionalism and voting behaviour to the activities of the social and economic elites, the Conservative Party, the anxieties of individual voters and pressure groups, and populist and economistic words and deeds in the Labour Party and trade unions. It is by no means certain, of course, that voters will identify dominant values with the Conservative Party nor translate such an identification into electoral support. The cues stemming from the Labour Party are decidedly ambiguous and many people have only a limited sensitivity to central values, etc, and do not see macrosocial agencies as crucial to their immediate concerns. We shall see below to what extent people really view political parties in these terms and act on such images.

Even if electors are insensitive to such pressures and images, however, the mutual identification of the Conservative Party and the dominant order could still have important effects on a Labour government. For, once elected, the Labour Party would be confronted by the dominant order itself, which, given Labour's populist, economistic, and occasionally socialist rhetoric, is most unlikely to be insensitive to *its* welfare under a Labour administration. Since the structure of power is pluralistic rather than monolithic and it is the economic and social centres that are dominant rather than the governmental system, the scope for attempts to frustrate and prevent radical change is correspondingly great.[27] Moreover, since Labour government tries to intervene more than a Conservative government in economic affairs, the opportunities for bargaining and blackmail are increased *pari passu*. When one also considers the ambivalence of the Labour Party and the usual confusion among the electorate about the dominant order and radical alternatives, then it would be surprising to find a Labour administration that successfully implements radical policies without precipitating major crises, confrontations, and instabilities.[28]

Indeed, when in office, the Labour Party has accommodated

even further in its programmes and policies to the traditional, dominant social and economic order then when it is out of power. This tendency is undoubtedly due in part simply to a failure to prepare for government when in opposition, a need greater in a radical than in a conservative party, so that it is relatively easy for the civil service and economic elites to impose their views by default. But it is also related to more explicit pressures emanating from domestic and overseas economic institutions and the press— both of which are naturally concerned to protect the dominant order of which they are part. Moreover, perhaps equally important is the party's own desire to establish its 'respectability' and 'fitness to govern.' In hegemonic societies, 'respectability' and 'fitness' are defined by the dominant elites—who can also wield various sanctions against those who are not respectable and prove unfit to govern. The result is to make a Labour government especially prone to caution and safety first in its political actions. Related to this desire is a general 'establishmentarian' attitude towards the governmental machinery. Thus, Labour seeks to use the existing machinery and personnel of government to prepare and implement its policies; it appoints directors and bankers to run nationalised industries; and it relies upon pressure groups for advice and delegated administration. In all of these cases it thereby creates additional pressures to encourage the abandonment of 'unsound' ideas and the dropping of 'impractical' innovations.[29] In turn, this accommodation leads to difficulties and estrangement among the ordinary party members and supporters, whose expectations are raised by populist and economistic rhetoric and who then see the party leadership betray them in government.[30]

This is not to deny that Labour governments have implemented policies that favour subordinate groups and classes nor that they have also failed to satisfy completely the dominant elites and institutions with whom they have co-operated and compromised. Indeed, it is to argue that the position of the Labour Party in British society is such that it cannot satisfy these elites *or* its natural supporters—it must disappoint both. As Worsthorne has written, 'a Labour Government will have to operate within a context of a governing class that has been threatened but not destroyed and replaced and a working class whose expectations have been awakened but not satisfied—within a context, that is, which allows it neither to fall back on the weight of tradition nor move forward behind the momentum of revolution.[31] Even when a world war had engendered national unity, fostered massive government intervention and planning, and produced a wide-spread popular desire for radical change, the Labour Party introduced few reforms that would not have been introduced by a Tory government and soon began to dismantle such controls as it had over the economy.[32] The major achievement of Labour since the last war has been in the field of liberalisation and not in the restructuring of political and economic power.

Thus we see that, while Labour voting can usefully be interpreted as deviant in terms of dominant values and is indeed treated as such by many dominant elites, the Labour Party itself is much more difficult to see unambiguously in these terms and is indeed itself ambivalent about the dominant order. Populism and economism play a major role in Labour rhetoric and have given rise to some redistributive measures. But the Conservative Party has also engaged in such activities and 'secular' support for the Tories is apparently widespread among the subordinate classes. Moreover, the actual performance of the Labour Party in office is more suggestive of commitments to the dominant order than it is of alienation and radical opposition. In short, an examination of the political parties and dominant order does not produce any definitive conclusions as to the motivation and orientation of those who support one or other major party. It would seem perfectly possible for those who are committed to the dominant value system to support Labour as well as the Conservative Party. It is this possibility that we shall investigate in the ensuing pages.

Finally, turning from traditionalism to civility, we find that Labour is also committed, and with less ambivalence than in the former case, to the fundamental civic values of British political culture. Its devotion to a parliamentary strategy is well-known and so, too, is its basically oligarchic structure.[33] Its commitment to a balanced constitution is well illustrated in Stewart's remark that good government:

> Must be strong enough to make itself obeyed and to carry out the duties of administration efficiently. Second, it must not be so strong that it can do just what it likes, and cannot be compelled to fulfil its part of the Social Contract.[34]

This view is found not only in the centre and on the right of the Party but also on the left. While the latter has always emphasised the need for popular participation and the importance of the electoral mandate, it has always coupled this with recognition of the need for decisive (Labour) government. It is none the less true that the Labour Party has been more aware of the conflicting demands of civility than the Conservatives. Whereas the former have continually debated the relationship between elected representatives and electors, particularly as this affects the party itself, the latter have rarely been concerned with this problem and have always stressed the importance of leadership and authority.[35] But the Labour Party has also tended to resolve the conflict between popular participation and governmental authority in favour of political leadership and autonomous government. Where it differs from the orthodox Tory doctrine of the constitution is in the Labour Party's greater commitment, not to popular participation, but to individual rights and liberties and, among liberal elitists at least, rational debate and decision-making. The basic values of civility are common to all major parties.

4.3 Conclusions

Overall, therefore, it would seem that Balfour's characterisation of the party system remains true today. He argued that 'alternating Cabinets, though belonging to different Parties, have never differed about the foundations of society . . . it is evident that our whole political machine pre-supposes a people so fundamentally at one that they can safely afford to bicker; and so sure of their own moderation that they are not dangerously disturbed by the never-ending din of political conflict.'[36] While rhetorical and symbolic differences certainly do exist, these are overridden by the parties' actual behaviour in office. This displays a common commitment to the managed economy, the welfare state, the parliamentary system, and the total social structure. Actual differences in policy and practice are marginal in comparison with this fundamental agreement on the foundations of society. This in turn is one manifestation of the institutional integration characteristic of British society. The 'never-ending din' should not be confused with actual reality.

4.4 Notes and references

1 A critical appraisal of six different models of the British power structure is presented in B Jessop, *Power Systems in Britain* (Harmondsworth: Penguin, forthcoming), Chapter 2. Main references for the neo-Marxist model employed below are: P Anderson, 'Origins of the present crisis,' in *Towards Socialism*, pp11–52; Miliband, *State*; R Miliband, 'The capitalist state—a reply to Nicos Poulantzas,' *New Left Review* (1970), 59, pp53–60; T Nairn, 'The British political elite,' *New Left Review* (1964), 23, pp26–53; and P Worsley, 'The distribution of power in industrial society,' *Sociol. Rev. Monograph* 8 (1964), pp15–34.
2 *cf* A Glyn and B Sutcliffe, *British Capitalism, Workers, and the Profits Squeeze* (Harmondsworth: Penguin, 1972), *passim*.

3 *cf* N Harris, *Competition and the Corporate State* (London: Methuen, 1972), *passim.*

4 On politicians, see W L Guttsman, *The British Political Elite* (London: MacGibbon and Kee, 1965), p27 and *passim*; M Rush, *The Selection of Parliamentary Candidates* (London: Nelson, 1969); A Ranney, *Pathways to Parliament* (London: Macmillans, 1965); and Hindess, *Decline of Working Class Politics*. On the Civil Service, see R A Chapman, *The Higher Civil Service in Britain* (London: Constable, 1970), pp121–5; and R K Kelsall, *Higher Civil Servants in Britain* (London: Routledge, 1955), pp124–6. On the judiciary, see P Abrams, 'Well-bred law,' *Sunday Times* (18 August 1963); and K Goldstein-Jackson, 'The judicial elite,' *New Society* (14 May 1970). On the bishopric and clergy, see A P M Coxon, 'An elite in the making,' *New Society* (26 June 1964) and D H J Morgan, 'The social and educational background of Anglican bishops,' *Br. J. Sociol.* (1969), xx, pp295–310. On academics and chancellors, see A H Halsey and M A Trow, *The British Academics* (London: Faber and Faber, 1971), pp216–24; and P Collison and J Millen, 'University Chancellors, Vice-Chancellors, and College Principals: A social profile,' *Sociology* (1969), iii, pp6–109. Finally, on the economic elites, see: Acton Society Trust, *Management Succession* (London, 1958); R V Clements, Managers (London: Allen and Unwin, 1958); G H Copeman, *Leaders of British Industry* (London: Gee, 1955); M. Barratt-Brown, 'The controllers of British industry,' in *Can the Workers Run Industry?*, edited by K. Coates, (London: Sphere, 1968); R Heller, 'Britain's top directors,' *Management Today* (March 1967); T Lupton and S Wilson, 'The social background and connections of top decision-makers,' *Manchester School* (1959), xvii, pp30–51; Public Schools Commission, *First Report*, Volume II, Appendix 8 (London: H M S O, 1968), p236.

5 There is some evidence that secondary socialisation within individual elites is important in attitudinal formation but it is far from clear-cut: see L Edinger and D Searing, 'Social background in elite analysis,' *Am. Pol. Sc. Rev.* (1967), lxi, pp428–45.

6 *cf* Parkin, *Middle-Class Radicalism*, p179.

7 *cf* L Sklair, 'Techno-economism: ideology of our times,' paper presented to B S A Conference, York, Easter 1972; and R Williams, Editor, *May Day Manifesto 1968* (Harmondsworth, Penguin, 1968).

8 *cf* A Roth, *The Business Background of M Ps* (London: Parliamentary Profiles, 1972), p24.

9 *cf* I Weinberg, *The English Public Schools* (New York: Atherton Press, 1967), pp127–53; and T J H Bishop and R Wilkinson, *Winchester and the Public School Elite* (London: Faber and Faber, 1968), pp41–7.

10 *cf* Hindess, *Decline*, and Rose, in *Sociology* (1968), p131.

11 *cf* Eckstein, in *Division and Cohesion*, pp241–8.

12 See J P Nettl, 'Consensus or elite domination: the case of business,' *Pol. Stud.* (1965), xiii (i), pp22–44.

13 *cf* Miliband, *State*, pp146–78.

14 *cf* L S Amery, *Thoughts on the English Constitution* (London: Oxford University Press, 1964), p15.

15 *Ibid*, p141; Nettl, *Mobilisation*, pp136–48; R T McKenzie, *British Political Parties* (London: Heinemann, 1963); R Butt, *The Power of Parliament* (London: Constable, 1968); R Jackson, *Rebels and Whips*

(London: Macmillan, 1968); and J P Mackintosh, *The British Cabinet* (London: Methuen, 1968).

16 *cf* Butt, *Parliament*, p403; B Crick, *The Reform of Parliament* (London: Weidenfeld and Nicolson, 1964), pp16–17; and I Gilmour, *The Body Politic* (London: Hutchinson, 1969), pp7 and 10.

17 *cf* Parkin, in *BJS* (1967), pp280 *et seq.*

18 Parkin, in *BJS* (1967), *passim*; and Nordlinger, *Tories*, pp214–15.

19 McKenzie and Silver, *Angels*, pp72–3.

20 Harris, *Competition*, *passim*.

21 *cf* Hindess, *Decline, passim*; and R Rose, 'The political ideas of English party activists,' *Amer. Pol. Sci. Rev.* (1962), lvi, pp360–71.

22 Gyford and Haseler, *Social Democracy*, pp17–22.

23 *Ibid.*

24 *cf* A Beattie, *English Party Politics*, (London: Weidenfeld and Nicolson, 1970), Volume II, pp238–40; R Miliband, *Parliamentary Socialism* (London: Merlin, 1964); R Skidelsky, *Politicians and the Slump* (Harmondsworth: Penguin, 1970); and, since the war, S Brittan, *Steering the Economy* (Harmondsworth: Penguin, 1971).

25 P Townsend and N Bosanquet, Editors, *Labour and Inequality* (London: Fabian Society, 1972).

26 On the unions, see: V L Allen, 'The ethics of trade union leaders,' *Brit. J. Sociol.* (1956), vii, pp314–36; *idem, Trade Unions and the Government* (London: Longmans, 1960); R Blackburn and A Cockburn, Editors, *The Incompatibles* (Harmondsworth: Penguin, 1967), esp. pp241–80; and H M Pelling, *A History of British Trade Unionism* (Harmondsworth, Penguin, 1963). On the co-operative movement, see: G N Ostergaard and A H Halsey, *Power in Co-operatives* (Oxford: Blackwell, 1965). On fringe movements, see G Thayer, *The British Political Fringe* (London: Blond, 1965); K Newton, *The Sociology of British Communism* (London: Allen Lane, 1969); and D E Apter and J Joll, Editors *Anarchism Today* (London: Macmillan, 1971), esp. pp84–104.

27 *cf* Anderson, 'Origins,' in *Towards Socialism*; Miliband, *Parliamentary Socialism*; and Parkin, in *Br. J. Sociol.* (1967).

28 *cf* P Worsthorne, *The Myth of Socialism* (London: Cassell, 1971); A Watkins, 'Labour in Power,' in *The Left* (London: Blond, 1966) pp167–80; T Nairn, 'The nature of the Labour Party,' in *Towards Socialism*, pp159–217.

29 *cf* A Rogow and P Shore, *The Labour Government and British Enterprise, 1945–51* (Oxford: Blackwell, 1955); C Jenkins, *Power at the Top* (London: MacGibbon and Kee, 1959), esp. pp19–40; and Watkins, in *The Left*, pp170–2.

30 *cf* Worsthorne, *Socialist Myth*, pp3, 105, and *passim*.

31 *Ibid*, p1.

32 *cf* Rogow and Shore, *Labour Government, passim*; Harris, *Competition*, pp131–5; and P Foot, *The Politics of Harold Wilson* (Harmondsworth: Penguin, 1968), pp50–99.

33 Anderson, 'Problems,' in *Towards Socialism*; McKenzie, *Political Parties*.

34 M Stewart, *The British Approach to Politics* (London: Allen & Unwin, 1965), p12.

35 *cf* S H Beer, *Modern British Politics* (London: Faber and Faber, 1965), *passim*; A H Birch, *Representation* (London: Macmillan, 1971) pp77 nd *passim*; and *idem, Representative and Responsible Government* (London: Allen & Unwin, 1964).

36   Lord Balfour, 'Introduction,' in *The English Constitution* (London: Oxford University Press, 1928), p*xxiv*.

Chapter 5

Dominant Values and Popular Beliefs

Even if the institutional and party political significance of traditionalism and civility were established beyond doubt, and we do not claim that this has been done, it would still be necessary to examine the extent to which traditional and civic orientations prevail among more peripheral members of our society. Moreover, since the purpose of the deference studies is to explain mass political behaviour, the degree of consensus is more relevant than that of institutional support. Likewise, although they do so mistakenly and to the neglect of institutional integration, the civility studies also emphasise the importance of the ordinary citizen's commitment to civic values. In the present chapter, therefore, we focus attention on the prevalence of deference, traditionalism, and civility, along with deviant values, among subordinate classes and political groups.

5.1 The pattern of beliefs in hegemonic societies

If we accept the hegemonic interpretation of stability in capitalist society, certain conclusions would seem to follow about the nature of beliefs, values, and expectations among the subordinate classes. The essential idea underlying this view is that the dominant elites of modern industrial society are able to maintain and to reproduce the distribution of power and rewards through a combination of institutional inertia and differential control over the values, beliefs, and feelings of subordinate classes. This control is exercised in manifold ways and tends to be cumulatively favourable to the dominant elites. Such institutions as the family, schools, the church, mass media, art, political parties, and language, all create and sutain commitment to dominant meaning systems and thus prevent the emergence and articulation of oppositional movements. Microsocial pressures have the same effect as these macrostructural processes. Unless the subordinate classes are

F

fully insulated or isolated from these influences, they will become committed to them in some degree—the precise extent depending on, *inter alia*, the extent of insulation and isolation.

Where the subordinate classes are neither fully insulated from, nor fully integrated into, the hegemonic order, then we may expect a measure of ambiguity, inconsistency, and confusion, in their attitudes and feelings. The two polar types are in fact unlikely to occur. It is by definition impossible for the subordinate classes to be completely incorporated into the centre since they lack essential requisites of central status. If they were completely insulated from contact with central institutions and personnel, then they would hardly belong to the same society. It is correspondingly important to consider the nature of the resulting ambiguities, etc, in popular belief systems. For these derive not only from the limited cultural resources of the periphery but also from its structural position.

Let us begin by examining the concept of 'commitment' in this connection. What exactly do we mean when we say that an individual is 'committed' to an institution, value, or belief? At a minimum, we would expect such a person to acknowledge his support for it: to say, for example, that he approved of the monarchy or felt private enterprise was good. Here we are really dealing with commitment to an institution, belief, or practice, as symbol. Beyond this, at deeper levels of commitment, we would expect two additional qualities. Firstly, we would expect the individual to display contextual knowledge of the institution and its legitimations, i.e. understanding of the values, beliefs, and practices associated with this institution and its connections with other institutions and aspects of society. Secondly, we would expect these commitments to have behavioural consequences that are favourable to, or at least compatible with, the institution in question. Furthermore, when we talk of commitment to a dominant value system, we imply commitment either to a majority of its elements or, at a minimum, to a majority of its key elements. That is, we would expect verbal affirmation, contextual knowledge, and behavioural consequences for all or most of the elements in the system. If the dominant value system is inconsistent, for example, as is the case with civility, then someone who is fully committed to it will be inconsistent in the same ways as long as it is transmitted as a package.

However, it is in the nature of socialisation and communication in class-stratified societies that belief systems are not successfully transmitted as unchanging, unbroken packages. Inequalities in linguistic and communicative competence, in the social distribution of knowledge, in locations within communication networks, and in the primacy of different needs and interests (derived in turn from inequalities in the distribution of power and rewards), all combine to inhibit successful transmission of meaning systems and to encourage the re-interpretation and innovation of elements within them. As the meaning system is transmitted from its original carriers, it becomes fragmented and its scope becomes narrower. Instead of wide-ranging ideologies that organise large amounts of specific information and imply orientations towards many different institutions and policies, there is a proliferation of belief-clusters among which there is little constraint, even of a logical kind. At the same time, the character of the key elements undergoes systematic change. They shift from the remote, generic, and abstract to the increasingly simple, concrete, and close to home.[1] While most research into these processes deals with the transmission of dominant values, it is reasonable to suppose that they also characterise the transmission of contracultural values. Both will become increasingly inconsistent and vague; and both will undergo fragmentation and concretisation as they are transmitted to groups increasingly remote from their original carriers.[2] Thus, just as the lower-class Conservative has a different belief system from a member of the ruling class, so the proletarian supporter of the Labour party will have a belief system structured differently from that of a socialist intellectual. In a sociological study, therefore, as opposed to a mere psephological survey, it is imperative to consider not only the party someone supports but also his reasons for so doing.

The transmission of dominant values to subordinate classes does not involve simply their fragmentation and concretisation, it also leads to their reinterpretation or extension to include additional elements. This is particularly likely where the recipients are not fully integrated into a dominant or a countercultural order. Faced with the conflicting messages in such a position, they will often reinterpret various values and produce a creative synthesis of dominant and countercultural elements. The more specific a value and the more relevant to everyday life, the harder it will be to maintain an interpretation compatible with the dominant meaning system. Symbolic institutions such as the monarchy and general values such as democracy are less likely to be re-interpreted in this way than are less remote and benign values and institutions such as big business and status attribution. On the other hand, commitment to these symbolic institutions and general values will be shallow—lacking in contextual knowledge and behavioural consequences. Other values are likely to be stretched or reinterpreted so as to make them realisable by subordinate classes in ways that would be derogated or unrecognised at the centre. And institutions that affect their daily life are likely to be rejected or at most accepted as inevitable rather than just.[3] Countercultural institutions and values will undergo similar processes of change and reinterpretation. Abstract, generalised, radical critiques of the power structure will be rejected or reinterpreted with the result that they become concrete, simplistic, and populist in nature. And oppositional organisations will tend to be viewed instrumentally or out of their radical context.

This discussion has a dual relevance—it affects the nature of peripheral beliefs and values *per se* and it affects the interpretation of voting behaviour. From what has been said it would seem that there is a wide range of beliefs compatible with hegemony and stability in a class-stratified society. Some people could have a mature grasp of the dominant value system complete with contextual knowledge and behavioural consequences. At the other extreme, some will be alienated from the dominant order and will participate only grudgingly in the ongoing macrostructural power systems and attempt to undermine them. In between would be the vast majority of people with a varying level of commitment to dominant and countercultural values. It would seem almost impossible, therefore, to refute the thesis that stability is due to hegemony, since almost any belief is compatible with the latter. However, the thesis implies more than this. It implies that there will be systematic variation in the incidence of these different types of belief system according to the structural location of the individuals concerned and the ongoing dynamics of the hegemonic society. And it also implies that, within this overall pattern of systematically structured variation, there will be uniformity of movement in public opinion and attitudes.[4] Instead of the polarisation characteristic of repressive states, members of an hegemonic society will react in similar ways to particular conflicts and problems because of the pervasive influence of the dominant value system. Changing attitudes will be most apparent among those neither fully integrated nor completely insulated; but some change will occur in all sections of the society. We shall test these implications below.

Secondly, this discussion also affects the explanation of voting behaviour. For, if affirmation of the dominant value system is to lead to conservative voting, people must connect their attitudes towards dominant but non-political institutions and values with support for particular political parties. The elector who has achieved so little grasp of politics that he may be termed a 'nature of the times' voter or, indeed, who lacks any issue consciousness as far as parties are concerned, will hardly be influenced by his orientations towards dominant values—supposing that he has them to any real degree.[5] In short, we have to examine not only commitment to these institutions but also the extent to which contextual knowledge exists to relate them to political behaviour. Where such knowledge is lacking, therefore, other factors must be found to explain voting behaviour. Moreover, unless we consider the inconsistencies and incoherences as well as the basic ideological nature of their outlook, we are likely to ignore potential instabilities in the political behaviour of the subordinate classes and to overstate the congruence between action and beliefs.[6] Thus consideration of the general nature of popular beliefs in hegemonic societies reinforces our earlier theoretical criticism of the deference studies, namely, that they ignore the mechanisms whereby deference is translated into political action. We have discussed some possible mechanisms in the preceding chapter and will refer to them in later pages.

5.2 Popular beliefs and traditionalism

We have already seen that the cues emanating from the political parties about the electoral implications of traditionalism are ambiguous and inconsistent, although they have tended, at least in the past, to encourage an association between attachments to traditional values and voting for the Conservative Party. We can now consider the extent to which such an association exists in electoral practice. This will also give some insight into the more general importance of traditionalism and civility in the popular belief system. In the next section we shall consider civic orientations more directly and then state our preliminary conclusions.

There are several types of survey evidence relevant to these these concerns. In addition to the studies oriented specifically to one or more aspects of deference, traditionalism, and civility, there are other sociological studies that deal with these matters tangentially or in which relevant data is due to spontaneous references. There is also an abundance of opinion poll data concerned with party preferences, leadership ratings, policy awareness, party images, and other political and non-political matters. In selecting material we employed two criteria. Firstly, preference was given to data analysed by class and party groups rather than overall proportions. Secondly, wherever possible, representative national samples were selected rather than single community studies. Data meeting these criteria provide a better insight into the nature of beliefs in hegemonic society than aggregate data and also show the link between orientations and political preferences. We can then proceed to supplement and refine them by reference to our own survey data. It is this latter task that will occupy the remaining chapters of the present book.

McKenzie and Silver report that 28 per cent of their first sample and 20 per cent of their later sample of working-class voters were ascriptive socio-political deferentials, that is, preferred a Prime Minister with a traditional upper-middle-class background. Nordlinger's study reports an average of only 16 per cent deference among urban working-class men, while Blumler *et al*, using the same operational definition, found only 5 per cent deferential in a 1969 Leeds quota sample. Finally, under a third of Samuel's 1959 sample of middle- and working-class voters in Stevenage stated a preference for political leaders drawn from families used to running the country, while only 13 per cent of a Grantham sample studied by Wolfinger *et al*, believed that MPs should be middle or upper class.[7] Moreover, in those cases where actual voting data are available, only about half of these deferentials voted Conservative with the rest voting Labour or Liberal. While this proportion is certainly greater than that of non-deferentials voting Tory, the overall proportions of deferentials cited and their apparently 'half-hearted' support for the Conservatives do not seem to give much credence to any assertions about the deferential character of the population nor about the importance of deference in Tory voting.

Other studies reveal even less deference but show this to be more strongly linked to Conservative voting since it is primarily Labour voters who do not mention deferential reasons when explaining their voting behaviour. Thus Goldthorpe and Lockwood, for example, found that their affluent Luton workers were overwhelmingly secular—only 17 per cent of regular Conservative voters gave deferential reasons for voting and none of the floating Tory voters did so. Similarly, Ingham found that only 16 per cent of his Bradford working-class Conservatives gave deferential reasons for their voting behaviour. Surveys conducted in the Bristol North-East constituency by Milne and MacKenzie also reveal a limited degree of deference: only 7 per cent of regular Conservative voters from both middle and working classes cited the superior abilities of their party leaders as a reason for voting in the 1951 election; and only 12 per cent did so in 1955.[8] The average level of deference across all voters in these four samples ranges between 3 and 4 per cent overall.

Opinion poll data are at best related only tangentially to the prevalence and incidence of deference. If we broaden the operational definition to a preference for education and experience in governing rather than an understanding of ordinary people, however, some insight can be gained. An ORC survey in 1968 shows that over one-third of the population is deferential in these terms and that Tory voters and the upper middle classes are the most deferential groups (see Table 5.1). Similar findings are reported for a 1970 survey.[9] In the Leeds survey reported above, Blumler *et al*, found very much the same incidence of deference by class and party group, while the Luton study showed non-managerial white-collar workers to cite deferential reasons for voting slightly more often than affluent workers.[10] These findings support the view that commitment to dominant values will be greater among higher socio-economic strata and among those that vote Conservative but they also suggest that, to the extent that ascriptive socio-political deference can be termed a dominant value, it is hardly consensual even within the upper middle class and is generally rejected in favour of preference for leaders who come from working-class backgrounds, have got on in the world, and understand ordinary people.

We now turn, therefore, to an examination of the evidence on the degree of traditionalism among the general population and its relation, if any, to voting behaviour. We shall be particularly concerned with attitudes towards dominant institutions considered both generally and with regard to specific criticisms; with views as to the legitimacy of the opportunity structures; with general images of society; and with radical alternatives to the dominant social, economic, and political order. This should provide a better test of our arguments than the data on ascriptive socio-political deference and will also permit more fruitful comparisons with our own research data.

The *monarchy* has been described as the most important symbol in British political culture[11] and it seems appropriate to begin an investigation of traditionalism with this most stable and enduring institution. The overall level of support for the monarchy is high by almost any criterion—successive surveys having shown that between eighty and ninety per cent of the population think Britain needs the Royal Family and believe it plays an important role in British life. The level of support is high in all classes and the

Table 5.1   CLASS, PARTY PREFERENCE, AND DEFERENCE

Item	MC		WC					
	AB %	C1 %	C2 %	DE* %	Con %	Lab %	Lib %	All %
Education and experience in governing more important than understanding ordinary people (ORC, August 1968)	52	38	34	31	41	32	34	36
Ditto (ORC, August 1970)	47	35	27	26	37	25	31	31
Prefer peer's son to clerk's son as political leader (Blumler *et al*, Leeds, 1969)	17	11	12	12	16	11	15	12
Prefer Old Etonian to ex-grammar school boy as political leader (ditto)	33	15	17	12	28	12	10	17
Prefer peer's son plus prefer Old Etonian as political leader (ditto)	11	2	6	3	7	4	5	4

* Most opinion poll data is analysed in terms of the Institute of Practitioners in Advertising (IPA) class categories. AB corresponds roughly to the professional and managerial occupational groupings, or upper middle class; C1 includes the remaining white-collar workers along with supervisory manual workers, such as foremen; C2 includes the skilled manual working class; DE is a residual category including unskilled manual workers and state pensioners (who may be retired working or middle class). Occasionally data is simply grouped into non-manual and manual, or middle (MC) and working class (WC) categories. The same abbreviations will be used in subsequent tables of this type.

main party groups but is higher in the top socio-economic strata and among Conservative and Liberal voters (see Table 5.2). The greatest disagreement seems to occur within the middle class between Conservative and Labour supporters. Butler and Stokes report that, whereas 72 per cent of subjectively working-class Conservatives thought the Queen and Royal Family were very important in Britain in comparison with 54 per cent of Labour supporters with the same class self-identity, only 32 per cent of the subjectively middle-class Labour supporters agreed with this assessment compared with 70 per cent of middle-class Conservatives.[12] A recent study also shows that it is among Labour supporters that support for a republic is greatest—25 per cent of Labour voters and only 8 per cent of Tories being entirely or largely favourable. The same Mass Observation survey found that hostility to a republic was strongest among those who attended church or chapel regularly, among Anglicans, and the upper and upper-middle classes; and that a monarchy was believed to be better than a republic for the religious life of the country, for moral and family life, for protection against extremism, and for political relations with other countries.[13] In short, there does seem to be widespread commitment to the monarchy in principle and this commitment does seem to be associated with Conservative voting, support for other dominant institutions, and with high social and economic status.

Table 5.2 ATTITUDES TO MONARCHY AND ARISTOCRACY

Item	*MC*		*WC*					
	AB %	*C1* %	*C2* %	*DE* %	*Con* %	*Lab* %	*Lib* %	*All* %
Monarchy should be allowed to continue, perhaps changing with times (ORC, March 1969)	88	84	86	82	91	80	87	85
Unfavourable to idea of a republic (Mass Observation, 1966)	81	72	66	66	84	59	75	70
Royal Family should not receive as much money as it does (NOP, February 1972)	29	45	52	53	32	63	48*	48
Royalty should not have so many privileges (ditto)	16	27	35	38	18	43	33*	32
People around the Queen drawn from too narrow a social class (ditto)	60	64	68	67	58	78	63*	66
Monarchy helps to preserve class differences and this is a good thing (ORC, June 1969)	21	21	19	21				21
Abolish hereditary titles (NOP, 1972)	41	55	57	57	43	67	53*	55
House of Lords should be abolished (ORC, November 1967)	11	15	27	30	12	39	17	23
Wrong for hereditary peers to vote on new laws (ditto)	57	58	60	53	48	71	56	57

* Including other, don't know; these NOP data refer to partisan identity not vote intention.

However, when we turn from commitment to the monarchy as a general and remote symbol to particular aspects of the monarchy, then we find some disaffection from the Queen and Royal

Family. Thus, one-third of the population believe royalty have too many privileges, one-half believe the Royal Family has too much money and should mix more with ordinary people, and two-thirds believe the people around the Queen are drawn from too narrow a social class. Furthermore, agreement with these criticisms is strongest among the subordinate classes and among Labour voters (see Table 5.2).[14] Whereas the monarchy as a symbol appears to be consensual, there is much more confusion and ambivalence about the monarchy in real life.

Less is known about popular attitudes towards the *aristocracy* and the *House of Lords* than about attachments to the monarchy. The data on ascriptive socio-political deference give some insight into this. Thus Nordlinger found that 28 per cent of his working-class voters preferred a peer's son to a clerk's son for Prime Minister—with Conservative voters twice as likely to favour the aristocratic scion.[15] And the Leeds survey conducted by Blumler *et al*, shows it is among the upper middle class and Tory voters that this preference is greater (see Table 5.1). Neither survey reveals much support for the aristocracy, however, and this is reflected in opinion poll data that show more than half the population supporting the abolition of hereditary titles (see Table 5.2). Commitment is again greater among the upper middle class and Conservative supporters. A similar degree of antagonism is found to the idea of hereditary peers voting on new laws although in this respect the upper middle class is as antagonistic as the rest of the population. Attitudes to the House of Lords are somewhat more favourable with only one-quarter of the population wishing for its abolition and hostility concentrated among the working-class and Labour voters.[16]

The *public schools* are another dominant institution identified with the Conservative Party and attachment to which supposedly leads to Conservative voting. It is certainly true that few people would like to see the public schools abolished or incorporated into the state system—in a recent survey less than one-third of interviewees agreed with these proposals—and that support tends to be concentrated among Conservative voters. However, as one moves from the general questions of abolition to more specific aspects such as the education of one's children or the choice of political leaders, attachment to the public schools declines among the upper-middle-class and Conservative voters as well as, albeit more sharply, the subordinate classes and Labour supporters. Thus less than half those interviewed would send their children to public school even if they could afford it and only a third believed fee-paying schools provide a better education than state schools (see Table 5.3). In addition, only one-third of Nordlinger's manual workers preferred an Old Etonian to a grammar school man as Prime Minister, while only one-sixth of the Leeds sample made this choice.[17] These data, even though they do support a deferential interpretation of a part of the Conservative vote, are perhaps more indicative of dissensus or rejection of public schools than they are of a widespread consensus. This is even more apparent in the case of education in the state sector. For, while Conservatives are certainly more attached to grammar schools and the eleven-plus exam, the overriding impression is one of dissensus and ambivalence (see Table 5.3).

There is a similar degree of dissensus among people today over the question of *Empire* and *Commonwealth*. Whereas two-thirds of the 1950 Greenwich sample agreed that Britain's foreign policy should be based on the principle of 'Empire first', about two-fifths of those interviewed in a 1972 national quota sample declared that they felt indifferent, ashamed, or angry about our Empire (see Table 5.3).[18] In both cases, however, it was among the upper middle classes and Conservative voters that support for the Empire was greatest, with the working-class and Labour voters most hostile. Likewise, McKenzie and Silver found that working-class voters were divided about fifty-fifty on the question of whether Britain had been too hasty in granting independence to the colonies. Conservatives tended to agree somewhat more, Labour voters somewhat less.[19] The data from Greenwich also show less support among Conservative than Labour voters and, incidentally, among the subjectively upper middle and middle classes than the working classes, for the policy of giving self-government to the colonies. Commitment to the Commonwealth is also the subject of dissensus—aggravated no doubt by attitudes to entry into Europe (see Table 5.3). Thus a recent NOP national survey showed that only three-fifths of Conservative, Labour, and Liberal voters believed the Commonwealth was a worth-while organisation, with two-fifths in each party group either disagreeing or unsure about the question.[20] Again, therefore, we find some slight support for an interpretation of Tory voting in terms of traditionalism and also some evidence that commitment to traditional institutions is greatest among the highest socio-economic stata. But it is support that must be interpreted within a context of widespread dissensus among the general population.

Popular attitudes towards the *Church and religion* are also relevant to the extent and political implications of traditionalism.

Table 5.3   ATTITUDES TO PUBLIC SCHOOLS, EDUCATION, AND EMPIRE

	MC		WC					
Item	AB %	C1 %	C2 %	DE %	Con %	Lab %	Lib %	All %
Do not abolish public schools nor include in state system (ORC, March 1968)	73	71	66	65	80	52	63	68
Would send own children to public school if could afford it (ditto)	59	51	43	38	58	32	33	45
Fee-paying schools provide better education than state schools (ditto)	48	44	33	29	45	25	31	36
Prefer grammar and secondary schools to remain separate (NOP, July 1967)					53	33	34	42
Eleven-plus examination is a good idea (ORC, October 1969)					37	34	34	34
Feel indifferent, ashamed, angry about our Empire (ORC, February 1972)	36	39	43	40	29	48	28	41
Britain's future lies with Commonwealth or America, not Europe (ditto)	27	33	43	52	32	48	35	41
Foreign policy should be based on Empire first (Benney *et al*, Greenwich, 1950)	85*	70*	65*	65*	78	65		70
Give self-government to colonies (ditto)	38*	44*	48*	48*	36	54		47

* Refers to subjective social class: (upper) middle *v* lower middle *v* working class *v* working class.

Here, too, there is considerable dissensus not only in the population as a whole but also within class and party groups. Thus, only half the respondents in a recent national random sample were certain of the existence of God nor was this belief related systematically to social class. The same survey employed a religiosity scale that included nine attitudinal variables and found 49 per cent of those interviewed scored five or more religious responses. There was only a slight positive correlation between class and this indicator of religious commitment.[21] As might be expected, symbolic religious institutions receive overwhelming majority support in precisely the same way as the monarchy. Martin reports that only one in fifteen people wish to abolish religious education in schools, that Sunday Schools attract almost universal approval, and that 'the form of the Coronation, prayers in the House of Commons, prayers in state schools, the provision of chaplains and the general coverage for the whole country provided by the Anglican clergy—all receive heavy majority support.'[22] This support for religion and the church at the symbolic level is not, of course, combined with extensive religious practice. It tends to be passive and is quite compatible with a certain scepticism about the ecclesiastical institution and a tendency to associate religious observance with hypocrisy.[23] However, among those who do translate religious belief into practice, there is a positive link between religiosity and Conservatism—a link which is particularly marked among the elderly, the middle classes, and Anglican believers.[24]

Turning from more traditional and symbolic institutions and beliefs to those that continue to exercise considerable power and have immediate relevance, we now examine attitudes towards *dominant economic institutions*. Attitudes towards nationalisation provide clues as to popular commitment to the idea of free enterprise and private property. Several studies reveal considerable disapprobation of nationalisation and a negative correlation between support for public ownership and Conservative voting.[25] The same generalisations apply to government control and planning of industry, although this is becoming increasingly acceptable both to industry itself and to the electorate. The change in attitude is well illustrated by the fact that, whereas three-fifths of people interviewed in 1967 felt competition was a better way of keeping prices down than control, three-quarters of the population agreed this year (1972) that the size of price rises should be limited by law (see Table 5.4). The 'nature of the times' has no doubt influenced these attitudes but it is not implausible to ascribe part of the change to a genuine, long-term acceptance of the corporate state. Some evidence for a real change can perhaps be found in the disproportionate upturn in support for government intervention, planning, and control, among the upper-middle-class and Tory voters so that the level of support is now much the same across different class and party categories.[26] This possibility would certainly be in line with the postulated emergence of a managerial, corporatist 'techno-economistic' value system that has replaced more traditional values.

Several studies reveal a degree of hostility towards big business although this is not as great nor as widespread as that towards

Table 5.4 ATTITUDES TO DOMINANT ECONOMIC
INSTITUTIONS

Item	AB %	C1 %	C2 %	DE %	Con %	Lab %	Lib %	All %
Nationalise all basic industries (Benney *et al*, Greenwich, 1950)*	13	22	37	37	7	49		33
More government control by nationalisation or share purchase (ORC, August 1969)	29	27	34	36	24	56	27	33
More government control and planning of industry (ORC, August 1968)	9	20	23	22	9	40	5	20
Size of price increases should be limited by law (ORC, July 1972)	67	74	80	74	74	76	78	75
Competition better than control for keeping prices down (NOP, March 1967)					79	49	74	62
Companies making too much profit (NOP, February 1971)	14	22	33	32	18	38	23	28
More people must buy shares if industry is to expand (RSL, February 1962)	48	47	48					48
Unscrupulous financiers on the Stock Exchange (ditto)	39	54	58					52
People have enough say in Banks, Finance Houses, and Building Societies (Gallup, September 1969)	26	23	25	16	25	20	23	25

* Analysed by subjective class: (upper) middle *v* lower middle *v* working *v* working.

trade unions. Less than a third of people in various samples agree that companies are making too much profit, for example, and a similar proportion feel that bankers and financiers have too much power (see Tables 5.4 and 5.6). More people are inclined to feel that there are unscrupulous financiers on the Stock Exchange, however, and that they do not have enough say in the way Banks, Finance Houses, and Building Societies run their operations. A recent Gallup poll, based on a national quota sample and conducted in 1969, found that almost two-thirds of the population felt that big business and the City have a lot of influence—ranking third to the Prime Minister and the trade unions.[27] Such rankings provide no indication as to how this influence is evaluated, however, and it is interesting to note that manual workers are less likely to see big business and the City as influential than are the upper middle class. Most sociological studies on the question of big business power focus on manual workers and generally report that about two-thirds of Labour voters and one-third of Conservatives believe it has too much power and influence.[28] More generally, almost all the available evidence shows that hostility to business, however measured, is greatest among the subordinate classes and Labour voters.

Such hostility is somewhat populist in nature, however, and is not always associated with disaffection from dominant institutions. Many of the same studies that demonstrate working-class opposition to big business power also show that most workers adhere to a harmonistic view of management–worker relations. Goldthorpe and Lockwood, for example, found that two-thirds of their affluent workers and three-quarters of lower white-collar workers believed management and workers were a team rather than on opposite sides. At the same time three-fifths of the car workers and almost two-thirds of lower white-collar employees also believed big business had too much power.[29] Similar inconsistencies are apparent in national survey data. Thus a recent Gallup poll found that four-fifths of those interviewed believed strong management was a good thing for the country while less than half thought strong unions were good. Similarly, only one in eight of a recent NOP national sample did not trust their own top management to have their employees' best interests at heart (see Table 5.5). This basic trust seems to be translated into political deference. Two-thirds of Conservative voters and of non-manual workers agreed early in 1968 that it would be good for the next government to appoint leading men from successful private and nationalised industries to run the country's economic and political affairs; more than half of manual workers and those who voted Labour also approved this suggestion.[30]

A combination of populist hostility to big business, the City, financiers, etc, with general support and trust of management and private enterprise is exactly the pattern of popular beliefs to be expected in an hegemonic society. Moreover, as suggested in the model outlined above, an examination of specific issues shows there is much disaffection from the dominant order. Thus only two-fifths of the population believe the top management of their organisition understands the difficulties they face at work. Under a third feel that people like themselves have enough say in the conditions under which they work and the policies pursued by their employers. Only one-fifth think they have enough control over the nationalised industries and financial institutions (see Tables 5.4 and 5.5).[31] The level of personal efficacy does not rise in any class or party group to 50 per cent and those who feel least effective are the working classes and, in most cases, Labour voters.

Turning to the *unions*, we find far less attachment to unionism than to management and private enterprise. While there is consensus on the value of strong management, for example, there is dissensus on that of strong unions and union participation in management (see Table 5.5). Moreover, when questioned in early 1969, less than one-third of a national random sample believed that unions exerted a good influence in this country and almost two-thirds believed unions had too much power. Similarly while few people believe that the government should exercise more control over industry, several surveys show that two-thirds of people believe the government should be tougher with unions.[32] A recent ORC survey also reveals that four-fifths of those interviewed agree that union leaders do not do enough to control militant shop stewards and also that militant union leaders and shop stewards have far too much power to disrupt the country's economy.[33] Manual workers, union members, and Labour voters are all less disaffected from unions but support is not consensual in any of the class or party groups. This is probably due to the importance of the mass media in generating concern about 'national issues,' such as unofficial strikes and the power of unions more generally, among all sections of the population. Blumler and Ewbank report that the mass media contributed significantly to the development of concern among rank-and-file unionists about unofficial strikes but did not affect the attitudes of shop stewards and union officials. They also show that rank and file involvement in unions is related strongly to immediate bread-and-butter issues rather than moral or organisational questions.[34] This influence would certainly account for the apparent contradiction between widespread antipathy to strikes and unions in general and the continuing involvement of large numbers of workers in unions and strike activity. Whatever the interpretation, it provides yet one more example of popular ambivalence and inconsistency in attitudes towards major institutions.

The same pattern can be found in attitudes towards the social and economic *class system* itself and the *opportunity structure* with which it is associated. There is a definite consensus on the existence of classes and of barriers between them. But this is combined with dissensus on the existence of class conflict or class struggle, on the actual desirability of large inequalities of wealth and privi-

Table 5.5   ATTITUDES TOWARDS MANAGEMENT AND UNIONS

| Item | NTU | | TU | | | | | |
	AB %	C1 %	C2 %	DE %	Con %	Lab %	Lib %	All %
Strong management good thing for the country (Gallup, May 1972)	82	82	79	78	86	75	86	80
Distrust top management to have my interests at heart (NOP, February 1972)	9	9	15	12	8	18		12
Top management out of touch with my difficulties at work (ditto)	31	38	46	48	29	49		43
Have enough say in conditions that we work in (Gallup, September 1969)	39	37	36	27	36	40	33	34
Have enough say in policies pursued by employers (ditto)	38	31	31	26	34	27	27	30
Unions should play part in management of firms (NOP, June 1968)	43*		64*		42	56		49
Strong unions good thing for this country (Gallup, May 1972)	39	39	54	49	35	64	33	47
Unions exert a good influence in this country (NOP, March 1969)	20	23	31	34	20	42	32	29
Unions have too much power (ditto)	75	73	59	50	72	46	69	62
Government should be tougher with trade unions (Harris, March 1970)	66*		60*		78	53	67	64
Approve union links with the Labour Party (NOP, June 1968)	37*		51*		25	64		40

*   Analysed by union membership: non-members *v* members.

lege, and on the reduction of class differences (see Table 5.6).[35] This dissensus is reflected in the evaluation of occupational prestige and in beliefs about the structure of opportunities in Britain. Manual workers are more likely than the middle classes to believe that social mobility is difficult, that the legal system is unfair and inefficient, that the courts are biased, that influence rather than hard work determines who gets ahead, that the elected representatives do not in fact rule Britain. Just as in the case of the sense of efficacy at work, therefore, it is the subordinate classes that feel least efficacious and appear to be most disaffected in respect of the social, legal, and political systems. Further evidence of this can be found in the differential evaluation of occupational prestige and importance. While all classes agree that doctors are important to the nation, for example, there is marked dissensus between classes on the importance of such occupations as engine driver, bus driver, and docker. There is a clear tendency for subordinate classes to elevate the prestige and significance of occupations characteristic of their own members notwithstanding their low status in terms of the dominant stratification system.[36]

Table 5.6   ATTITUDES TO SOCIAL AND ECONOMIC CLASS

Item	*AB* %	*C1* %	*C2* %	*DE* %	*Con* %	*Lab* %	*Lib* %	*All* %
There are different social classes in Britain today (NOP, February 1972)	93	95	92	87	95	92	89	91
Class barriers exist (ditto)	78	75	77	71	78	74		75
Easy to move into higher class (ditto)	40	32	32	27	28	28		32
Class interests conflict (Martin, Greenwich and Hertford, 1950)†	36	42	48	48	39	48	39	45
Large inequalities in wealth and privilege are wrong (Benney *et al*, Greenwich, 1950)*	34	49	53	53	37	58		50
Approve wealth tax on those with £75,000 or more (ORC, August 1969)	40	50	58	69	49	74	59	58
Strongly approve reduction of class differences (RSL, 1962–3)	24	35	44	42	27	50	39	39
Doctors are important to the nation (BMRB, 1960)	80	87	84	88				85
Engine drivers are important to the nation (ditto)	39	47	53	71				56
Dockers are important to the nation (ditto)	28	28	38	48				38

*   Greenwich data analysis by subjective class: (upper) middle *v* lower middle *v* working *v* working.

†   Liberals and Conservatives grouped in Greenwich and Hertford data.

There is also a tendency for disaffection from these three systems to be more marked among Labour than Conservative voters—particularly so in respect of the reduction of class differences.[37] The greater class-consciousness of manual workers and Labour voters is reflected in the fact that two-thirds of middle-class

Table 5.7 ATTITUDES TO THE OPPORTUNITY STRUCTURE

Item	AB %	C1 %	C2 %	DE %	Con %	Lab %	Lib %	All %
System of law and justice is fair and efficient (Gallup, September 1969)	64	63	55	53	63	59	42	57
Judges independent and not influenced by government (ditto)	77	72	68	60	73	65	59	67
Courts impartial and do not favour the rich (ditto)	72	61	51	45	64	48	42	54
Everyone is equal in court (NOP, February 1972)	50	40	37	36	40*	29*		39
Influence rather than hard work determines who gets on (Gallup, September 1969)	62	76	79	79	75	77	78	76
Bankers and financiers have too much power (ditto)	30	34	29	24	29	32	41	29
TUC has too much power (ditto)	59	54	42	40	54	32	47	46
People like ourselves have no influence (ditto)	51	51	57	64	58	56	58	57
Rich and aristocrats rule Britain, not elected representatives (NOP, February 1972)	10	20	26	32	14*	33*	25*	25

* NOP data refer to party identity rather than vote or vote intention; liberal includes other, don't know.

Conservatives in Butler and Stokes' national survey did not see politics as the representation of class interests nor the expression of class political norms. In contrast, two-fifths of working-class Labour identifiers saw politics as the representation of opposing class interests, almost one-half saw it as representing simple class interests, a twentieth as an expression of class political norms, and less than one in ten did not relate politics to class.[38] However, even in the case of those who viewed politics as class conflict or opposition, very few seem to have more than a trade-union conscious level of class awareness. It is sufficient to see the Tories as more for the monied class or middle class, the Labour Party as more for the workers, with some awareness of conflicting interests in resources, for a voter to be classified as having such a model. Any interpretation of political behaviour in terms of class awareness must bear this limited degree of consciousness in mind.

Overall, therefore, there is only limited support for an interpretation of Labour voting purely in terms of traditionalism and deference. On the one hand, we find extensive support for general symbolic or remote dominant institutions and values that spreads across all classes and party groups. On the other hand, we find a large measure of dissensus on more immediate, less abstract issues related to the dominant order. In most cases, it is true, Labour voters are more disaffected or ambivalent than Conservative voters but it is also true that disaffection and ambivalence characterise many of the latter. However, there is some support for the theory of stability outlined above. The upper middle class that provides the bulk of recruits to the dominant elites is markedly more committed to the dominant order than the working class. The latter is more disaffected and ambivalent about the *status quo* and its belief system is structured in the way one would expect in an hegemonic society. We now turn to an examination of civic orientations to assess the hegemonic and civility models more precisely.

5.3　Civic dispositions

The civic culture is supposedly most effective in producing stability if it occurs within the context of a general commitment to the total community and its symbols.[39] Such a commitment does seem to exist in Britain. Almond and Verba, for example, report that half of their national sample interviewed in 1959 spontaneously mentioned governmental and political institutions when asked about things of pride in Britain.[40] A high level of political allegiance is also reported by Rose and Mossawir for their survey of Stockport in 1964—almost three-quarters positively endorsed the general arrangements for governing the country with Parliament, Prime Minister, and Cabinet. As one might expect, the reasons offered for this support were somewhat confused—three-quarters said it is the best system known, two-thirds that it was the kind people wanted, and two-thirds that one had to accept it whatever one thought. There was similar support and inconsistency for obedience to the law.[41] The data already cited on attitudes towards dominant institutions and values at the symbolic level can also be interpreted to show that there is a general, albeit confused, commitment to the overall social and political order.

Not only does there seem to be general acceptance of the political order but people also seem to accept a limited role within that order. A 1969 Gallup poll, for example, found that two-thirds of those interviewed believed Britain was a democracy and that democracy was understood to mean that everyone has a vote, elections are free, there is freedom of speech, and there is individual liberty. Very few people spontaneously mentioned the idea that democracy involves popular influence over the government and, even when prompted, only two-thirds agreed with this definition in comparison with 89 per cent who agreed that democracy was a system in which everyone has the right to vote. Moreover, it is the upper middle class that is most likely to mention such popular influence when prompted, rather than subordinate classes.[42] The comparative lack of emphasis on popular control as such is probably a reflection of successful institutionalisation of the dominant version of the civic culture. Thus Butler and Stokes found that three-quarters of their national sample believed that having elections makes the Government pay a good deal or at least some attention to what the people think—a belief which is an important element in the elitist theory of democracy. This general affirmation of a key legitimating belief was not combined, however, with any great contextual knowledge of the political system. Only one-eighth of the sample had a well-developed understanding of popular control through a competitive party and election system, while two-fifths had not crystallised a general understanding or belief in popular control through these means.[43] This, in turn, may be due to a positive acquiescence in powerlessness. Thus Nordlinger, for example, reports that two-thirds of those manual workers in his sample who felt they had little influence over the government and a third of those who felt they had no influence were in fact satisfied with this situation.[44] However one interprets these data it is apparent that important elements of the civic culture are accepted, if not fully understood, by members of subordinate classes.

Further support for this view is to be found in popular attitudes towards voting and political participation. There is a general consensus on the importance of voting and on the individual's duty to vote in national and local elections (see Table 5.8).[45] A number of studies also report that there are high levels of subjective political and administrative competence. Four-fifths of Almond and Verba's British sample said they expected equal treatment with everyone else in their contacts with the police and government officials. The same proportions expected some consideration to be given to expressions of their own viewpoint in such contacts. Furthermore, over three-quarters of their respondents also felt they could do something to change an injust regulation imposed by a local authority; while three-fifths felt they could effect an unjust national decision. Nordlinger reports similar figures for his manual workers.[46] In both samples, about a third also believed that, if they actually made an effort to influence such decisions, they would probably succeed in so doing.

There also seems to be widespread acquiescence in independent governmental authority as well as acceptance of the other key elements of the civic culture. Thus Nordlinger found that his working-class voters generally approved of independent government action in opposition to public opinion. Overall, 50 per cent gave unqualified approval to such action when performed by the 'opposition' party government and 70 per cent gave unqualified support to such action by their own party in government. Moreover, the most frequently cited reason for giving such approval was the argument that governments should lead. Similarly, Rose and Mossawir found that 90 per cent of their Stockport sample believed one should obey the law because it is generally sensible and two-thirds also mentioned that laws are made by people who know what one ought to do. Finally, there is some evidence that strong leadership and an ability to make unwelcome decisions— both factors that suggest an acquiescent outlook—are particularly desired qualities in political leaders.[47]

If one considers these data with those cited in the preceding four paragraphs, therefore, it would seem that the average citizen is committed to the political order as a whole, to his limited role within it, and to the legitimacy of the administrative, legal, and governmental systems. But it is also clear from data cited in the preceding section that this is not an adequate description of popular attitudes towards the social order. For, as we move from acceptance of general beliefs and commitment to abstract values to specific aspects of the political opportunity structure, we find increasing dissensus and disaffection. A degree of inconsistency is also apparent if we consider attitudes towards independent governmental authority in the light of attitudes towards government by referendum and beliefs about the adequacy of popular influence over the way the government runs the country (see Table 5.8). In general such disaffection and dissensus is particularly marked in the subordinate classes, who are thus shown once more to have confused and ambivalent attitudes towards the dominant social, economic, and political order. In all three respects there is a discrepancy between feelings about particular aspects of the system and an apparent commitment to the overall power structure. These two sets of attitudes are able to co-exist because there is only limited contextual grasp of the dominant and deviant meaning systems and because few occasions arise on which a confrontation between the two is necessary for immediate action.

Table 5.8 CIVIC ORIENTATIONS BY CLASS AND PARTY

Item	AB %	C1 %	C2 %	DE %	Con %	Lab %	Lib %	All %
Britain is a democracy (Gallup, September 1969)	76	72	70	59	69	77	63	68
Britain is becoming less democratic (ditto)	55	51	47	49	59	40	52	50
People like us have enough say in way government runs country (ditto)	22	29	27	21	24	34	13	25
Prefer referendum to a government decision on important issues (ditto)	62	74	69	66	71	58	77	68
Doesn't matter if I don't vote at general elections (ditto)	11	9	13	17	8	10	21	13
Approve compulsory voting (ditto)	35	43	41	31	42	36	33	37
Lives are governed by secret plots of politicians (ditto)	29	31	34	37	36	33	23	34
Political demonstrations should be banned (NOP, February 1970)	10	28	34	44	29	35	28	32
Demonstrations by strikers should be banned (ditto)	24	32	33	41	33	33	35	34
Should be illegal to refuse job on racial grounds (ORC, August 1968)	45	45	37	43	35	50	51	42
People choose who is to rule them at elections (NOP, February 1972)*	53	47	46	47	58	43	44	47

* NOP data refer to party identity; liberal includes other, don't know.

Finally, we shall look at another aspect of civility, namely, attitudes towards various civil liberties and rights. While these do not, significantly enough, receive much attention in the models employed by Nordlinger and Almond and Verba, they are none the less important elements in the more general elitist theory of democracy. It is partly because they despair of the average citizen's civility in this respect that elitist theorists stress the importance of an elite that is committed to the maintenance of civil liberties as well as to firm government more generally. What they often ignore, of course, is that civil liberties are often invoked to legitimate inequalities in power and rewards and to resist demands for reform.[48] The evidence seems to support the elitists—the subordinate classes are more likely to agree that demonstrations, for example, should be banned even where it is strikers that are demonstrating (see Table 5.8). This tendency is probably related to the limited contextual grasp of democratic principles that is found among subordinate classes in combination with the important part played by the mass media in generating concern about particular issues. Where the weight of the media is thrown behind civil liberties, as in the case of racial discrimination, there are fewer differences between classes. This suggests that popular disregard for civil liberties is less a permanent attribute of the periphery and more an artefact of particular structural and communicative networks.[49]

5.4   Preliminary conclusions

We have now presented some empirical observations, both statistical and discursive, with which to confront our earlier theoretical remarks. Although the evidence is by no means unambiguous and clearcut it is none the less possible to state certain preliminary conclusions about deference, traditionalism, and civility, and their relationship to voting behaviour and political stability in Britain. This is the task of the present section and will conclude the present chapter. In the succeeding chapters we shall be concerned to present data from our own surveys in order to refine and illustrate these conclusions. A final chapter will then place the main issues in comparative context and look forward to further research problems.

Firstly, ascriptive socio-political deference does not appear to be consensual nor does it seem to contribute greatly to Conservative voting among the working class. Even among the middle class, which seems to be more deferential, its effect is not much greater. Ascriptive socio-political deference, however measured, is expressed by no more than a third of the population and the proportions in some studies are considerably less than this. It is also limited in political impact—on average only one in two of those who state deferential attitudes actually translate them into voting behaviour. Indeed, there is more support expressed for the introduction of businessmen into political life than there is for an ascriptive ruling class, public school alumni, or aristocratic politicians. It is true that deference is much more often cited spontaneously by Conservatives than Labour voters but spontaneous expressions of deference are comparatively few in number. In short, however important it may be in a small proportion of cases, all the indications suggest that such deference is unimportant in determining political behaviour as a whole.

This means that alternative bases of working-class Conservatism must exist. One such base is traditionalism. But even this more general form of deference seems to be linked only weakly with electoral support. On the one hand, there is consensus across all classes and party groups on dominant values, elites, and institutions at the symbolic level, e.g. monarchy, capitalism, top management, institutionalised religion; on the other hand, specific criticisms of the dominant order also tend to cut across class and party groups. In both cases, certainly, it is the subordinate classes and Labour voters who are most alienated but the differences, such as they are, do not suggest that traditionalism is the key factor in explaining political partisanship. This could mean that many voters are insensitive to the dominant value system and/or that Labour support is not incompatible with traditionalism. The evidence presented in the preceding chapter certainly suggests that the latter alternative is possible. However, differences between Labour and Conservative voters on these attitudes are generally greater than those between classes. Since about half of the Conservative vote derives from the working class, therefore, this suggests a genuine causal link between traditionalism and partisanship rather than simple co-variation explicable solely in terms of the greater commitment of the middle classes to dominant institutions as well as to the Tory Party.[50] This is a possibility that deserves further investigation.

Moreover, if traditionalism seems to account for only a limited amount of voting behaviour, the role of class consciousness appears to be similarly restricted. Attitudes towards the distribution of wealth, the reduction of class differences, nationalisation, etc, are somewhat more strongly related to class position and to voting than are attitudes towards symbolic institutions such as the monarchy or institutionalised religion. But even so the percentage differences between party groups on these issues would seem to indicate that class consciousness accounts for only a quarter of the variation in voting behaviour.[51] As in the case of traditionalism, there is less variation across classes than there is across the Labour and Conservative Party supporters. Thus there is some evidence that class awareness is causally related to electoral support.

These attitudinal data must be interpreted cautiously, however, since they may understate the influence of traditionalism and class consciousness at the same time as they overstate the general extent of both. In the case of deference, for example, an examination of spontaneous references revealed a stronger link with partisanship even if it also revealed the restricted scope of deference in the general population. This suggests that commitment to deference is rather shallow for many people and that they may also lack a well-developed contextual grasp of its implications. It certainly suggests that many people who express deferential attitudes rank other factors more highly in choosing a political party or in choosing an appropriate justification for a traditional party preference. Butler and Stokes' research into class awareness and party identity is capable of a similar interpretation. It shows that more than 90 per cent of working-class Labour supporters mentioned class norms or interests in their description of different parties whereas only one-third of middle-class Conservatives did so. When combined with our attitudinal data this suggests that many of those who appear to hold-class conscious beliefs do not in fact have a well-articulated or crystallised class ideology and so fail to translate them into political action, justification, or evaluation. Thus, while well-developed class-consciousness may be less prevalent than indicated, the relationship between such awareness —even if only economistic in nature—and political behaviour may well be stronger than these data indicate. Moreover, although there are no corresponding data for traditionalism about spontaneous references and party images, it is likely that similar considerations apply. Our discussion of the nature of popular beliefs in hegemonic society certainly implies that confusion and ambivalence exist and will therefore reduce the apparent strength of such relationships.

Finally, these data also support the hegemonic interpretation of stability somewhat more than they do that of the civility model. It is true that many people do accept the democratic myths propagated in Britain and that such support exists on both sides of the main party cleavage. But this support is combined with much greater ambivalence and disaffection than is encompassed within the civic culture model. Moreover, the incidence of such characteristics accords with the class theory of stability, being greatest among the subordinate classes. None the less, it is difficult to eliminate the civility thesis solely on empirical grounds—partly because it is so vague—and theoretical considerations must also be employed in its rejection. The model will be considered once more when our own survey data are presented in a later chapter.

Thus, while some progress has been made in evaluating the two themes of deference and civility, there is still considerable scope for further investigation. For example, although it has been possible to demonstrate the postulated ambivalence and disaffection in popular attitudes, it remains to be seen exactly how this is affected by different structural contexts and how electoral choices are mediated in ambivalent situations. The role of residential communities, union membership, local tradition, and occupational communities, for example, cannot be readily investigated with this sort of data. Secondly, the data so far presented do not provide much information about the relation between party choice and traditionalism within particular classes. If we are to investigate the origins of working-class Conservatism and middle-class Labour voting in any detail, it is the latter sort of analysis that must be conducted. Likewise, more detailed analyses are required if we are to consider the connections, if any, between civility and traditionalism. Fourthly, while there is some evidence that traditionalism and class consciousness both contribute to the determination of electoral behaviour, it remains to assess their importance not only in relation to each other but also relative to other factors. This can only be done with survey data specifically gathered for such an examination. The use of scales rather than individual items should provide a better indication of depth of commitment to the dominant order and some insight into the importance of contextual knowledge can be gained through open-ended questions. Both techniques were employed in our own research. Finally, the relative merits of the hegemonic and civility theories of stability also need further investigation. When these questions have been answered we shall be in a better position to draw firm conclusions about the causes of voting behaviour and political stability in Britain.

5.5 Notes and references

1 *cf* P Converse, 'The nature of belief systems in mass publics,' in *Ideology and Discontent*, edited by D E Apter (Glencoe: Free Press, 1964), pp206–61; for some methodological problems involved in the study of popular beliefs, see *idem*, 'Attitudes and non-attitudes: continuation of a dialogue,' in *Quantitative Analysis of Social Problems*, edited by E R Tufte (London: Addison-Wesley, 1970), pp168–89.
2 The main exception to this generalisation occurs where an intellectual group adopts and refines deviant beliefs and values of subordinate classes.
3 *cf* Mann, in *Am. Sociol. Rev.* (1970).
4 *cf* Lipset, *Political Man*, pp33–4.
5 For a discussion of different levels of political awareness in relation to voting behaviour, see A Campbell *et al*, *The American Voter* (New York: Wiley, 1964), Chapters 8 and 9; and Butler and Stokes, *Political Change*, Chapter 9.
6 *cf* J A Westergaard, 'The rediscovery of the cash nexus,' in *Socialist Register 1970*, edited by J Saville and R Miliband (London: Merlin, 1970), pp111–38.
7 McKenzie and Silver, *Angels*, pp159 and 227; Nordlinger, *Tories*, pp 65–8; Samuel, in *New Left Rev.* (1959); Wolfinger's data as cited in Kavanagh, in *Government and Opposition* (1971), p341. King has criticised the

representativeness of the McKenzie and Silver sample owing to the disproportion of Conservatives relative to their numbers in all urban constituencies: this will tend to inflate the proportion of deferential voters. See
his review in *New Society* (17 October 1968). Nordlinger interviewed only
male manual workers who voted Labour or Conservative in 1959 and who
intended to vote the same way when interviewed: since *Angels* shows that
constant Tories are more deferential, this is likely to overstate the effects
of deference.

8 J H Goldthorpe *et al*, *The Affluent Worker: Political Attitudes and
Behaviour* (London: Cambridge University Press, 1968), pp18–20; G K
Ingham, 'Plant size: political attitudes and behaviour,' *Social. Rev.* (1969),
xvii, pp235–49; R S Milne and H C MacKenzie, *Straight Fight* (London:
Hansard Society, 1954), p120; *idem*, *Marginal Seat* (London: Hansard
Society, 1958), p158.

9 Data provided by Opinion Research Centre: both samples had over
1,000 respondents. The overall percentage in August 1970 was 31 per cent
and there was a similar distribution by class and party.

10 Data from Leeds provided by Dr Blumler; for a description of the
sample and methods, see J. G. Blumer *et al*, 'Attitudes to the Monarchy:
their structure and development during a ceremonial occasion,' *Pol. Stud*
(1971), xix, pp149–71. Luton data reported in Goldthorpe *et al*, *Affluent
Worker*, pp18–20.

11 Rose, *Politics*, p51.

12 Butler and Stokes, *Political Change*, p114.

13 L M Harris, *Long to Reign Over Us?* (London: Kimber, 1966), *passim*;
data based on a 1965 national quota sample (N = 1005).

14 Data provided by National Opinion Polls from their extensive survey
into social class conducted in February 1972, with national random sample
of adults: see *NOP Political Bulletin* (June 1972 and July 1972). See also
Blumler *et al*, in *Pol. Stud.* (1971). Other survey data provided by Opinion
Research Centre.

15 Nordlinger, *Tories*, p67.

16 Data on House of Lords provided by NOP from their class survey and
ORC from a monthly survey.

17 Nordlinger, *Tories*, p67; other data provided by ORC and NOP
from their regular monthly surveys.

18 M Benney and P Geiss, 'Social class and politics in Greenwich,' *Br. J.
Sociol.* (1950), i, pp310–27; M Benney and R H Pear, *How People Vote*
(London: Routledge, 1956), p141. ORC data based on national quota
sample of 1,083 adults interviewed 16–20 February 1972.

19 McKenzie and Silver, *Angels*, pp152–3.

20 *NOP Political Bulletin* (January 1969).

21 Independent Television Authority, *Religion in Britain and Northern
Ireland* (London: ITA, 1970).

22 D Martin, *A Sociology of English Religion* (London: Heinemann,
1967), pp56–7.

23 *Ibid*, p57.

24 *cf* Butler and Stokes, *Political Change*, pp124–34; and J M Bochel and
D T Denver, 'Religion and voting: a critical review and a new analysis,'
Pol. Stud. (1970), xvii, pp205–19.

25 See, for example, Abrams *et al*, *Must Labour Lose?*, pp31–6; Benney
and Pear, *How People Vote*, p141; Butler and Stokes, *Political Change*,

pp176–80; McKenzie and Silver, *Angels*, p207; Nordlinger, *Tories*, pp 158–9; R Rose, *Influencing Voters* (London: Faber, 1967), pp182–3. Milne and MacKenzie argue that nationalisation is one of the few differences in principle between the major parties and has become symbolic of the parties' whole outlooks: see *Straight Fight*, p137.

26 Data supplied by ORC from monthly surveys; see also *NOP Political Bulletin* (March 1967 and February 1971). Between August 1968 and August 1970, ORC found a general increase in electoral support for government control and planning: 28 per cent supported such action in 1970 compared with 20 per cent in 1968. Support among ABs rose from 9 to 27 per cent, among Tories from 9 to 26 per cent; proportionate increases were less in remaining classes and dropped among Labour voters.

27 Two interesting surveys into attitudes towards share owning and the Stock Exchange have been commissioned by the Wider Share Ownership Committee: see WSOC, *Sharing the Profits* (London: Garnstone Press, 1968) and Research Services Limited, *Savings and Attitudes to Share Ownership* (London: February 1962). Other data provided by Gallup, from their 1,000 quota sample study of power in Britain, and by ORC and NOP, from their monthly surveys.

28 See, for example, Butler and Stokes, *Political Change*, pp166–70; Goldthorpe *et al*, *Affluent Worker*, pp26–7; Ingham, in *Sociol. Rev.* (1969), pp243–4; McKenzie and Silver, *Angels*, pp126–33; Nordlinger, *Tories*, p109; I C Cannon, 'Ideology and occupational community,' *Sociology* (1967), i, pp165–85; and S Hill, 'Dockers and their work', *New Society* (17 August 1972).

29 J H Goldthorpe *et al*, *The Affluent Worker: Industrial Attitudes and Behaviour* (London: Cambridge University Press, 1968), pp73–5; and *idem*, *Affluent Worker: Political*, pp26–8.

30 Data from Gallup's power survey; *NOP Political Bulletin*, (July 1972); and data provided by Gallup from a monthly survey.

31 Data from NOP's class survey and Gallup's power survey.

32 On government toughness with unions, see, for example, the Harris Poll reported in the *Daily Express* (18 March 1970) and the ORC poll reported in *The Times* (8 September 1972).

33 *Ibid.*

34 J G Blumler and A Ewbank, 'Trade unionists, the mass media, and unofficial strikes,' *Br. J. Ind. Rel.* (1970), viii, pp32–54. Goldthorpe *et al*, *Affluent Worker: Industrial*, also show that workers' involvement in unionism is instrumental in character.

35 A recent Gallup poll reports data similar to those found in Martin's survey: 58 per cent of those interviewed in May 1972 thought there was a class struggle in this country; half those who supported the Tory Party and two-thirds of Labour voters agreed, 56 per cent of the ABC1 class and 66 per cent of the C2s also agreed. Data provided by Gallup; *cf* F M Martin, 'Social status and electoral choice in two constituencies,' *Br. J. Sociol.* (1952), iii, pp231–41.

36 The British Market Research Bureau data on occupational importance are presented by M Abrams, 'Some measurements of social stratification in Britain,' in *Social Stratification*, p139; see also, M Young and P Willmott, 'Social grading by manual workers,' *Brit. J. Sociol.* (1956), vii, pp337–45, and Parkin, *Class Inequality*, pp93–5. Young and Willmott also report that those who made their judgement according to social contribution rather than dominant values were influenced by their left-wing political attitudes.

37 *cf* M Abrams, 'Social class and politics,' in *Class,* edited by R Mabey (London: Blond, 1966), pp19–32. Abrams notes that there is widespread complacency about the educational system among those who strongly support reductions in class differences and suggets this is because they fail to connect the educational system with the structure of class differences; in contrast the middle classes are opposed to such a reduction and are likely to think the educational system is satisfactory (p31).

38 Butler and Stokes, *Political Change,* pp80–92.

39 Almond and Verba, *Civic Culture,* pp31, 102–5, 483–5; cf E A Shils, *Political Development in the New States* (Hague, Mouton), pp58–9.

40 Almond and Verba, *Civic Culture,* pp102–5; such pride was more frequently expressed by those with higher education.

41 R Rose and H Mossawir, 'The significance of an election,' *Pol. Stud.* (1967), xv, pp174–201.

42 Data provided by Gallup; a brief presentation of some data from this survey is reported in 'Is Britain still really democratic?' *Weekend Telegraph* (26 October 1969).

43 Butler and Stokes, *Political Change,* pp32–4.

44 Nordlinger, *Tories,* pp100–2.

45 Almond and Verba, *Civic Culture,* p169; P Abrams and A Little, 'The young voter in British politics,' *Br. J. Sociol.* (1965), xvi, pp95–110; and Rose and Mossawir, in *Pol. Stud.* (1967).

46 Almond and Verba, *Civic Culture,* p185; Nordlinger, *Tories,* p114. Almond and Verba found subjective competence to be positively correlated with educational length, which provides some indication of class position.

47 Nordlinger, *Tories,* p83; Rose and Mossawir, in *Pol. Stud.* (1967), p191.

48 *cf* Young, in *Berkeley J. Sociol.* (1967), pp6–9.

49 *cf* Pateman, in *Brit. J. Pol. Sci.* (1971), *passim.*

50 In almost every case class differences are less than party differences: main exceptions are attitudes towards 'Empire First,' Common Market, price increases, and work conditions, that is, specific policies or issues.

51 Percentage differences generally about 25 per cent.

Chapter 6

The Surveys:
Their Purpose and Design

We have now presented theoretical critiques and empirical data for two themes in the study of British politics. The research discussed below is certainly not intended to provide definitive solutions to all, or even a few, of the theoretical issues considered in preceding pages. Nor is it intended to supersede the data already presented on the nature and content of British political cultures. Indeed, even with a large budget to finance both detailed historical research and also surveys of dominant elites and the non-elite, it would not be possible to resolve these issues for all time. The present research, in contrast to such a major and ambitious undertaking, is intended simply to supplement and refine the data already considered. It is neither national in scope nor simply descriptive in focus. For we were not concerned with straightforward description of the extent of commitment to particular ideas and institutions but rather with the factors that influence these commitments and also their impact on political behaviour. These two concerns suggested the need for local surveys in specially chosen constituencies rather than for a large, nationwide survey that would probably only have provided the sort of data that already exists in abundance. We shall describe the actual surveys—their location and major items—in this chapter; in later chapters we shall then present our findings.

6.1 The constituencies chosen

The relationship between theory and research is dialectical in nature—and this is particularly apparent in the present case. It was difficulties in class theory that gave rise to the research into deferential voting; in turn, difficulties with the deference approach have given rise to our reformulation of class theory. Moreover, the research intended to test this reformulation led to additional modifications and thus necessitated a second set of surveys. Likewise, it was dissatisfaction with the civility studies that led to their articulation with class theory. Subsequent research suggested the need for even more revision than had been expected and so explicit concern with civility was dropped in the second stage surveys. Additional research will no doubt suggest the need for even more modification and reformulation of the theoretical approach we have adopted. In the present section, however, we are concerned to present only an account of the two surveys and five constituencies in which our own research was conducted.

For reasons already stated it was decided not to draw a national sample for our research. In the original study, on the contrary, it was decided to focus on a number of quite different constituencies in a single region. Three constituencies were chosen to represent an established working-class community, a mixed residential area, and a solidly middle-class suburb.[1] These constituencies were Stepney, Wood Green, and Wanstead and Woodford, respectively. All three are situated in north-east London. By taking three different types of constituency and including items on class and union membership we were able to study the effects of those factors believed to be most crucial in determining attitudes towards dominant institutions and values. Their general proximity eased administrative burdens and eliminated regional variation when assessing residential community effects. But it also meant that we were unable to explore the importance of regional variations and of rural–urban differences; and were unable adequately to control for the conversion and transplantation effects due to the considerable migration within Greater London.[2] Thus, when the opportunity arose to conduct further research into these problems, it was thought desirable to examine these other effects along with the more recent theoretical developments. In a second set of surveys, therefore, a rural agricultural constituency and a north-eastern mining constituency were selected for investigation. These were the Isle of Ely and Easington, respectively. These constituencies are both predominantly rural but their history and social structure are markedly different. This enables a comparison of the effects of urban and industrial constraints on commitments and voting behaviour when results from these constituencies are compared with those from London. We shall now consider the five constituencies in more detail.

The choice of constituencies in the first surveys was limited by three main factors: they had to be within the same general area, of contrasting types, and preferably within easy reach of

Cambridge. We took Woodford as the representative middle-class suburb because social data from an earlier survey by the Institute of Community Studies was already available.[3] This confirmed the middle-class character of the constituency but also pointed to the continuing influx of East Enders who come because 'the suburb is desirable and by so doing make it less desirable for the people who were there before.'[4] The Institute had also studied a working-class community, Bethnal Green, but we chose Stepney instead because it once had a Communist MP and we hoped to examine the relative civility of the small number of Communist voters who remain.[5] In many ways, however, Stepney is very similar to Bethnal Green. It is an old-established and in some ways declining community close to the City and Port of London. It is predominantly working class in composition and many of the non-manual workers are publicans or shopkeepers and thus, as in Bethnal Green, 'more akin to the working-class people they serve than to the professional men and women with whom they are classified.'[6] Both have also experienced an influx of immigrants and aliens for many decades with the resulting racial and ethnic conflicts and social disorganisation. While the former have not affected political behaviour recently,[7] the general poverty of environment and community life is reflected in abnormally high rates of mental illness and of abstention in national and local elections.[8] Finally, Wood Green was chosen because it is in the same general area as the other two constituencies and is intermediate between them on most indices of social and economic structure (see Table 6.1). The survey work in these three constituencies was conducted in 1968 and is described in the next section.

In the later surveys, conducted in 1972, we decided to examine rural rather than urban areas and to look at other regions. In contrast to the anonymous and mobile world of city life, however mediated in practice by neighbourhood and kinship contacts, small towns and villages are supposedly well-integrated and more likely to have local status systems based on interaction rather than conspicuous consumption.[9] These are conditions more favourable to deferential voting of some kind and thus particularly important in a study of such voting behaviour. However, rural conditions can be combined not only with agriculture and light industry but also with such traditional proletarian pursuits as mining, fishing, or forestry. It therefore seemed worth-while to examine both a rural agricultural area and also a rural mining area. While the Isle of Ely happily combined a rural and agricultural character with proximity to Cambridge, the choice of a mining area was

H

Table 6.1 CHARACTERISTICS OF FIVE CONSTITUENCIES

Characteristics	Constituency				
	Easing-ton %	Ely %	Stepney %	Wood-ford %	Wood Green %
Professional and managerial workers	6	15	6	32	11
Manual workers[a]	84	74	78	37	66
Mine workers	53	*	*	*	*
Farm workers[b]	3	26	*	*	*
Unemployed men[c]	3	2·5	4·4	1·7	3
Owner-occupiers	26	44	3	68	39
Council tenants[d]	50	28	52	13	34
Households without cars	70	46	78	44	64
Households with two or more cars[e]	2	8	2	11	4
Lab Vote, 1966	81	42	76	26	61
Con Vote, 1966 [f]	19	46	17	56	39

[a] Sample Census, 1966, Tab. 6. [d] Sample Census, 1966, Tab. 8.
[b] Sample Census, 1966, Tab. 5. [e] Sample Census, 1966, Tab. 13.
[c] Sample Census, 1966, Tab. 4. [f] Butler and King, 1966, pp313–18.
* Less than 1 per cent.

more difficult. Easington was eventually selected because it is in an entirely different region, has a disproportionately high Labour vote, shares the militant Durham mining tradition, and contains a large number of pit villages.[10] As with docking in Stepney, however, agriculture in the Isle of Ely and mining in Durham are both declining occupations and provide a decreasing proportion of the total employment in the two areas. While this means that these three occupational groups do not constitute too great a proportion of our total sample, the more general character of these constituencies does mean that none of our communities and few of the manual workers in the sample are representative of those areas and those workers supposedly most prone to *embourgeoisement* and the resulting changes in political and economic attitudes.[11] Since the actual extent of *embourgeoisement* is open to doubt, however, the implications of this are difficult to determine. The main effect is likely to be some understatement of the proportion of workers who are neither solidly 'deferential' nor solidaristically proletarian in outlook.

6.2 Samples and techniques

The sampling frames for this research comprised the electoral registers for the five constituencies. A systematic random sample was drawn from these registers to provide 300 respondents in each constituency and the sampling fractions varied accordingly. As we desired to relate the structural location of respondents to commitments to traditionalism, deference, civility, etc, and to voting, it was decided to include only men in the sample. There is greater variation in the structural location of men than women and exclusion of the latter also eliminated the need to control for sex when analysing the results. In a larger survey, one would obviously extend the scope of the analysis to include women.

Questionnaires in the first surveys were dispatched by post in three waves of 100 per constituency in the period July to August, 1968: the wave pattern facilitated administration and permitted more immediate personal following-up of non-respondents. After three weeks a reminder was sent and, two weeks later, a second questionnaire was posted to non-respondents. After a further period of three or more weeks, a one-in-three sample of non-respondents were visited in an effort to ascertain the reasons for non-response and to elicit a reply wherever possible. Where such a reply was forthcoming, it was weighted threefold in the sample. The response rates for different constituencies are presented in Table 6.2.

Table 6.2 SURVEY RESPONSE RATES BY CONSTITUENCY

	Easing-ton	Ely	Stepney	Wood-ford	Wood Green
Initial returns*	172	177	135	168	155
Follow-up returns†	21	12	15	15	27
Refusals	90	82	85	91	74
Moved, demolished	9	8	38	17	31
Deceased, sick	8	11	22	9	10
Language problems‡	—	—	5	—	3
Total, *N*	300	300	300	300	300

* This includes 69 interviews in Ely and 23 in Easington.

† Follow-up returns have been weighted threefold to reflect the one-in-three sampling ratio of non-respondents.

‡ This figure includes only those whose stated reason for non-response was a language problem and not all those who might reasonably be thought to have such difficulties.

Postal techniques involve several well-known drawbacks that tend to counteract their obvious cost and time advantages. In particular, they are associated with lower response rates than interviewing because of the disproportionately low response from the less articulate and from those with lower socio-economic status. Secondly, they are incompatible with carefully structured sequences of questions (since people can read the whole schedule before replying) and also with complete control over which member of a household actually replies.[12] In both stages we tried to overcome the first and last of these difficulties through a personal follow-up of the non-respondents and through the inclusion of certain items allowing a check on who in fact replied.[13] The actual response rates achieved were quite reasonable—ranging from 64 per cent of the effective sample in Stepney to 71 per cent in Wood Green. Moreover, in the second stage surveys, we delivered almost all of the Ely schedules in person and attempted to conduct interviews then or at a later date, whereas the Easington schedules were posted and treated in the same way as the first-stage constituencies. The fieldwork for this stage took place in April and May of 1972. It is interesting to note that the response rates in these two second-stage samples were practically the same but that the Ely sample tended to be more representative of the target population (see Table 6.3). More generally, the actual response was poorer for manual workers and the elderly among demographic groups and, among political groups, poorer for non-voters. This last difference is difficult to interpret since men are more likely to vote than women and since the dead and mobile neither vote nor reply to surveys. Even so, there is clearly significant under-representation of non-voters. The comparison of the Ely and Easington surveys shows that the main drawback in the postal technique is likely to be slightly greater unrepresentativeness rather than lower response rates and this must be borne in mind when interpreting the data below. None the less, this research is primarily analytical rather than descriptive in purpose and such unrepresentativeness is perhaps less of a handicap for this reason. This is especially so where class is controlled and non-voters are exluded from analysis.

Notwithstanding any problems with our samples and techniques, confidence in our data is reinforced, not only by the mutual confirmation revealed when our two surveys are analysed separately, but also, and more significantly, by the similarity of our findings, where comparisons can be made, with those of other surveys based on large national samples with better response

Table 6.3   TARGET AND SAMPLE CHARACTERISTICS

Characteristics	Easing-ton Tgt %	Easing-ton Act %	Ely Tgt %	Ely Act %	Stepney Tgt %	Stepney Act %	Wood-ford Tgt %	Wood-ford Act %	Wood Green Tgt %	Wood Green Act %
Non-manual	16	27*	26	27	22	30*	62	68†	34	43
Manual	84	73	74	73	78	70	38	32	66	57
15–29 yr	27	34†	27	25	21	25†	18	19†	18	21
30–44 yr	27	30	27	29	30	28	26	32	26	26
45–59 yr	25	18†	25	29†	28	34†	34	31†	30	26
60(+) yr	21	18	21	17†	21	13*	21	18	25	27
Non-voters	24	10*	24	14*	49	9*	23	8*	33	9*
Con vote	19	24†	46	46	17	22*	56	51	39	34†
Lab vote	81	76	43	45	76	75	26	36*	61	63
Other vote	—	—	11	9	7	3*	18	13*	—	3
Miners‡	36	38	—	—	—	—	—	—	—	—
Farming	3	3	26	23	—	—	—	—	—	—

*   Difference significant at 0·01 level using two-tailed test.
†   Difference significant at 0·10 level using two-tailed test.
‡   Figure differs from that in Table 5.1 because allowance is made for decline in those employed in mining: see data for Durham in *Annual Abstract of Statistics* (1971), p159.

rates and more sophisticated methods of analysis. In this latter respect, for example, our results are completely at one with those analysed in Chapter 3. It is to be hoped, therefore, that the approach developed in these pages will be employed in subsequent research with more 'respectable' samples.

Finally, we also conducted forty relatively unstructured interviews with selected respondents from Ely and Easington to refine and supplement the original survey data. We were thus able to ask questions that could not usefully be included in a postal questionnaire and also to probe further into matters of interest. Special effort was made to contact 'deviants' in this final survey—that is, persons such as Conservative miners, Labour farm workers, middle-class Labour voters, radical Conservatives in either class, and so on. We also interviewed some of the less 'deviant' respondents in both constituencies. Data from these interviews will be used to illustrate and refine the results from the original surveys.

6.3   Main items and scales

The questionnaires employed in this research were relatively long —the first comprised a total of 109 items, the second included 91 items, and both ranged from agree/disagree statements through check-lists of various kinds to open-ended questions on attitudes and background data. The questionnaire was originally pretested in Cambridge with a systematic random sample of 100 electors—half of whom were interviewed and half of whom received the questionnaire by post. At this stage the scales were constructed and items which elicited a 'don't know' response of 10 per cent or more were revised or eliminated. The response rate from the postal pilot was 60 per cent and this encouraged us to proceed with the postal technique in the first survey. Experience with the questionnaire in the first survey led to some further modifications in the second survey and theoretical considerations led to the inclusion of several additional items. We shall now describe the main items and scales to be employed in the subsequent analysis.

The deference item needs little introduction. It has already been employed in the deference studies and consists in one question which asks the respondent to state a preference for a Prime Minister with an upper-middle-class background or one who is upwardly mobile from the working class. This item was modified, however, through the inclusion of an open-ended alternative giving people the opportunity to say that there is no difference between the two possible premiers and/or to state other criteria for their selection. This modification enables us to examine the relationship between civility and deference more fruitfully: we shall be able to see, for example, whether the civil are more or less likely to be deferential than meritocratic, more or less likely to state alternative criteria of evaluation, and so forth.

Traditionalism is a set of items assessing attitudes towards the traditional social and moral order. It was based on Parkin's analysis of the dominant institutional order and does not include any items specifically related to political institutions. This is necessary if we are to correlate civility and traditionalism without introducing distortions due to an overlap between their two domains of measurement. The emphasis placed in these items on institutions rather than values ought also to be explained. In a society in which values are diffuse and ambiguous and are symbolised in institutions, it is easier to assess commitment to these values through support for institutions than through direct measurement of value orientations. It will be obvious that the traditionalism scale measures only the minimal level of commitment to institutions, that of verbal affirmation. It does not attempt to measure contextual knowledge or behavioural consequences.

In the unstructured interviews with selected respondents we did attempt to investigate these aspects and to relate them to voting behaviour and other attitudes. The actual items included in this scale, with the traditional mode of response in parenthesis, are as follows:[14]

1   Private enterprise is essential to the well-being of society and the prosperity of all (agree)
2   The aristocracy are a privileged minority who have no place in a democratic society (disagree)
3   Britain gave far more to her Empire than she ever received from it (agree)
4   The Royal Family play an important role in British life (agree)
5   Christianity is the best basis for government and personal morality (agree)
6   Public schools provide the best sort of education (agree)
7   War is justified when other ways of settling international disputes fail (agree)

The traditionalism scale measures verbal commitment to a traditional social and moral order rather than to some more modern value system. This is in accord with the usual theoretical arguments and with the fact that it is this order with which the Conservative Party is identified and into which most people were socialised. However, it does not allow for the possibility that the dominant elites now emphasise somewhat different legitimating values and institutions and have rejected some of the older, more jingoistic beliefs and values. To investigate whether the newly emergent 'techno-economistic' value system was also associated with structural location and political behaviour, therefore, we included four new items in the second questionnaire. In conjunction with the item on private property and private enterprise these formed a cumulative, five-item scale designed to measure techno-economism. These four items were as follows:

1   Big business has too much power today (disagree)
2   Science and technology will help mankind to solve its problems without the need for revolution (agree)
3   Further economic growth will not really help us to overcome the problems facing the world today (disagree)
4   More opportunities should be given to successful businessmen to play a major role in government (agree)

In addition to measuring commitment to the overall social and economic order, it was necessary to measure the extent of class or status consciousness among our respondents. The combination of the traditionalism (and techno-economism) score with the extent of such consciousness can then be used to provide an indicator of 'trade-union consciousnesss.' Six items were employed to measure attitudes towards various aspects of the social and economic stratification system. They were combined to form a cumulative scale that included the following items (the class conscious or 'egalitarian' mode of response being indicated in parenthesis):[15]

1   There is little opportunity for talented people to get on in Britain (agree)
2   Some people are superior and deserve special rewards and privileges (disagree)
3   The government should take more steps to reduce social and economic inequalities (agree)
4   The idea of class struggle has no bearing on our current problems (disagree)
5   Too many people in this country are either poor or have trouble managing (agree)
6   Profits should go to the workers and not just to those who happen to own shares in industry (agree)

In addition to these items, one question was included to determine the class self-identity of respondents from a choice of upper, middle, working, other, or none.

Finally, in the first questionnaire only, several items were included to measure verbal commitment to the civic culture. As we noted in Chapter 3, civility is an exceedingly ambiguous and multidimensional value system and/or theoretical model. The measurement of civic orientations is correspondingly difficult. There are two possible approaches—to develop a cumulative scale covering the various aspects of civility or to measure each aspect separately. In the end we employed both approaches. When a gross or overall indicator of civility is required we have employed a simple aggregate scale that does not discriminate between different types of civic orientation. For more detailed analyses, however, we disaggregated this scale and examined items individually. Because of the complex nature of civility the scale was correspondingly long—including eleven items and tapping five different aspects. The latter were as follows: (i) affirmation of the overall legitimacy of the political order; (ii) recognition of the need for prudent and responsible government as well as responsive government; (iii) acceptance of one's own civic duties, that is, to take a moderate interest in political matters and to vote regularly; (iv) recognition of the rights of fellow-citizens to political participation and to the benefits of government; and (v) commitment to the idea of a public interest which ought, at least occasionally, to take precedence over self-interest. The items intended to measure the extent of such orientations were these:

1   It is sometimes necessary to put country before party (agree)
2   So many other people vote in general elections that it doesn't matter much to me whether I vote or not (disagree)
3   Politics is much more important to me than anything else (disagree)
4   It isn't so important to vote when you know your party doesn't have a chance of winning (disagree)
5   Everyone should take some interest in the economy and governmental affairs (agree)
6   Our system of government may need some reform but basically it is fair and just (agree)
7   The whole of politics is a fraud and betrayal of public trust (disagree)
8   Instead of criticising politicians, we should try to understand their problems a bit more (agree)
9   Only those with a definite minimum of intelligence and education should be allowed to vote (disagree)
10   A government should do what it thinks right even if the majority of people disagree (agree)
11   Quite honestly, the majority of people aren't qualified or informed enough to vote on today's problems (disagree)

In addition to these items, some of which were also included in the second questionnaire, we also measured people's professed interest in politics and recorded voting behaviour.

All these items were distributed systematically throughout the body of the questionnaire and some allowance for response set was made by including items that required both agree and disagree responses for someone to gain a score at either extreme of a scale. 'Don't know' responses were assigned alternately to the agree and disagree categories for the purposes of cumulation but are treated as such for the analysis of individual items. In addition, scores on all four scales were trichotomised so that about a third of respondents were classified into each of the three categories of commitment to central values and institutions.[16] This is not only facilitates analysis and tabulation, but also further reduces the distortions due to response set and the particular choice of items for the different scales.[17]

6.4   Summary and conclusions

The research described below is based on two different sets of surveys conducted in 1968 and 1972, respectively. In the first surveys, we chose three different London constituencies to represent a long-established working-class community, a mixed residential area, and a solid middle-class suburb. In the second surveys, two rural areas in different regions were selected for investigation: one of these was predominantly agricultural in tradition, and the other was a traditional mining area. Systematic random samples were then drawn from the electoral registers of each constituency to provide a total of 1,200 male electors. These were then circulated with a questionnaire and a one-in-three sample of those who failed to reply were visited. The effective response rate averaged 67 per cent across the five constituencies. The working classes, the elderly, and non-voters, were all significantly under-represented in almost all these constituencies but the overall pattern of response is reasonable given the analytic intent of the research. The bulk of the present analysis hinges on four new scales measuring traditionalism, techno-economism, egalitarianism, and civility. Each of these is a cumulative scale comprising several agree-disagree items and they have all been trichotomised to facilitate analysis and tabulation. In the following chapters we present the results gathered in these surveys.

6.5   Notes and references

1 The sampling frame employed is that constructed by Moser and Scott from a factor analysis of 1951 Census data: see C A Moser and W Scott, *British Towns* (Edinburgh: Oliver and Boyd, 1961).
2 Willmott and Young, for example, report that 15 per cent of all people living in Woodford were born in the East End, 26 per cent in the inner Essex boroughs of Leyton, East Ham, West Ham, and Walthamstow (now parts of the GLC), and 20 per cent elsewhere in greater London: only 12 per cent were born in Woodford itself. See P Willmott and M Young, *Family and Class in a London Suburb* (London: New English Library, 1967), p14. Unfortunately, no question about length of residence and place of birth was included in the first questionnaire.
3 *Ibid*.
4 *Ibid*, pp16–17.
5 *cf* M Young and P Willmott, *Family and Kinship in East London* (Harmondsworth: Penguin, 1962). P Piratin was elected for the Mile End

division of Stepney in 1945; in 1966 the CP candidate won 7·3 per cent of the total vote and in 1970 he won 5·7 per cent of the vote.

6   *Ibid*, p94; *cf* J H Robb, whose study of working-class anti-semitism in Bethnal Green classified traders as working class because of their low level of education, see *Working-Class Anti-Semite* (London: Tavistock, 1954).

7   *cf* N Deakin, 'GLC elections', *Race Today* (May 1970); for earlier electoral history, however, see: H M Pelling, *Social Geography of British Elections* (London: Macmillan, 1969), pp45–6; P Thompson, *Socialists, Liberals, and Labour* (London: Routledge, 1967), pp238–41; and, for the 1930s, R Benewick, *Political Violence And Public Order* (London: Allen Lane, 1969).

8   *cf* Psychiatric Rehabilitation Association, *Mental Illness in Four London Boroughs* (London: PRA, 1969); Butler and Pinto-Duschinsky, *Election 1970*, p361.

9   See particularly Lockwood, 'Sources of variation in working class consciousness,' *Sociol. Rev.* (1966), xiv, pp249–67; and M Stacey, *Tradition and Change* (London: Oxford University Press, 1960).

10   *cf* W R Garside, *The Durham Miners* (London: Allen & Unwin, 1971), *passim*; Pelling, *Geography*, pp334–8; and D E Butler and R Pinto-Duschinsky, *The British General Election of 1970* (London, 1970), pp427f.

11   *cf* J H Goldthorpe *et al*, *The Affluent Worker*, 3 volumes (London: Cambridge University Press, 1968–9), *passim*.

12   *cf* C A Moser, *Survey Methods of Investigation* (London: Heinemann, 1969), pp175–84.

13   Thus, an item on sex and an item on age allowed us to eliminate two women and three children from the respondents.

14   The first questionnaire employed slightly different versions of some of these items: see Jessop, in *Br. J. Pol. Sc.* (1971), for the original version.

15   The first questionnaire employed slightly different versions of these items and had an item ('everyone has enough money nowadays') in place of that on workers and profits: see *ibid*.

16   For traditionalism, the cutting points were: $0–2 =$ radical, $3–4 =$ intermediate, and $5–7 =$ traditional; for egalitarianism, they were $0–2 =$ inegalitarian, $3 =$ intermediate, and $4–6 =$ egalitarian; for techno-economism, $0–2 =$ low, $3 =$ intermediate, and $4–5 =$ high; and, for civility, $0–6 =$ incivil, $7–8 =$ intermediate; and $9–11 =$ civil. The cutting points for all but techno-economism are based on distributions for the 1968 sample only; this means that a third of respondents for the combined samples do not necessarily fall into each category on a scale.

17   *cf* J A Galtung, *Theory and Methods of Social Research* (London: Allen & Unwin, 1967), p391. Galtung ignores the fact that trichotomised ordinal variables are very difficult to use in partial correlation analysis.

Chapter 7

The Deferential Subject

Deference is almost universally acclaimed as a feature of English political culture. From Bagehot onwards commentators have echoed the sentiment that we are a deferential nation. Until recently, however, there had been little systematic investigation of this assertion nor, indeed, any careful delineation of the character and quality of these deferential attitudes. As we argued above, there are at least four types of deference mentioned in these commentaries and they are not always clearly distinguished. The recent empirical studies show, moreover, that ascriptive socio-political deference is not as common as has often been implied even if it is quite markedly related to Conservative voting. In this chapter, therefore, we consider further the problems involved in the deference theme and introduce some data from our own survey to throw more light on the extent and significance of deference in popular consciousness. Although the present research is not strictly comparable with the earlier studies, there is sufficient similarity in design and method to warrant comparisons and contrasts between the results.

7.1 The extent and impact of deference

We turn first to an examination of the extent of deference—or, more precisely, the extent of ascriptive socio-political deference. Not one of the earlier studies found more than a third of the electorate to voice such deference and the average proportion is less than a quarter in the deference studies proper and under one twenty-fifth in the other studies. Only 12 per cent of our own sample, when asked to choose between two candidates for prime ministerial office, stated a preference for a man with an elite background and almost half (49 per cent) preferred the candidate from a working-class background. Further, more than a third either saw no difference between them or stated alternative criteria of evaluation—such as their abilities, their policies, their character, their sincerity, or simply their party. This latter proportion is similar to that found by Nordlinger among working-class voters: an average of just over a quarter of the male urban workers in his study replied spontaneously that both candidates were equally good and/or that their selection depended on other things.[1] The proportion of ascriptive socio-political deferentials, however, is the lowest yet reported in a study concerned explicitly with deference and it is, moreover, greater for the middle-class or non-manual respondents than for the manual working-class subjects in the sample (see Table 7.1). The middle classes are also significantly more likely to mention alternative criteria of evaluation. For a nation as reputedly deferential as the English, these are not high levels of ascriptive socio-political deference. Indeed, deference to the upwardly mobile, to the man who gets ahead on merit rather than accident of birth, would seem to be more normal.

Table 7.1 DISTRIBUTION OF DEFERENCE BY CLASS

Type of deference	Non-manual subjects %	Manual subjects %	Total %	N
Ascriptive	14	10	12	107
Meritocratic*	40	57	49	436
No difference	17	17	17	151
Depends on . . .†	25	14	19	167
(Ability, policies)	(12)	(5)	(8)	(70)
(Character, etc)	(8)	(5)	(6)	(53)
(Other criteria)	(5)	(4)	(5)	(44)
DK/NA	4	2	3	26
Total, %	100	100	100	
Total, numbers	406	481	887	

* That is, subjects stating a preference for the prime minister who has been upwardly mobile from the working class.

† Those respondents who stated alternative criteria of choice and hereafter termed 'qualified seculars' or 'seculars'.

Moreover, among working-class respondents, deference to an elite political leader was not strongly related to Conservative voting in the 1966 election as compared with earlier elections (see Table 7.2). The earlier studies show that only half of working-class deferentials actually voted Conservative and, indeed, that only a third of younger deferentials did so.[2] The proportions in other studies not concerned explicitly with deference is even less.[3]

In our own sample, taking only the vote for the two major parties, three-fifths of these deferentials supported Labour compared with four-fifths of the meritocratic deferentials. Furthermore, those seeing no difference between the two candidates were almost as favourable to the Conservatives—dividing two-to-one in support of Labour compared with the four-to-one division among the meritocratic deferentials and the three-to-two division among the ascriptive socio-political deferentials. Not only is deference more widespread in the middle classes, however, it is also more strongly related to Conservative voting. Three-quarters of the middle-class ascriptive deferentials voted Tory in contrast to only three-eighths of the meritocratic deferentials. But those who stated alternative criteria of evaluation were also favourable to the Conservatives— they gave about two-thirds of their votes to that party. It is worth noting that there were such marked differences in the voting behaviour of those who saw no difference between the candidates, those who stated some secular criterion of evaluation, and those who preferred the candidate from the working-class background. For all three categories would be labelled 'seculars' or 'prag- matists' in the earlier studies on deference. This procedure is hardly justified in the light of this research and it increases the probability of showing deferentials (a small and homogeneous group) to be different from 'seculars' (a large and heterogeneous group).

Similar relationships were found for vote intention in the next general election among the 1968 sample and also for actual voting in the 1970 general election among the second sample. The relationship between deference and Conservatism was stronger in both cases—this reflects the decline in Labour fortunes at the time both samples were drawn and also a possible decline in ascriptive socio-political deference between 1968 and 1972. Even so, more of such deferentials in the working class intended voting Labour in 1968 than intended to vote Conservative. Indeed, there was less defection to the latter party and less uncertainty or wavering among these deferentials than in any other group of working-class deferentials. This suggests that working-class ascriptive deferen- tials who vote Labour weight other factors more strongly than having an elitist political leadership since they are more resistant to adverse swings than are the meritocratic deferentials.[4] The relationship was again stronger in the middle class. In terms of voting intention the ascriptive socio-political deferentials divided six-to-one in favour of the Conservative Party compared with a three-to-two division among the meritocratically deferential

Table 7.2 VOTING IN 1966 BY DEFERENCE AND CLASS

Middle class

Type of deference	Con %	Lab %	Lib %	DNV %	Total %	N
Ascriptive	68	18	2	11	101	56
Meritocratic	32	52	6	9	99	145
No difference	42	39	9	9	99	64
Depends on . . .	60	27	5	8	100	84
Total, number	162	135	20	32		349
Average, %	46	39	6	9		

Working class

Type of deference	Con %	Lab %	Lib %	DNV %	Total %	N
Ascriptive	40	56	2	2	100	45
Meritocratic	16	72	3	9	100	250
No difference	26	53	4	16	99	68
Depends on . . .	15	70	2	13	100	54
Total, number	83	280	12	42		417
Average, %	20	70	3	10		

group. In the second sample, as well, the relationship between deference and voting was also strengthened. In the latter survey, however, the proportion of deferentials proper was lower in both classes and this could be due to a disproportionately greater ebbing away of such deference among Labour sympathisers as other criteria are emphasised in the dominant value system. This suggestion is reinforced by the fact that, while the overall proportion of deferentials in the second sample was lower, the contribution of deferentials to the total Conservative vote in both classes was greater. Within the working class, two-thirds of the ascriptive deferentials voted Conservative compared with only one-seventh of the meritocratic deferentials. In the middle class only one of the fifteen deferentials voted Labour compared with three-in-five of the meritocratic deferentials.

So far we have concerned ourselves only with voting and voting intentions. It could reasonably be argued that this concern leads to an understatement of the strength of any relationship between deference and partisanship since a certain number of voters will support a given party without feeling any firm attachments to it. Both the major deference studies report that deferentials are more partisan in support of the Conservative Party than secular voters. We can examine this question more directly by considering the reported party identifications of respondents in our second sample. We find that none of the middle-class ascriptive socio-political deferentials identifies with the Labour Party, while almost half of the meritocratic deferentials do so (see Table 7.3). The relation is not so strong in the working class but it is still present with ascriptive deferentials more than five times as likely as meritocratic deferentials to identify with the Conservative Party. In fact, there are more working-class ascriptive deferentials who have a Conservative partisan identity than there are such deferentials who actually voted Conservative in 1970. Thus the data on partisan attachments support the findings on voting behaviour—as, indeed, one would expect in the light of the strong correlations reported in the literature between party self-identification and support for different parties in elections.[5]

Table 7.3 CLASS, DEFERENCE, AND PARTY IDENTIFICATION

Party identity	Middle class, %				Working class, %			
	ASPD	*MD*	*ND*	*QS**	*ASPD*	*MD*	*ND*	*QS*
Con	82	24	48	50	38	7	20	16
Lab	0	49	32	19	31	70	40	63
Lib	6	6	8	2	6	4	3	3
None	12	21	12	26	19	17	34	13
DK/NA	0	0	0	2	6	2	3	5
Total, %	100	100	100	99	100	100	100	100
Base, *N*	17	67	25	42	16	138	35	38

* ASPD—ascriptive socio-political deferential; MD—meritocratic deferential; ND—no difference; QS—qualified secular. This scheme will be used in subsequent tables in this chapter.

Overall, however, there is little evidence to suggest that this type of deference is an especially important source of Conservative support among the working class. On this both the present research and earlier work are in agreement. In the middle classes, however, ascriptive socio-political deference is more widespread and is also more strongly related to Conservative voting and party attachments. But it still does not provide the bulk of Conservative support in the middle class. Even if we assume that such deference is a cause rather than a correlate of voting behaviour, it does not explain or account for much of the observed variation. Its greater significance in the middle class can be explained in terms of the presence of fewer cross-pressures on the middle-class Conservative to vote for another party. Within the working class a greater number of ascriptive socio-political deferentials will feel constrained to vote against their leadership preferences. Thus, in our combined sample, Conservative support is drawn disproportionately from those deferentials who do not belong to unions, who live in agricultural or middle-class constituencies, who are older rather than younger, and who worked in small plants.[6] In saying this, however, we are simply confirming what our reappraisal of the deference studies has already suggested and the new data we can offer on the non-manual worker in no way upsets that analysis. If we are looking for a more general explanation of Conservatism, then it may pay us to examine other types of deference. This we shall do in the following chapter.

7.2 Structural location and personal attributes

We now turn, however, to an examination of the structural location and personal attributes of different types of deferential and non-deferential electors. This analysis is necessarily restricted by the paucity of deferentials in the two samples—we cannot push cross-tabulations too far without undermining the numerical basis of comparative proportions and percentages. Nor can we establish with any certainty that structural location or personal attributes contribute causally to the acceptance or rejecton of deferential attitudes. For such an analysis would require cross-temporal data on the coincidence and emergence of these attitudes and suggested independent variables. None the less, if we do find that deference correlates in the expected ways with structural location and with personal attributes, then some indirect support will have been demonstrated for the underlying causal model we have adopted.

Ascriptive socio-political deference seems to be firmly institutionalised in the dominant value system and thus we may expect the expression of deferential orientations to be correlated with social and economic status. But the deference studies are not very helpful on the origins of deferential attitudes. They concentrate overmuch on such personal or individual variables as income, age, sex, or class identity and neglect structural factors such as residential community, factory size, type of employment, union membership, and so on. The data may be summarised briefly in these generalisations—women are more deferential than men, the old than the young, the lower paid than the higher paid, home-owners than tenants, regular savers rather than non-savers, those employed in large firms rather than small firms, workers without personal contacts with their employers rather than those with such contacts, the irreligious rather than the religious, the subjectively 'middle class' among the lower paid rather than the subjectively 'working class' in this income group, and, possibly, those in the south of England rather than the north.[7] Several of these relations are weak (income, self-class, *embourgeoisement*, size of plant, contacts with employers, religiosity, and region) while three are also counter-intuitive (plant size, employer contact, and religiosity). Moreover, the rationale behind these analyses is not clear—little attention going to the 'deviant' Labour-voting deferentials and several possible structural analyses going unreported. For example, there is no analysis of deference by union membership, region, or organisational involvement, although these independent variables were included in one or both of the key deference studies. There is still considerable scope, therefore, for an investigation of deference and its origins—especially if we spread our net to include the hitherto neglected middle classes.

Our model of hegemonic society suggests that deference will be related to social and economic status. Moreover, those who are insulated from the dominant values by virtue of non-commercial employment, union membership, or residence in a predominantly working-class community, may reasonably be expected to be less deferential. Plant size can also be expected to have this effect. Exposure to the dominant order also occurs through the school system and it is reasonable to expect that alumni of public and grammar schools will be more deferential than those who attended elementary or secondary schools. Finally, if it is true that ascriptive socio-political deference is a declining force in the dominant value system, then younger respondents should be less deferential as they will have been less exposed to deferential values of this type. In this section we shall put these hypotheses to the test. The relevant percentages are shown in Table 7.4.

It has already been shown that socio-political deference is associated with occupational prestige and responsibilities within the middle class itself. Whereas one-sixth of those in higher managerial and professional occupations prefer the elite background candidate, only one-ninth of routine non-manual workers do so. Indeed, with the highest occupational group, Hall-Jones class one, 23 per cent of respondents preferred this candidate. More generally, we see that the lower the socio-economic status, the more favourable people are to the candidate from the working-class background. As anticipated, union membership and residence in a predominantly working-class constituency are also associated with increased meritocratic deference and lower rates of preference for the elite background prime minister.

Plant size and type of employment were also linked to variations in deference. These variables were measured directly only in the 1972 sample. We found that, whereas middle-class employees in nationalised industries and in state or local authorities had only 4 per cent deferentials, 17 per cent of the self-employed and 14 per cent of the commercially employed preferred Mr X. There was also a slight association between type of employment and such a preference in the working class.[8] Likewise, whereas 15 per cent of non-manual workers in firms with twenty or fewer employees were ascriptive socio-political deferentials, among those employed in firms with more than 250 workers only 11 per cent shared this attitude. Within the working class, moreover, the proportion of such deferentials in the larger plants was only half that for those employed in the very small firms.[9]

Schooling and age have less clearcut effects upon deferential attitudes—especially in the working class. This may well be due to the overriding importance of other, more immediate structural influences in the latter case and, in the case of the middle class, to the masking effects of variation in qualified secularism. This varied with length of education and there was also a strong association between type of school and length of education. For example, 18 per cent of those in the middle class who left school when they were fifteen or younger gave alternative criteria of evaluation; fully 40 per cent of those who stayed on beyond eighteen were qualified seculars. If we consider only the rate of ascriptive socio-political deferentials to meritocratic deferentials in this class, however, then we do find a degree of support for the hypotheses outlined above. Thus, among those who attended secondary or elementary school, this ratio was one-to-three; it was more than one-to-one for those who attended public school. Similarly, among the youngest respondents one-in-five of those who expressed a choice for either candidate selected the elite background man; conversely, the oldest middle-class respondents divided one-to-two in his favour. For the working class, however, the relationships were very weak and not significant.

Finally, we shall consider the relationship between deference and religion. Although McKenzie and Silver report an apparently odd negative association between religious involvement and a

Table 7.4 STRUCTURAL LOCATION AND PERSONAL ATTRIBUTES OF DEFERENTIALS

Independent variables	Middle class, %					Working class, %				
	ASPD	MD	ND	QS	N	ASPD	MD	ND	QS	N
Hall-Jones SES										
1+2 or 6	17	30	18	32	(122)	11	56	15	15	(230)
3+4 or 7+8	14	42	17	24	(181)	10	58	18	13	(251)
5	11	49	16	18	(88)	—	—	—	—	—
Union member										
Member	9	50	16	25	(121)	9	62	16	13	(280)
Non-member	17	38	19	26	(270)	12	55	18	15	(196)
Constituency										
Woodford	21	34	18	27	(126)	19	51	19	10	(52)
Isle of Ely	15	36	17	31	(86)	12	56	18	14	(102)
Wood Green	18	39	20	22	(79)	9	55	25	11	(102)
Stepney	6	52	19	23	(50)	14	60	12	13	(99)
Easington	6	55	15	23	(65)	3	64	13	20	(126)
Schooling										
Elem/sec	17	52	17	14	(178)	9	58	14	10	(349)
Grammar	11	31	21	37	(149)	11	67	9	13	(46)
Public	28	25	8	39	(36)	10	60	20	20	(10)
Age group										
Under-29	10	43	14	33	(84)	10	58	14	18	(105)
30–44	16	37	22	25	(106)	11	58	17	14	(136)
45–64	15	44	13	27	(160)	9	57	20	13	(175)
65+	18	36	33	13	(50)	12	63	18	8	(52)

preference for the elite background prime minister, data from our first sample reveal a positive association on three different measures of religious commitment. In the middle class, for example, almost a quarter of Anglicans chose this candidate in contrast to only a seventh of atheists and agnostics. Similarly, 22 per cent of those who had attended church within the previous six months were deferential to Mr X compared with 15 per cent of others. Thirdly, among those scoring high on a religiosity attitudinal scale, 22 per cent were deferential; this compares with 14 per cent among those scoring low on the same scale.[10] The relationships within the working class were in the expected direction only on the last two of these variables but both of these relationships were as strong as in the middle class.[11] The unexpected negative association between religious affiliation and deference in the working class could well be due to the greater willingness of manual than non-manual workers to claim nominal membership of the established church when their actual religious commitment is very weak or non-existent. When one employs more rigorous measures, the relationship is in the expected direction.

Overall, therefore, the relations between structural location and personal attributes, on the one hand, and deferential orientations, on the other hand, do support our interpretation of commitment to dominant values. We found that ascriptive socio-political deferentials tend to be drawn disproportionately from the higher social strata, non-union members, residents in predominantly middle-class or agricultural areas, those employed in small firms and organisations, those employed in commercial concerns, the alumni of public or grammar schools, and the religious. These relationships tend to be stronger for the middle classes than the working classes but are generally weak even for the former respondents. This weakness is probably due to three factors—the low percentage of deferentials proper in both classes, the inadequacies of the ascriptive socio-political deference item itself, and the wide variation in the proportions of different categories who are seculars. The last two factors are related. The deference item cuts across the social and political aspects of culture but a third of the respondents did not translate their social attitudes into a preference for one or other candidate for prime ministerial office. They either expressed indifference between them or stated alternative criteria for making a choice. All three factors make it more difficult to discover the relationships between social location and deferential orientations. The employment of a scale such as 'traditionalism,' however, avoids this problem and, as we shall see in our next chapter, commitment to the traditional social and moral order is more noticeably related to social location and personal attributes.

7.3 Social and political thought of deferentials

We shall now examine some concomitants of deference—class self-identity, egalitarianism, traditionalism, political interest, and civility. Following this, we shall summarise the findings of the present chapter and then proceed to investigate the nature, distribution, impact, and origins of traditionalism.

There are three different views about the relationship between deference and class self-identity. In his analysis of working-class consciousness, Lockwood suggests that the deferential worker claims to be nothing grander than 'working class' and thus shares the same nominal identity as the traditional proletarian.[12] Mark Abrams goes further and argues the deferential orders of whom Bagehot wrote are coterminous with subjectively working-class Conservative voters.[13] On the other hand, Parkin argues that deferential attitudes and a middle-class self-identity are both correlated with working-class Conservatism since all three phenomena are aspects of socialisation into the same central value system. Some support for this can be found in Runciman's discovery that, among working-class voters, middle class self-identity only has an effect on Conservative voting when an orthodox, traditional meaning is given that identity.[14] McKenzie and Silver also find that, at least among the lower income Conservatives, deferentials are more likely to identify themselves as middle class. Nordlinger found no significant differences in this respect between deferentials and pragmatists.[15] Finally, Rose takes a middle line between these two opposing positions. He says that the deferential may regard himself as either working class or middle class and that both identities are compatible with the dominant motive of deference to the upper classes.[16] Just as earlier research is vague and inconsistent on this topic, so too is the present survey. For, among the working-class deferentials, we find both those who identify with the middle class and those who believe they are working class. The latter outnumber the former but those who identify with the working class are also less prone to choose the elite-background prime ministerial candidate. In short, there is some support for all three views. Within the middle class, on the other hand, not only are the subjectively 'middle class' more prone to ascriptive socio-political deference but they also make up the greater number of such deferentials (see Table 7.5). Thus, we see once again that the middle-class respondents conform to the theoretically anticipated pattern—taking Parkin's view in the present case—more than do the working classes. We shall discuss the significance of this finding at the end of the chapter.

Table 7.5 DEFERENCE BY SELF-CLASS AND OCCUPATION

Type of deference	Non-manual, %			Manual, %		
	M C	*W C*	*None**	*M C*	*W C*	*None**
Ascriptive	24	9	17	15	9	12
Meritocratic	29	55	28	51	60	50
No difference	19	17	10	17	16	23
Depends on . . .	29	19	45	17	14	15
Total, per cent	101	101	100	100	99	100
Base, *N*	(147)	(197)	(42)	(41)	(343)	(66)

* Legend: M C—those identifying themselves as upper or as middle class; W C—those identifying themselves as working class; None—those declaring they do not think in these terms and not mentioning alternative class-identities.

We can explore the inter-relations between deference and the dominant value system in two further ways. If deference is an integral part of the dominant cultural order, then it should be linked to other dominant values as well as to middle-class self-identity. Thus, there should be a positive correlation between preference for an upper class prime minister and commitment to other hierarchical, elitist values. Similarly, there should also be a correlation with support for other dominant social, economic, and moral institutions. We can test both hypotheses by comparing the scores of such deferentials on egalitarianism, traditionalism, and techno-economism, with those of others in the same class. There is indeed such a link in both classes in each case. Thus, in both the middle and the working classes, traditionals are four times as likely to choose the upper-class candidate as are the radicals; and they are correspondingly less likely to choose the upwardly mobile, working-class candidate. Likewise, in the case of egalitarianism, there is a slight link between status-hierarchical attitudes in the working class and deference towards someone at the top of the central stratification system. This link is stronger in the middle class—here the class conscious are also most likely to choose the upwardly mobile person. From Table 7.6 we can also see that indifference and qualified secularism are not related to traditionalism in either class; nor to inegalitarianism in the working class. This reinforces our earlier remarks about secularism and the translation, or otherwise, of commitments to the dominant institutional order into preferences for a prime minister. Earlier we found that there were marked variations in voting behaviour between types of 'pragmatic' electors, although previous studies categorised them as one. Now we find that there is little homogeneity in their degree of commitment to traditional values and institutions. It remains to be seen whether socio-political deference —ascriptive or meritocratic—is a major intervening variable in voting behaviour or simply an incidental concomitant of traditional Conservatism. In either event, moreover, it is still necessary to discover the ways in which other voters translate—if at all —attachments and hostilities to the dominant order into the choice between political parties.

Table 7.6 EGALITARIANISM, TRADITIONALISM, AND DEFERENCE

Type of deference	Egalitarianism, %			Traditionalism, %		
	Inegal	Med	Egal	Trad	Med	Rad
Non-Manual						
ASPD	22	18	7	24	10	6
MD	24	40	56	31	44	56
ND	23	17	14	18	20	13
QS	31	24	22	27	26	24
N	(130)	(103)	(158)	(154)	(155)	(82)
Manual						
ASPD	13	14	8	17	9	4
MD	57	53	61	49	64	57
ND	17	18	17	21	14	21
QS	13	14	14	13	13	19
N	(60)	(125)	(295)	(144)	(225)	(104)

There are similar variations by deference in commitment to the increasingly dominant techno-economistic value system. Not one of the ascriptive socio-political deferentials in either class scored 'low' on techno-economism. One-in-six of meritocratic deferentials in both classes, on the other hand, did record such a score. There are corresponding differences at the top end of the scale. Three-quarters of middle-class ascriptive deferentials scored 'high' but only one-third of meritocratic deferentials. Likewise, within the working class, whereas almost half of the former deferentials scored 'high,' under a third of the meritocratic deferentials did so.[17] In the case of three different indicators of attachment to the dominant institutional order, therefore, ascriptive socio-political deference appears to be linked in with a more general world view. In both the classes under consideration the deferential voter is more 'conservative' as well as more 'Conservative.'

Many writers have tended to treat the working-class Tory—especially the deferential Tory—as politically ignorant and apathetic and as socially unaware.[18] However, not only do the two major studies show that the Conservative manual worker is more strongly committed to his party than the Labour supporter, but also that the deferential is more partisan than the secular. In addition, McKenzie and Silver purport to show that deferentials are as politically knowledgeable and self-confident as seculars.[19] But partisanship is not incompatible with ignorance and the items employed in both the studies have a distinctly Tory flavour. Thus McKenzie and Silver argue that the Labour voter is less partisan because he agrees with the Conservative worker that the Tory Party is more patriotic, more likely to keep up the Empire, and more likely to ensure the country's prosperity. They do not include items on matters that are plausibly more salient to Labour voters—such as the party that is likely to do more for the working class. They do show Labour supporters to be more partisan in assessing the party closer to the interests of everyone in the country.[20] There are similar problems with the index of political knowledge employed in both studies. This is based upon the ability to name political leaders. Yet the Tory Party is peculiarly identified with an emphasis on leadership and deferentials, by definition, are oriented primarily to the qualities of leadership. It would seem only reasonable, therefore, to expect deferentials to perform better on such a test and not just as well as seculars. Yet fewer deferentials than seculars actually identified all three party leaders in the McKenzie and Silver survey.[21] Finally, it is perhaps significant that deferentials in this survey were one-and-a-half times more likely than seculars to say that people like themselves had no say in how the country was run. Nordlinger found that Tory deferentials were more likely to say that people like themselves had no influence on government and also that such deferentials were less satisfied with this situation than pragmatists.[22] In short, the data on partisanship, knowledge, and political efficacy are decidedly ambiguous and difficult to interpret. This contrasts with the more clearcut data on the social conservatism and general traditionalism of deferentials compared with seculars. In this respect as well, therefore, there remains scope for further investigation.

We turn finally to consider the extent of political interest and civility among deferentials. It will be recalled that several writers have treated the working-class deferential as politically apathetic and ignorant. Others have argued that, apathetic or not, he is certainly also politically deferential. However, our own data show that, in both the middle and the working class, deferentials are in fact more often interested in politics than uninterested and also more interested than meritocratic deferentials. This interest carries over into voting behaviour. Conservative ascriptive socio-political deferentials in both classes are more likely to express an interest in politics than are those same deferentials who vote for the Labour Party.[23] Whatever the reasons for this relationship it is certainly not compatible with the argument that deferentials are apathetic. Those who do tend to be uninterested, indeed, seem to be disproportionately *indifferent* to the choice of candidates in both classes (see Table 7.7). Within the middle class, those who stated an alternative criterion of candidate evaluation were also more likely to be interested in politics. Political interest probably produces qualified secularism rather than vice versa; while, conversely, lack of interest probably leads to indifference in the choice of prime minister. Political interest may also make people more sensitive to their political environment so that, other things being equal, the greater their interest, the more likely they are to share the political attitudes and voting habits of the local community. This might explain the relation between interest and ascriptive deference in the middle class—among whom merito-cratic deferentials tend to be less politically interested—and, given the structural location of working-class deferentials, the greater interest of these individuals as well. Such an hypothesis would also explain the tendency for working-class meritocratic deferentials to be more interested than average in politics. There are too few deferentials, however, to be able to test this inter-pretation.

In contrast to their greater interest, middle-class deferentials are disproportionately low-scoring on civility. Within the working class, however, they do tend to be more civil also. The explana-tion for this apparently anomalous finding is to be found in the pattern of responses to civility items. Middle-class deferentials are disproportionately incivil because they distrust majority

Table 7.7 POLITICAL INTEREST, CIVILITY, AND DEFERENCE

Type of deference	Civility*, %			Political interest†, %			
	Low	Med	High	None	Low	Med	High
Non-manual							
ASPD	33	15	13	5	19	13	22
MD	48	38	43	62	47	39	29
ND	12	24	19	24	15	21	10
QS	8	22	26	10	18	27	39
N	(52)	(77)	(101)	(21)	(93)	(224)	(51)
Manual							
ASPD	11	7	22	5	10	11	21
MD	57	51	43	51	56	61	72
ND	21	42	17	30	22	15	5
QS	10	10	17	13	12	11	12
N	(61)	(98)	(69)	(37)	(169)	(219)	(43)

* Civility items were included only in the first survey.
† Political interest was included in both surveys.

opinion and reject the rights of the ill-informed and ill-educated to participate in elections; they are not incivil by virtue of any lesser political deference or greater political alienation.[24] The civic orientations of this group are thus quite consistent with an elitist choice for prime minister. The lesser civility of working class meritocratic deferentials cannot be traced to particular orientations—it is simply the product of slight but cumulative differences in response to various civility items. Variations such as these reinforce our earlier remark that civility is a difficult concept to employ in research and that its multidimensional nature necessitates disaggregation of component parts it it is to be useful. When this is done we shall frequently find that one or other component is associated particularly strongly with distinctive attitudes towards other dominant institutions and values. The link between middle-class deference and distrust of the majority is just one example of this covariation; others will be reported in later chapters.

7.4 Summary and conclusions
In this chapter we have examined several aspects of deference and secularism in the light of previous studies and our own survey. We were particularly concerned with the extent, impact, and location of ascriptive socio-political deference. The main results can be summarised briefly as follows.

Such deference is limited in extent in all studies and meritocratic deference is more normal. Only one-eighth of our respondents chose the political leader with an elite background and almost half chose the man who had been upwardly mobile from the working class. Furthermore, over a third were either indifferent in the matter or stated alternative criteria of selection. We also found that such deference had a limited impact on working-class voting although it was more strongly related to voting in the middle class. The social location and personal attributes of ascriptive socio-political deferentials are consistent with the argument that structural centrality and exposure to dominant values and institutions have important effects on commitment to 'ruling ideas.' They were drawn disproportionately from the highest social strata, small firms, commercial concerns and the self-employed, non-union members, public and grammar schools, those resident in predominantly middle class or agricultural constituencies, the religiously involved, and the elderly. Lastly, we examined some concomitants of deference and found some evidence for the view that ascriptive socio-political deference is related to other dominant values and attitudes. Those who scored 'high' on inegalitarianism, traditionalism, and techno-economism, for example, were also more prone to choose the upper-class prime-ministerial candidate. Those with a 'middle-class' self-identity were also more likely to make this choice.

However, the fact that many subjectively 'working-class' voters in both classes were ascriptive socio-political deferentials and also committed to traditionalism, inegalitarianism, and techno-economism, suggests these data cannot just be explained in terms of the middle class (objective or subjective) being more committed to middle class values. Rather, there seems to be a good case for interpreting them in terms of centrality and exposure to central values. The greater strength of relationships in the middle class is then due to the greater coincidence of the two sets of variables—centrality and exposure—for this class compared with the working class. There are fewer cross-pressures on the former to disturb or reduce the expected relationships. Moreover, for the same reasons, the middle classes are more likely to have a contextual knowledge of central values, with the result that they are also more likely to translate them into political action. Among working-class voters, however, the combination of cross-pressures, limited exposure, and limited commitment (including limited contextual understanding) is likely to reduce the strength of relations even where some commitment to dominant values is expressed. Further support for this interpretation can be found in the social location of class deviants. Within the middle class those least committed to the central values are those who, whatever their socio-economic status, are the least exposed to the central order. And, within the working class, it is again those most insulated from such contacts or exposure who are least committed to conservatism and the Conservative Party.

Given the degree of support for this interpretation provided by our data, it is perhaps surprising that ascriptive socio-political deference is so limited in extent. In this respect at least traditional values have not been communicated successfully to the periphery —although one must admit that deference to the upwardly mobile is not exactly a countercultural value. None the less, while ascriptive socio-political deference is generally limited in extent, it does seem to form part of a more widely held value system includ- ing traditionalism, inegalitarianism, techno-economism, Con- servativism, and 'middle-class' self-identity. It seems useful, therefore, to investigate the extent, impact, social location, and concomitants, of other components of this value system.

Such an investigation should not only prove theoretically interesting but should also be more satisfactory on methodological grounds. For the deference items which form the operational bases of the deference studies are inadequate in two respects—not all those who are 'deferentials' in the broad sense actually translate their social commitments into preferences for an upper class political leader and thus, secondly, the item provides insufficient deferentials for rigorous analysis. Purely on operational grounds, therefore, we could argue in favour of the traditionalism or inegalitarianism scales as measures of deference since they avoid the problem of 'deferentials' who do not express their deference in political leadership preferences and since they can also be split up so as to provide sufficiently large numbers of socio-cultural and socio-economic deferentials for more extensive analysis. In this way the analysis will be made more fruitful theoretically and the deference item can be retained for the measurement of that aspect of deference it alone can measure—ascriptive socio-political deference.

7.5 Notes and references

1 Nordlinger, *Tories*, p67. Calculated using the weighting index: the actual percentage was 27·4.
2 *Ibid*, p67; and McKenzie and Silver, *Angels*, pp156, 224.
3 A Liberal candidate stood in 1966 only in the Isle of Ely and in Wan- stead and Woodford; this complicates the analysis to some extent but the main points hold for each class in each constituency.

4 Further support for this argument is found in the fact that in the first sample ascriptive socio-political deferentials who voted Labour in 1966 are less likely ever to have voted Tory than are such deferentials who voted Conservative ever to have voted Labour (18 and 30 per cent, respectively, have voted for the other party at least once).

5 *cf* Butler and Stokes, *Political Change*, pp36–8.

6 For, example, whereas half the trade union members who expressed a preference for the elite prime minister voted Labour, less than a third of non-members did so. Likewise, whereas half of those with a working-class background voted Labour in 1966, only a tenth of those with a middle-class father did so. None of those employed in small or medium-sized plants voted Labour, whereas a third of those employed in large plants did so. More than half those resident in Easington, Stepney, and Wood Green voted Labour, only a quarter of those from Woodford and Ely.

7 On sex differences, see McKenzie and Silver, *Angels*, pp187f; on age, *ibid*, pp183–5; and Nordlinger, *Tories*, p68; on income, savings, and home-ownership, *Angels*, pp92–7 and 185–6; on class identity, *ibid*, pp196–200, and *Tories*, pp175–83; on plant size, employer contact, see Nordlinger, in *New Society* (13 October 1966); and on religion, see *Angels*, pp194–5. Regional differences may be inferred from a comparison of Nordlinger's national data and those of Blumler *et al*, for Leeds: Nordlinger reports a national average of 16 per cent deference and Blumler *et al*, using the same operational definition, found only 5 per cent among Leeds men in a 1969 quota sample (personal communication).

8 Eleven per cent of the commercially employed, 9 per cent of those in state and local authority organisations, preferred 'Mr X.'

9 Ingham also found his deferentials to be concentrated in one small plant rather than his two large firms: see Ingham, in *Sociol. Rev.* (1969), p242. For our own sample, the percentages were 14 and 7, respectively, for small and large plants.

10 This scale is described in Chapter 10, note 27.

11 Nineteen per cent of church-attenders, 11 per cent of non-attenders, are deferential; 20 per cent of those scoring 'high' on religiosity, 14 per cent of low-scorers, were deferential.

12 Lockwood, in *Sociol. Rev.* (1966), p252.

13 Abrams, *Public Opin. Q.* (1961), p345.

14 Runciman, *Relative Deprivation*, pp170–87.

15 McKenzie and Silver, *Angels*, p197; Nordlinger, *Tories*, p164.

16 Abrams and Rose, *Must Labour Lose?*, p87.

17 Middle class A S P Ds were 77 per cent techno-economist, M Ds were 34 per cent; in the working class these figures were 44 and 29 per cent, respectively

18 For example, N Birnbaum writes of them as 'the most economically, intellectually, and psychologically restricted manual workers. Their Toryism may well be a classical case of what Engels called 'false consciousness'— in so far as it is conscious at all.' See N Birnbaum, 'Great Britain: the reactive revolt,' in M Kaplan, Editor, *The Revolution in World Politics* (New York: Wiley, 1962), p52.

19 McKenzie and Silver, *Angels*, pp121–6 and 193–4.

20 *Ibid*, pp113–20. Abrams and Rose, *Must Labour Lose?* report that Labour voters do not rank highly in party evaluation either respect for British traditions or being out for the nation as a whole; prosperity and raising everyone's standard of living are more important and are associated with greater partisanship (p12). Westergaard makes a similar criticism in his article in *Socialist Register, 1970*.

21 McKenzie and Silver, *Angels*, p193n; they were also less likely to score nil on the political awareness scale.

22 Nordlinger, *Tories*, pp97–103.

23 In the working class, 14 of the 18 ASPDs who voted Tory were (very) interested, compared with 13 of the 25 who voted Labour; in the middle class, 29 from 34 Tory ASPDs and 5 from 11 Labour ASPDs were thus interested.

24 For example, 42 per cent of middle-class ASPDs and 70 per cent of MDs disagreed that only those above a certain minimum of education should vote.

Chapter 8

Traditionalism, Social Structure and Voting

Traditionalism, although it comprises a major element in British political culture, has scarcely been investigated in political survey research. This is especially surprising because of the many indications, both theoretical and empirical, that it may be an important influence in many respects. The role of traditionalism in the maintenance of social and political stability has been adumbrated not only by left-wing polemicists such as Anderson and Nairn but also by Tory philosophers such as Burke and Hailsham.[1] Studies of party images have shown that a major component in their construction is a general traditionalism factor.[2] It has been suggested that the greater partisanship of Conservative voters in support of their own party and in opposition to other parties, which is now well-established in sociological research, occurs because 'Conservatives are probably twice-armed—by their ordinary party loyalties and by an extra element of confidence in their party's embodiment of the enduring values of British society and culture.'[3] The Conservative Party itself, as we saw earlier, has tried to identify itself exclusively with the traditional social, economic, and moral order. It has been argued that traditionalism produce Conservative voting and inhibits the implementation of radical change by left-wing governments. As with deference in its narrower sense, therefore, traditionalism has been held to have a wide variety of consequences.

Yet evidence as to the actual importance of traditionalism is rarely cited in support of any of these arguments. Moreover, such evidence as is cited derives largely from studies into quite other matters. Thus even Parkin, in his major theoretical discussion of the role of traditionalism in the genesis of voting behaviour and the difficulties faced by left-wing governments, is forced to rely on a motley collection of references not one of which actually examines attitudes towards the dominant order. The evidence he mentions is equally compatible with an interpretation of voting behaviour based only on class consciousness, structural mediation, or simple inherited party loyalties. The data we have marshalled in preceding chapters does provide somewhat more direct support for his reformulation of the deference thesis but it is hardly conclusive and does not suggest that traditionalism is a major element in the causation of electoral behaviour. There must remain some doubt, therefore, as to the general role and relative importance of traditionalism in the determination of voting, party identities, governmental performance, and political stability. Accordingly, in this chapter, we present some more direct evidence on some of these issues from our own survey. We shall be particularly concerned with the impact of traditionalism and techno-economism and the ways in which their effects are mediated through structural channels. Following our presentation of these data, attention will be turned to the origins and concomitants of traditionalism, to the structural location and the social and political thought of those with different scores on the traditionalism scale.

8.1 Traditionalism and voting behaviour

We have already seen that there is a moderate degree of association between support for several traditional institutions and electoral support for the Conservative Party. Moreover, we have also seen that ascriptive socio-political deference, which is now established as an apparent cause of such support, is quite strongly related to traditionalism. It is now time to discuss evidence that is more directly relevant to any assessment of the relations between voting behaviour and the latter type of deference, that is, deference to traditional values and institutions. If the Conservative Party is more closely identified with the traditional social and moral order, and if socio-cultural commitments are expressed for one reason or another in political choice, then there should be a positive correlation between traditionalism and Conservative voting. This is indeed the case.

In both the middle and working classes, those who score low on traditionalism are disproportionately Labour in their reported vote for the 1966 general election (see Table 8.1). The correlation is stronger for non-manual workers than manual workers. Thus, whereas traditionalism explains two-thirds of the variation in the two-party vote for the middle class, for the working class it accounts for just under a third. Disaggregation of the scale improves its explanatory power in both classes relative to the grouped, trichotomous scale, but this still does not affect the

K

comparative weakness of the relation within the working class. Thus, while all of those who scored nil on the traditionalism scale voted Labour in 1966, under half of those manual workers with the maximum possible score voted Conservative in contrast to 89 per cent of top-scoring non-manual workers. In short, use of the disaggregated scale explains almost 90 per cent of the variation in the middle class two-party vote, but only 43 per cent of the working class variation. Although this version of the scale best brings out the explanatory power of traditionalism, it will not be used in our subsequent analysis because it provides too few cases in each cell and also discriminates against other, less sophisticated measures in analysing the relative importance of different attitudinal and structural factors in the determination of voting behaviour. However, the full power of this variable should not be forgotten in the following pages.

Several studies have suggested that Liberal voting provides a transit point in shifts of party allegiance and also a more palatable means of protesting against one's own major party than voting for the other major party.[4] In this study there is a tendency for middle-class 'radicals' and working-class traditionals to be disproportionately Liberal in party choice. This suggests Liberalism also provides a means of alleviating conflict between the implications of socio-cultural commitments and class voting norms.

Table 8.1 TRADITIONALISM, CLASS, AND 1966 VOTE

Middle class

Tradm score	Con %	Lab %	Lib %	DNV %	Total %	N
Trad	71	16	5	8	100	151
Med	36	47	6	11	100	141
Rad	15	62	8	15	100	78
Total, N	171	138	22	39		370
Average, per cent	46	37	6	11		

Working class

Tradm score	Con %	Lab %	Lib %	DNV %	Total %	N
Trad	32	57	6	5	100	133
Med	18	70	2	10	100	195
Rad	6	73	3	17	99	94
Total, N	83	282	14	43		422
Average, per cent	20	67	3	10		

The same general pattern is apparent for vote intentions at the next general election for the 1968 sample and for the reported 1970 election vote for Ely and Easington. Some indication of the effects of traditionalism can be discerned in the fact that, although this was an unfavourable period for Labour, no more radicals intended to vote Conservative in 1968 than actually did so in 1966. Among both traditionals and those intermediate on this scale, however, a swing to the Tory Party was quite obvious. Similarly, an analysis of the floating vote showed that vote changes were more common among those intermediate on traditionalism than among those at either extreme of commitments. Among those old enough to have voted in at least two elections, only a quarter of traditionals and a third of radicals had supported another party; in contrast, 44 per cent of those with intermediate scores had supported another party on at least one occasion.[5] But these relationships suggest that traditionalism does exercise some sort of constraint over electoral behaviour.

Another way of looking at this same question is through party identification and its relationship to traditionalism. Party identities are more stable than voting behaviour over time so that evidence as to a strong relationship would suggest that traditionalism is more than fortuitously associated with political behaviour.[6] The relationship that exists is indeed in the expected direction and is as strong as that between traditionalism and voting behaviour in the preceding two elections (see Table 8.2). In the middle classes, for example, traditionals are three times as likely to identify with the Conservative Party, radicals three times as likely to identify with Labour, as their opposite numbers. Similarly, within the working class, whereas more than a quarter of traditionals identify with the Tory Party, only one-in-twenty-five radicals share this political identity. The tendency for working-class traditionals to vote Liberal is reflected in their greater identification with that Party. Likewise, radicals in both classes are not only more likely not to vote in general elections, but also more likely to withhold identification from a political party. Perhaps this occurs because they are more alienated from the party and electoral systems as well as the social and moral order. In any event this tendency provides part of the explanation for the continuing electoral success of the Conservative Party since those unlikely to vote Tory are also unlikely to vote at all.

We have already seen that ascriptive socio-political deference is associated with Conservatism and that it is positively correlated with traditionalism in both classes. It seems wise, therefore,

Table 8.2   CLASS, TRADITIONALISM, AND PARTY IDENTI-
FICATION

Party identity	Middle class, %			Working class, %		
	Trad	Med	Rad	Trad	Med	Rad
Con	61	30	19	27	8	4
Lab	17	42	54	42	71	68
Lib	8	2	8	13	1	—
None	15	25	38	15	17	26
DK/NA	—	2	—	3	4	2
Total, per cent	101	101	99	100	101	100
Base, N	66	60	26	71	104	53

to examine the relative importance of deference and traditionalism
in the determination of voting behaviour. We see that the latter
does in fact account for much of the impact of ascriptive socio-
political deference (see Table 8.3). In the working class, none of
those deferentials who were also radicals voted Conservative in
the 1966 general election; conversely, almost half of those who
expressed both types of deference did support that party. Similarly,
three-quarters of middle-class radical deferentials voted Labour
compared with only one-eighth of traditional ascriptive socio-
political deferentials. Traditionalism had a parallel effect on the
voting behaviour of meritocratic deferentials—accounting for
60 per cent of the variation in the middle class and for about a
quarter in the working class. The implication of these data is clear
—it is not so much ascriptive socio-political deference *per se* that
produces Conservative voting but traditionalism or affirmation
of dominant values and institutions. While the deference studies
point in the right direction, therefore, they identified the wrong
type of deference in seeking to explain as much variation as
possible in working class political behaviour.

It was argued in our second chapter that traditionalism is in
fact quite compatible with a limited class or 'trade union' consciousness. It may well be therefore that the relation between
voting and traditionalism, which is not perfect, is actually spurious
and explicable in terms of differential class and status consciousness. Such an interpretation is implied in much of the literature
on British politics—characteristic of which is Pulzer's argument
that 'class is the basis of British party politics: all else is embellish-
ment and detail.'[7] Conversely, it may be that traditionalism not
only accounts for much of the observed variation in voting

behaviour by deference but also accounts for the observed variation in terms of class consciousness. While not directly stated in
his reformulation of the deference thesis, this could be one interpretation of Parkin's analysis of voting and commitments to the
dominant value system. It is more reasonable to expect, however,
that, while class or status consciousness will not fully interpret
the relationship between traditionalism and voting behaviour,
neither will traditionalism fully interpret that between class
consciousness and electoral choice. Rather, class consciousness
can be expected to account for much of the deviation from the
theoretical 'norm' for different categories of traditional. For at
least some people who are committed to the overall social,
economic, and moral order will none the less be trade-union
conscious and so available for mobilisation by the Labour Party.
Similarly, at least some of those who are either insensitive to the
dominant order or disaffected from it could still share the status
conscious attitudes associated with the Conservative Party.
Before proceeding to investigate these possibilities it would be
appropriate to look simply at the impact of egalitarianism on the
voting behaviour of our sample.

There is indeed a strong association between inegalitarianism
and Conservatism (see Table 8.4). The effect is again more marked
in the middle class than the working class but it accounts for a
quarter of the variation even in the latter case. Likewise, those who

Table 8.3 PERCENTAGE OF THE TWO-PARTY VOTE GOING
TO LABOUR BY CLASS, TRADITIONALISM, AND
DEFERENCE

Type of deference	Middle class, %			Working class, %		
	Trad	Med	Rad	Trad	Med	Rad
ASPD	12	36	75	48	61	100
MD	31	62	94	69	85	92

are more disaffected from the dominant economic and social
order are also more likely to abstain in elections. The same
relationships are apparent for voting intention in the first sample
and for 1970 vote in the second sample. In each case, however,
egalitarianism is less strongly related to electoral behaviour than
is traditionalism.[8] Thus egalitarianism cannot account fully for
the impact of traditionalism even if it proves to account for most
of its effect in both classes. Let us see if the latter possibility
occurs.

Both traditionalism and egalitarianism seem to have strong independent effects in both middle and working classes (see Table 8.5). In the middle class, for example, traditionalism is one and a half times as important as egalitarianism but together they account for 80 per cent of the variation in the two-party vote. Similarly, in the working class, almost half of the variation is explained by their joint effects and traditionalism is slightly more important.[9] While this confirms our theoretical argument that the political impact of traditionalism will be modified by class consciousness—a possibility ignored by Parkin—half of the variation in the working-class vote still remains unexplained by their joint effects. This suggests that for the working class at least traditionalism and general class consciousness are less important than might at first be thought. Since class position itself still explains a quarter of the variation in voting after these two variables have been controlled, it may be that some other correlate of class position is a major determinant of voting behaviour.[10] We shall explore several possible structural factors in our next section.

If, as these data indicate, voting is partly determined by attitudes towards dominant values and institutions, then commitments to the emergent central value system of techno-economism should also be correlated with voting behaviour. This is indeed

Table 8.4   EGALITARIANISM, CLASS, AND 1966 VOTE

Middle class

Egalm Score	Con %	Lab %	Lib %	DNV %	Total %	N
Ineg	68	21	5	6	100	126
Med	45	33	9	12	99	97
Egal	28	54	5	14	101	147
Total, N	171	138	22	39		370
Average, per cent	46	37	6	11		

Working class

Egalm Score	Con %	Lab %	Lib %	DNV %	Total %	N
Ineg	39	55	0	5	99	56
Med	23	69	3	5	100	116
Egal	14	68	4	14	100	250
Total, N	83	282	14	43		422
Average, per cent	20	67	3	10		

Table 8.5   PERCENTAGE OF THE TWO-PARTY VOTE GOING
TO LABOUR BY CLASS, TRADITIONALISM, AND
EGALITARIANISM

| | Middle class, % | | | Working class, % | | |
	Ineg	*Med*	*Egal*	*Ineg*	*Med*	*Egal*
Trad	10	21	31	53	71	62
Med	40	59	69	63	77	89
Rad	38	73	90	80	76	98

the case. In both classes techno-economism is related to Conservative support reported for the 1970 election (see Table 8.6). The strength of the relation is very similar to that between traditionalism and Conservative voting. The same relationship is apparent for voting in 1966 and Liberal Party identities were drawn disproportionately from middle-class electors alienated from the techno-economistic order and from working-class voters who are committed to this order. This reproduces the relationship found between Liberalism and commitments to the traditional dominant order. Indeed, the general relationships are so similar that it would be worth while examining whether

Table 8.6   TECHNO-ECONOMISM, CLASS, AND 1970 VOTE

Middle class

Tech Score	Con %	Lab %	Lib %	DNV %	Total %	N
Tech	72	18	—	10	100	71
Med	37	42	—	21	100	38
Anti	23	63	—	14	100	35
Total, N	73	51	—	20		144
Average, per cent	51	35	—	14		

Working class

Tech Score	Con %	Lab %	Lib %	DNV %	Total %	N
Tech	35	49	—	17	101	66
Med	17	68	—	15	100	75
Anti	6	67	—	26	100	78
Total, N	41	136	—	42		219
Average, per cent	19	62	—	19		

traditionalism can explain that between techno-economism and voting, or vice versa.

The relative effects of traditionalism and techno-economism are difficult to determine owing to the strong correlation between the two variables (see below) and the resulting problem of multi-collinearity.[11] None the less, it seems that techno-economism has effects at least as strong as, and possibly stronger than, traditionalism in both classes (see Table 8.7). Together these variables account for almost nine-tenths of the variation in the middle-class vote and three-fifths of that in the two-party vote among the working class. The greater influence of techno-economism may be due to the greater contemporary political relevance of techno-economistic issues than traditional institutions such as the monarchy, Christianity, public schools, or empire. Certainly the issues of economic growth, technology, international trade, monopoly, and the appropriate relationship between government and economy, have received more attention in recent political debate than more traditional political topics, such as republicanism, disestablishment, abolition of public schools, and the end of empire. It is likely that traditionalism will become decreasingly relevant politically, therefore, and that voting behaviour will become more closely linked to positions on techno-economistic questions if not to a voter's general attachment to techno-economism.

Table 8.7 PERCENTAGE OF THE TWO-PARTY VOTE GOING TO LABOUR BY CLASS, TRADITIONALISM, AND TECHNO-ECONOMISM

	Middle class, %			Working class, %		
	Tech	Med	Anti	Tech	Med	Anti
Trad	11	46	13	43	70	73
Med	38	58	92	83	84	85
Rad	0	60	100	0	85	100

Overall, therefore, traditionalism does appear to be strongly related to voting behaviour and party identity—more so certainly than seemed to be the case in our analysis of opinion polls. This discrepancy is probably due to differences in measurement techniques rather than to peculiarities in our samples. For, whereas the poll data referred to simple approval or disapproval of single institutions, the traditionalism scale is both cumulative and trichotomous. Thus it provides not only a better guide to an individual's overall level of commitment to the traditional order but also allows more scope for variation in voting behaviour by virtue of its division into three rather than two categories. Consequently, had a greater difference not been apparent in this particular survey, we would have had some cause for questioning the political influence of commitments to the dominant order. However, their political impact was strongly in the expected direction and was apparent in four different tests of the relationship. Moreover, not only was traditionalism linked with Conservative support in terms of actual voting in two elections, vote intention, and party identification, but commitment to the emergent techno-economistic order was similarly related in all four cases. Thus some sort of connection between orientations to dominant values and electoral behaviour would seem to be established.

However, several further points must be made in qualification of this conclusion. Firstly, neither traditionalism nor techno-economism fully account for the variation in voting behaviour even within the middle class where their impact is stronger. While the disaggregation of both scales improves this situation, especially in the middle class,[12] there is still considerable deviation from the theoretical norm within the working class. Moreover, it still remains necessary to account for the voting behaviour of those who have an intermediate score on traditionalism and thus, at least in terms of the traditionalism thesis, predisposed towards neither the Conservative nor the Labour Party. Part of the explanation in both cases is to be found in the impact of general class and status consciousness. Thus, where someone committed to the traditional order is also class conscious, he is more likely to vote Labour than one who is both traditional and status conscious. Conversely, radicals who do not hold class conscious beliefs are more likely to vote for the Conservative Party. Such beliefs also affect the votes of persons who are neither traditional nor radical. None the less, in the working class, the combined effect of class consciousness and traditionalism still leaves half the variation in Labour and Conservative voting unexplained. This could be due to some voters' insensitivity to dominant values, to the ambivalent position of the Labour Party within a traditional-radical schema, to the economistic appeals of the Conservative Party, to the influence of more specific material or symbolic interests, to the mediating effects of social interaction or organisations, or to some other factor. We consider some of the latter possibilities below. Finally, although we have demonstrated that a relationship does exist between commitment to the dominant order and voting behaviour, we have not yet established how the relation develops nor whether it is really a cause of voting behaviour or is explicable in terms of other factors or as a causal link running in the opposite direction. These possibilities are also considered below.

8.2 Structural mediation and voting

Many different structural factors have been found to vary with party support. They include house-ownership, union membership, residence, plant size, income, type of employment, unemployment history, length of education, type of schooling, social mobility, religion, church attendance, parental partisan self-image, age, and so forth. However, it has also been argued that some of these factors are related to commitment to dominant values. It is imperative, therefore, to consider whether or not the relationship between traditionalism and voting is spurious and explicable in terms of these other factors, is independent of them, or, perhaps, actually explains their effects. In addition, the answer to this question will help to resolve the problem concerning the determinants of voting among those 'intermediate' persons socio-culturally predisposed to neither major party. It is at least possible that structural factors of one kind or another mediate their voting behaviour and explain much of its variation. Ten such factors are examined in the following pages.

Parkin argues that Conservative support will be strongest when involvement in the deviant subcultures of the industrial workplace and the working-class residential community are at their weakest.[13] We can consider this hypothesis by examining the impact of constituency, union membership, plant size, and parental occupation. Those who reside in predominantly working-class constituencies, who belong to unions, who work in large factories or offices, and who had working-class parents, may reasonably be thought to be more integrated into these deviant subcultures. In each case those who are more integrated in our sample are also more likely to vote Labour. None the less, traditionalism still has important independent effects when each of these variables is controlled and continues to explain more of the variation in voting behaviour. Among middle-class respondents, for example, traditionalism accounts for about three-fifths of the observed variation, while none of these structural factors accounts for more than a quarter of the variation (see Table 8.8a). Likewise, within the working class, traditionalism accounts for between one-fifth and two-fifths of the variation, whereas only plant size also accounts for more than a fifth of this variation. Together these variables explain up to three-quarters of the middle-class two-party vote and up to two-thirds of the working-class vote. As we shall see later, and as the numerical bases in the accompanying table indicate, there is also an obvious positive correlation between each of these structural variables and traditionalism. Overall, then, these results suggest that involvement in deviant subcultures does indeed generate disaffection from dominant values and also that, even among those who are less influenced in this way, it predisposes people to vote for the Labour Party.

In his critical review of the deference literature, Kavanagh argues that it ignores the vital extraneous variable of parental

Table 8.8a LABOUR VOTE BY CLASS, TRADITIONALISM, AND STRUCTURAL LOCATION

Structural variable	Middle class			Working class		
	Trad	Med	Rad	Trad	Med	Rad
Constituency						
Ely	9%	35%	80%	57%	78%	79%
	(33)	(20)	(10)	(30)	(23)	(14)
Woodford	13%	41%	56%	60%	65%	89%
	(46)	(32)	(16)	(10)	(20)	(09)
Wood Green	10%	72%	90%	66%	69%	80%
	(21)	(29)	(21)	(32)	(42)	(10)
Stepney	53%	62%	100%	62%	84%	100%
	(15)	(13)	(08)	(24)	(38)	(22)
Easington	29%	74%	75%	78%	92%	100%
	(17)	(23)	(04)	(23)	(50)	(22)
Union-Memb'p						
Non-Union	15%	46%	72%	54%	71%	80%
	(101)	(74)	(36)	(63)	(66)	(23)
TU-Mbr	29%	74%	91%	77%	78%	98%
	(31)	(43)	(23)	(56)	(107)	(52)
Plant Size						
Small	9%	45%	100%	38%	71%	50%
	(32)	(22)	(01)	(16)	(07)	(04)
Medium	11%	14%	88%	72%	92%	83%
	(09)	(07)	(08)	(18)	(13)	(12)
Large	35%	75%	57%	60%	87%	100%
	(17)	(16)	(07)	(25)	(69)	(21)
Father's SES						
Non-manual	10%	31%	69%	48%	64%	100%
	(58)	(35)	(26)	(23)	(14)	(06)
Manual	27%	67%	84%	67%	83%	90%
	(60)	(60)	(25)	(86)	(135)	(62)

Table 8.8b   LABOUR VOTE BY CLASS, TRADITIONALISM,
AND PATERNAL PARTY IDENTITY AND AGE

	Middle class			Working class		
	Trad	Med	Rad	Trad	Med	Rad
Paternal Party						
Con	4%	13%	75%	36%	25%	100%
	(27)	(08)	(08)	(11)	(04)	(03)
Lab	55%	79%	75%	85%	95%	96%
	(11)	(19)	(04)	(20)	(41)	(24)
Age Group						
—44 years	14%	57%	77%	59%	75%	83%
	(36)	(49)	(35)	(37)	(84)	(41)
45 or more	20%	56%	81%	62%	87%	100%
	(96)	(37)	(21)	(20)	(85)	(34)

party loyalties. He suggests that much of working-class Conservative support is simply inherited and that parental loyalties
may also explain deferential attitudes.[14] Less than three-fifths of
the national sample studied by Butler and Stokes, however,
actually remembered that their father voted Labour or Conservative. Moreover, only three-fifths of those whose parents
supported the party not dominant in their class continued to
support that party themselves.[15] This suggests that inherited party
loyalties may not be so important in explaining working-class
Conservatism. In our own sample, parental loyalties accounted
for about two-fifths of the variation in both classes for those who
could recall that their father voted for one of the major parties.
Traditionalism was just as important in the working class and
explained more variation within the middle class (see Table 8.8b).
Moreover, within that half of the middle-class sample whose
fathers were Liberal or left no partisan recollections, traditionalism accounted for 40 per cent of the variation. Similarly, it
accounted for 20 per cent of the variation among the two-fifths
of the working classes in this category. While there is also a
positive correlation between parental loyalties and traditionalism,
as Kavanagh suggests, neither voting behaviour nor socio-cultural
commitments are fully explained by paternal partisanship.

Studies of voting behaviour consistently report that those who
hold a middle-class self-image are more likely to support the Tory
Party than those who see themselves as working class.[16] Runciman
has shown that the adoption of a middle-class self-image among

manual workers is related to such social factors as income, age, religion, length of education, parental occupation, and region, but still retains some of its significance when each of these variables is separately controlled. He finds that a middle-class identity is most influential where it is associated with the adoption of middle-class norms.[17] Although traditionalism does not necessarily imply the acceptance of middle-class attitudes towards class and status, it does involve affirmation of general middle-class values and institutions and it is related to Conservative support. It will be worth examining, therefore, the relative importance of these two variables. As one might expect, the results of such a comparison parallel those for the relative effects of traditionalism and egalitarianism. Thus, within the middle class, traditionalism explains almost three times as much variation as the possession of a middle-class self-image and the two variables jointly account for well over three-quarters of the variation. Among the manual workers, on the other hand, class self-image is relatively more important although traditionalism still explains more of the two-party vote. Together they account for almost half of the vote. This provides further confirmation of our argument that the effects of traditionalism will be modified by the nature and degree of class consciousness.

Age is also well-established as a covariant of voting behaviour with the elderly more likely to support the Conservative than the Labour Party. The most likely explanation of this is held to be the hardening of partisanship in later years in conjunction with the relative immaturity of the Labour Party within the British party system.[18] An additional factor may be that traditionalism was not only more firmly institutionalised in the past but also more relevant politically. This would mean that only those firmly insulated from exposure to the dominant value system would be likely Labour voters. But, as traditionalism became less strongly promulgated and politics became more secular, increasing numbers of people would become available for mobilisation by the Labour Party. The structural location of the initial Labour electoral successes supports this argument. In combination with the immunising effects of habit and maturity, therefore, our argument would suggest that traditionalism accounts for most of the variation typically reported for age. This is indeed the case. Within the middle class, for example, traditionalism accounts for twenty times as much variation as age and is also fairly strongly correlated with the latter. Moreover, within the working class, age is actually negatively correlated with Conservatism once the influence of traditionalism is controlled. The usual positive correlation persists, however, if we control techno-economism rather than traditionalism in both classes. This provides further support, therefore, for our argument that traditionalism is becoming less relevant to political life.

The effects of traditionalism also persist when other important structural factors are considered. For example, while experience of unemployment is positively associated with Labour voting in both the middle and working classes traditionalism none the less explains more than three times as much of the middle-class bipartisan vote and thirty times as much of the working-class vote (see Table 8.9). Similarly, although those employed in nationalised industries and public service organisations are more prone to support Labour than those employed in commercial organisations and the self-employed, more of the variation in the two-party vote is still explained by socio-cultural commitments. The same is true of house ownership versus tenancy. While this variable discriminates between Labour and Conservative supporters in both classes, and especially so in the working class, it none the less accounts, even in the latter case, for less variation than traditionalism (see Table 8.9).

Further education and secondary education beyond the minimum have also been found to correlate with Conservative voting in the working class; for the middle class, on the other hand, further education is generally associated with Labour sympathies.[19] In our second sample, too, further education seems to have these effects—especially in the working class. Again, however, traditionalism remains more influential (see Tabel 8.9). Finally, while those in the first sample who were Anglicans or scored high on a religiosity scale were more prone to support the Conservative Party, none of the influence of traditionalism was eliminated by controlling this variable. Thus, however one seeks to interpret the influence of traditionalism by controlling for this or that variable, it does not prove possible to show that the relationship between traditionalism and Conservatism is spurious and capable of interpretation in terms of some third variable.

None the less, it could perhaps be argued that traditionalism appears to be important because it is measured by a cumulative scale and is associated with many different structural variables that are also linked to Labour and Conservative voting, whereas these latter variables are held constant separately and are measured by a single item only in each case. If the structural factors were combined into a single measure, however, their effects might

Table 8.9 LABOUR VOTE BY TRADITIONALISM, CLASS, AND FOUR VARIABLES

	Middle class			Working class		
	Trad	Med	Rad	Trad	Med	Rad
Employment						
Employed	15%	54%	69%	56%	83%	92%
	(46)	(41)	(13)	(34)	(39)	(25)
Unemployed	31%	67%	100%	59%	91%	88%
	(13)	(09)	(03)	(22)	(32)	(12)
Type of employment						
Communal	5%	47%	40%	53%	85%	83%
	(41)	(32)	(05)	(34)	(40)	(18)
Public	53%	73%	82%	68%	87%	95%
	(17)	(15)	(11)	(25)	(39)	(19)
House ownership						
Owner	16%	52%	85%	38%	67%	87%
	(43)	(29)	(13)	(16)	(18)	(16)
Tenant	25%	65%	33%	64%	90%	90%
	(16)	(20)	(03)	(44)	(61)	(20)
Further education						
Yes	24%	59%	75%	11%	77%	89%
	(17)	(22)	(08)	(09)	(13)	(09)
No	17%	52%	75%	65%	87%	89%
	(42)	(27)	(07)	(34)	(66)	(28)

Note: data derived from second sample only and relating to 1970 election

outweigh that of traditionalism. This view can be tested by comparing the impact of traditionalism and scores on a structural position scale. Like traditionalism, this is a seven item scale that applies to middle as well as working class. It is intended to measure the extent to which a person is exposed to situations and experiences that facilitate the development and acquisition of deviant values and beliefs and, conversely, inhibit the acquisition of dominant orientations. To qualify for the highest score, a person must (i) live in a city, large town, small industrial town, or mining village; (ii) work in a factory, or organisation with more than 250 employees; (iii) belong to a union; (iv) live in a council or pit house; (v) have a working class father; (vi) have been unemployed at some time for more than a month; and (vii) either belong to a club or organisation in a city, large town, small industrial town, or pit village, *or* not belong to one in a small country town or village, so that in neither case is he exposed to the influence of dominant values. The lowest score is obviously achieved by those who have none of these ideal typical characteristics.

Structural position would seem to account for all of the variation in the bipartisan vote in both classes. None of those with a zero score voted Labour; all of those with the top score did so. Within the middle class there was a steady increase in Labour support with each increase in the structural position score. The same trend was apparent, with the exception of a large jump between zero and one on the scale, for the working class (see Table 8.10). This result suggests that structural position outweighs the influence of traditionalism—in the case of the working class by a large margin and by a smaller margin in the middle class. While use of this index of structural position demonstrates the power of a sophisticated class model, the correlation between structural position and electoral support for Labour is not perfect. This is especially noticeable in the working class, where only one person scored zero and 43 per cent of those with the next lowest score cast Labour votes. Moreover, even given the great explanatory power of structural position, it is still necessary to ask how it relates to traditionalism and what determines the vote among persons with 'intermediate' scores on either variable.

Table 8.10   STRUCTURAL POSITION, CLASS, AND LABOUR VOTE

Class	Structural position score							
	0	1	2	3	4	5	6	7
Middle	0%	27%	39%	41%	57%	73%	71%	100%
	(09)	(34)	(23)	(22)	(14)	(11)	(07)	(02)
Working	0%	43%	50%	62%	77%	82%	90%	100%
	(01)	(07)	(14)	(26)	(43)	(40)	(40)	(07)

Note: data derived from second sample only and related to 1970 election

A comparison of the effect of structural position and traditionalism shows that they both exercise strong independent effects on voting behaviour. They are equally important in the middle class and together explain more than 90 per cent of the variation even in their grouped versions. Structural position is more important in the working class, however, accounting for a third as much variation in the bipartisan vote. None the less, in the latter class as well, the two variables interact cumulatively to account for almost three-quarters of the vote. The most likely explanation for such a class differential is the interaction of a partial asymmetry in the political implications of traditionalism and radicalism together with different class norms of voting behaviour. In both classes alienation from the dominant order much more strongly implies opposition to the Conservative Party than commitment thereto implies support for that party. Moreover, whereas the political norm for the working class is support for Labour, Conservatism is expected of the middle class. Working-class traditionals, who are already in an ambivalent position, will thus be subjected to additional cross-pressures by their general class position. Exposure to situations and experiences favourable to deviant, Labour values will reinforce these pressures so that structural position will account for a considerable amount of variation within the working class. Within the middle class, on the other hand, the class norm reinforces the tendency for traditionals to vote Conservative. Accordingly, such exposure operates against the class political grain and will probably have most influence on those intermediate in their attitudes towards the dominant order. This seems to be the case for the two classes in the present study.

Table 8.11 PERCENTAGE OF TWO-PARTY VOTE GOING TO LABOUR BY CLASS, STRUCTURAL POSITION, AND TRADITIONALISM

SP*	Middle class			Working class		
	Trad	*Med*	*Rad*	*Trad*	*Med*	*Rad*
Low	8%	16%	100%	20%	75%	50%
	(39)	(19)	(08)	(10)	(08)	(04)
Med	33%	63%	20%	58%	76%	88%
	(12)	(19)	(05)	(31)	(21)	(17)
High	50%	89%	100%	78%	87%	94%
	(08)	(09)	(03)	(18)	(52)	(17)

* Low = 0, 1, 2; Med = 3 and 4; High = 5, 6, 7 on SP Index.

Similar considerations apply to the more general question of the structural mediation of voting behaviour. We argued above that those who are intermediate on traditionalism should be particularly susceptible to structural influences such as union membership, residential community, plant size, and so forth. For it is among persons whose electoral choice is not 'overdetermined' by attitudes to the dominant order that mediating structural factors will play crucial determining roles. An examination of the tables presented in the present section shows, however, that, while this is indeed the case with the middle-class vote, it is not true of manual workers. Thus, in twelve tabulated comparisons, the structural factors held constant account for most variation within the 'intermediate' category on seven occasions for the middle class. Only age, subjective class, unemployment experience, and type of employment produced more effect among radicals or traditionals. Among the working class, however, this is true in only three cases from twelve—for eight other comparisons it is the traditionals who are most influenced by the structural variables. The reason for this class difference is almost certainly that outlined in the preceding paragraph, namely, the interaction of class norms and the partial asymmetry between the political implications of radicalism and traditionalism.

Thus traditionalism does indeed have important effects on the voting behaviour of manual and non-manual workers. However we try to interpret these effects in terms of other factors it still persists with varying tenacity. The structural location of voters in terms of exposure to deviant and dominant beliefs also has important effects. The influence of such commitments is independent of structural position and interacts with it to produce an even larger amount of variation. This is only to be expected. Even where the sense of civic obligation is strong, voters predisposed towards a particular party by virtue of their general attitudes and beliefs must still be mobilised to support it rather than another political party. The differential strength of party machines in a given area and their emphasis on various issues as well as the national election campaigns of the different parties are obviously relevant here. But the strength of union organisation, political traditions mediated through informal interaction in the residential and occupational communities, inherited party loyalties and family feuds, and the like, will also be relevant. Thus, where a given party is weak on the ground it will be less effective in mobilising the votes of electors predisposed towards it in terms of general attitudes and beliefs; conversely, where a party is strong on the ground, it may be able to mobilise support from those who, elsewhere, would be likely to vote for the opposing party. It is precisely because of subtleties such as these in the electoral mobilisation process, over both the long term and the immediate campaign, that there can be no single explanation for electoral behaviour. None the less, traditionalism does seem to be a necessary part of any general explanations of voting behaviour in Britain. But its impact will vary from elector to elector according to their exact location within the total social, economic, and political structure.

Exactly similar considerations apply to the effects of techno-economism and of class consciousness.

8.3 Causal models of the conservative vote

Our analysis of voting behaviour has so far relied on relatively simple statistical tools appropriate to the evaluation of ordinal and nominal data. It may be useful, however, to apply more sophisticated techniques in an exploratory fashion to examine questions of causality and covariation in greater detail. The techniques involved are those developed by Wright, Simon, and Blalock for the evaluation of causal models in non-experimental research. Although these methods were originally designed for use on interval scale data they can be applied to less rigorous material provided due caution is paid to the problems this involves.[20]

There are several other assumptions involved in the employment of these techniques in addition to that of interval levels of measurement. These assumptions are: one-way causality, no correlations between error terms, no correlation between a given independent variable and the error term of another variable, and no external variables causing covariation between two independent variables internal to the causal system.[21] These are quite exacting assumptions. It is difficult, for example, as in the case of egalitarianism and traditionalism, to decide whether two variables are related in a reciprocal or unidirectional fashion. And we have no real way of knowing whether error terms or external variables are distorting the relations between our variables. None the less, it may still be worth employing these techniques as a guide to the interpretation of our results and as an indicator of further avenues of research.

The basic method involved in these techiques is quite simple. Different causal models are constructed to connect the variables in the causal system and predictions are then derived from these various models as to the strength of given correlations and partial correlations. These predictions are typically that a given correlation will be zero if variables causally prior to it, or intervening between it and the dependent variable, are controlled. In the simple causal model W–X–Y–Z, for example, we would predict that the partial between W and Z will be zero if either of the intervening variables X and Y are controlled. More elaborate models can be constructed, either on the basis of *a priori* reasoning or in a purely exploratory fashion, and their implications tested as well. The validity of the causal models will depend not only on the accuracy of the prediction equations but also on the variables included in, or excluded from, the causal system. If other variables were included, or certain variables excluded, the causal model might have to be changed. There is thus no single 'correct' model that can be demonstrated to be superior to all others.[22]

From the preceding analysis several variables have emerged as important in the determination of voting behaviour. Among those included in both samples are parental class, constituency, union membership, social class, traditionalism, and egalitarianism. Paternal party loyalties, techno-economism, structural position, and size of plant also proved to be important determinants as measured for the second sample. These will provide the starting point for our analysis. For the joint sample the dependent variable will be the two-party vote in the 1966 election; the 1970 vote will provide the dependent variable in the second sample. We begin with an analysis of the combined samples.

While there are a large number of different causal models that can be constructed from the seven variables, parental occupation obviously precedes all other variables and social class should precede union membership. An examination of the zero-order correlations in Table 8.12 also provides some clues as to the appropriate causal model. After considerable experimentation with different models, that which finally emerged as the model best fitted to the data confirmed the results of the preceding analysis. It shows that the effects of egalitarianism and traditionalism on voting behaviour not only persist when each is held constant for the other, but also that they are independent of various structural influences such as constituency, union membership, and social class. Conversely, each of these latter variables also exercises an independent influence on voting behaviour. Only parental occupation retains no significant independent influence on voting and, as we shall see below, such influence as it does have is probably the result of its association with paternal party loyalties rather than class *per se*. The other interesting result that emerges from this analysis is that neither social class nor constituency have immediate effects on the level of traditionalism but work their effects indirectly through egalitarianism and union membership. This reinforces the argument that an inferior social and economic position is insufficient in itself to produce disaffection from the dominant order and must therefore be combined with insulation from that order to have this effect. It also suggests that the clustering of those with similar social and economic positions in predominantly one-class communities has more impact on the

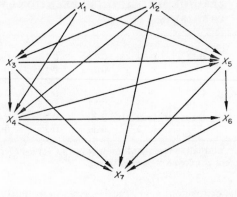

$$r_{12} = 0\cdot 11$$

$$r_{16\cdot 345} = -0\cdot 01$$

$$r_{17\cdot 3456} = 0\cdot 08$$

$$r_{26\cdot 45} = 0\cdot 03$$

$$r_{36\cdot 45} = 0\cdot 01$$

$$R_{7\cdot 56} = 0\cdot 46$$

$$R_{7\cdot 256} = 0\cdot 52$$

$$R_{7\cdot 2356} = 0\cdot 56$$

$$R_{7\cdot 23456} = 0\cdot 57$$

$$R_{7\cdot 123456} = 0\cdot 58$$

Figure 8·1 SEVEN–VARIABLE CAUSAL MODEL OF CONSERVATIVE VOTING IN 1966

development of corporate or collective consciousness than on the overall level of attachment to the dominant order. If general antipathy is to develop, then exposure to organisations or structures that channel such disaffection is required. This implication will be considered more fully in a later chapter. Lastly, we may note that the combined effect of all six independent variables on voting behaviour was only one and a half times as great as that of traditionalism and egalitarianism alone.[23] This underlines the importance of these two variables as indicated in the preceding analysis.

We now turn to a consideration of causal models for the middle and working classes in the second sample. More variables are utilised in this analysis and the likelihood of error is correspondingly greater. But exploration of this kind can still prove useful in understanding the general nature of the relationships involved. In this analysis, eight independent variables will be considered—the relevant zero-order correlations are presented in Table 8.13. The final models again tended to confirm the results of the earlier analysis. Thus traditionalism, egalitarianism, and techno-economism continue to exercise independent effects on voting behaviour

Table 8.12   ZERO-ORDER RANK CORRELATIONS FOR SEVEN
             VARIABLES

	1	2	3	4	5	6	7
1	—	0·11	0·33	0·30	0·18	0·07	0·11
2	0·11	—	0·19	0·20	0·19	0·10	0·31
3	0·33	0·19	—	0·19	0·25	0·09	0·19
4	0·30	0·20	0·19	—	0·22	0·20	0·30
5	0·18	0·19	0·25	0·22	—	0·26	0·35
6	0·07	0·10	0·09	0·20	0·26	—	0·38
7	0·11	0·31	0·19	0·30	0·35	0·38	—

Note: in this and all subsequent matrices, the rank-order correlation
coefficient employed is Kendall's τc.

Legend
1   Parental occupation: non-manual—deceased—manual
2   Constituency: Ely—Woodford—Wood Green—Stepney—Easington
3   Social class: non-manual—manual
4   Union Membership: non-member—member
5   Egalitarianism: inegalitarian—medium—egalitarian
6   Traditionalism: traditional—medium—radical
7   1966 vote: Conservative—Labour

within both classes. This is equally true whether it is the remaining
two attitudinal variables held constant in each case or the effects
of structural factors. Secondly, the structural variables themselves,
as represented principally in the structural position index but also,
in the case of the middle class, by union membership, also retain
an independent influence. Thirdly, in both cases, the strength of
the relationship is greater in the middle class than the working
class. This is apparent not only in the zero-order correlations but
also in the size of the multiple correlation on the two-party vote—
the largest fifth-order multiple for the middle class explains three
times as much variation in voting as does the comparable multiple
in the working class.[24] The reasons for this consistent difference
between classes have already been discussed. In addition to the
general confirmation thus provided for the preceding analysis,
several other points emerge from an examination of these models.

Firstly, paternal party preference appears to account fully for
the influence of parental class on voting in both classes. Perhaps
this means that social mobility is irrelevant to political loyalties
but alternative explanations do exist. In this study, as in others,
the upwardly mobile are recruited disproportionately from Conservative working-class homes;[25] and, in addition, only those who
have not been mobile away from the influence of the local political
environment and who have thus been less exposed to stimuli

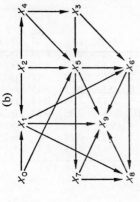

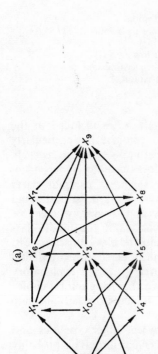

(a)

r_{02} = 0·09	$r_{15\cdot023}$ = 0·10	$r_{46\cdot23}$ = −0·13
r_{04} = 0·04	$r_{17\cdot6}$ = 0·04	$r_{47\cdot263}$ = 0·07
r_{06} = 0·01	$r_{18\cdot367}$ = 0·06	$r_{48\cdot5}$ = 0·03
r_{07} = 0·03	$r_{27\cdot36}$ = −0·08	$r_{49\cdot35}$ = 0·08
$r_{08\cdot5}$ = −0·11	$r_{28\cdot56}$ = 0·02	r_{562} = −0·10
$r_{09\cdot15}$ = −0·03	$r_{29\cdot56}$ = 0·02	r_{573} = −0·06
$r_{14\cdot2}$ = −0·03	$r_{38\cdot567}$ = 0·00	

(b)

r_{02} = 0·06	$r_{13\cdot2}$ = 0·00	$r_{28\cdot15}$ = 0·10
r_{03} = 0·03	$r_{14\cdot2}$ = 0·05	$r_{29\cdot15}$ = 0·08
r_{04} = 0·02	$r_{15\cdot2}$ = 0·09	$r_{36\cdot5}$ = 0·09
$r_{06\cdot5}$ = 0·03	$r_{17\cdot5}$ = 0·07	$r_{37\cdot5}$ = 0·02
$r_{07\cdot5}$ = −0·02	$r_{23\cdot4}$ = 0·05	$r_{38\cdot56}$ = 0·09
$r_{08\cdot5}$ = −0·10	$r_{26\cdot15}$ = 0·09	$r_{47\cdot5}$ = 0·04
$r_{09\cdot15}$ = 0·04	$r_{48\cdot5}$ = 0·04	$r_{49\cdot5}$ = 0·07
$r_{46\cdot35}$= 0·01	$r_{58\cdot67}$= 0·04	$r_{67\cdot5}$ = 0·03

FIGURE 8·2 CAUSAL MODELS OF CONSERVATIVE VOTING IN 1970
(a) Middle class and (b) Working class

Table 8.13   ZERO-ORDER RANK CORRELATIONS FOR TEN
VARIABLES

Working class

	0	1	2	3	4	5	6	7	8	9
0	—	0·17	0·06	0·03	0·02	0·19	0·05	0·02	0·07	0·12
1	0·30	—	0·32	0·07	0·19	0·21	0·28	0·11	0·24	0·29
2	0·09	0·23	—	0·21	0·46	0·41	0·19	0·20	0·20	0·24
3	0·24	0·31	0·28	—	0·51	0·42	0·14	0·10	0·17	0·21
4	0·04	0·05	0·34	0·29	—	0·49	0·10	0·13	0·13	0·20
5	0·40	0·32	0·45	0·52	0·36	—	0·13	0·20	0·13	0·29
6	0·01	0·25	0·33	0·35	0·06	0·07	—	0·05	0·37	0·28
7	0·03	0·14	0·08	0·36	0·15	0·14	0·40	—	0·30	0·24
8	0·04	0·13	0·17	0·24	0·08	0·15	0·27	0·24	—	0·28
9	0·16	0·46	0·31	0·48	0·23	0·36	0·48	0·35	0·46	—

Middle class

0	Parental occupation: non-manual *v* deceased *v* manual
1	Parental party loyalty: Conservative *v* other *v* Labour
2	Constituency: Ely *v* Easington
3	Union membership: non-member *v* member
4	Plant size: less than 20 *v* 21–250 *v* more than 250
5	Structural position: low *v* medium *v* high
6	Techno-economism: high *v* medium *v* low
7	Egalitarianism: inegalitarian *v* medium *v* egalitarian
8	Traditionalism: traditional *v* medium *v* radical
9	1970 vote: Conservative *v* Labour

encouraging desertion of familial loyalties are included in the sample.[26] The combination of these two factors is thus particularly favourable to the minimisation of social mobility effects as such. Other studies demonstrate that it does have an independent influence.[27] Secondly, as Kavanagh suggests, parental party loyalty is also associated with deference—albeit to the traditional social and moral order—in both classes. However, whereas its effect is direct in the case of manual workers, in the middle class it is mediated through union membership and class consciousness. Furthermore, the effects of traditionalism persist when parental party preference is controlled. However great the explanatory power of such preferences, therefore, whether for electoral choice or attachments to the dominant order, it is by no means absolute or exhaustive.

None the less, the association between father's politics and union membership in the middle class is interesting. This probably arises from a combination of circumstances. Occupational choice is linked more strongly with opportunities for union membership in the middle class than in the working class, owing to the greater unionisation of manual occupations. Moreover, where such opportunities do occur, an element of optionality is more often present than in the case of the working class. And both the initial choice of occupation and the decision to join a union are probably influenced by socialisation experiences and general political values. It is probably for the same reasons that union membership retains an independent influence upon voting in the middle class, whereas its effects are subsumed under general structural location for manual workers. Certainly, there is evidence to suggest that the factors inclining people to Labour also incline them to join unions and that this self-selection is strongly involved, and especially so in the middle class, in the greater propensity of union members to vote Labour.[28] Lastly, we may note that constituency has a continuing effect on union membership in the middle class whereas its association with plant size seems a sufficient explanation of its effects in the working class. This is most probably a reflection of differences in occupation, especially agricultural versus industrial and bureaucratic, in the two constituencies—differences that are greater for the middle class than the working.

The implications of these causal models should not be over-emphasised because of the various difficulties involved in the implication of causal modelling.[29] None the less, the results do largely confirm the preceding analysis and also tell us something about possible causes of traditionalism, egalitarianism, and techno-economism in different classes. We shall consider these possibilities along with others in a later chapter. Before proceeding to such an analysis, however, we shall look more closely at the party loyalties of traditionals and radicals, and of deviant and non-deviant voters, as they emerged in open-ended questions and interviews with the second samples. Only then will we be able to give a comprehensive overview of the relations between traditionalism and politics as they appear in the present study.

8.4 Notes and references

1 *cf* Anderson, 'Origins,' in *Towards Socialism*; T Nairn, 'The fateful meridian,' *New Left Review* (1970), 60, pp3–35; E Burke, *Reflections on the Revolution in France* (Harmondsworth: Penguin, 1968); and Q Hogg, *The Conservative Case* (Harmondsworth: Penguin, 1959), *passim*.
2 Trenaman and McQuail find that traditionalism-radicalism is a major factor underlying party images, accounting for 45 per cent of variation in the images held by Leeds and Pudsey samples: Tory identification with the upper class and British traditions contrasted with Labour identification with the working class, opposition to the class system, and the welfare state. See J Trenaman and D McQuail, *Television and the Political Image* (London: Methuen, 1961), pp41 and 52–3. B G Stacey and R T Green conducted

a factor analysis of attitudes among a motley collection of Coventry voters and found three main factors to be associated with Conservative voting— elitism *v* egalitarianism, patriotism *v* internationalism, traditionalism *v* reformism: *idem*, 'The psychological bases of political allegiance among white-collar males,' *Br. J. Clin. Soc. Psychol.* (1968), vii, pp45–60. *cf* Butler and Stokes, *Political Change*, pp367–72, on the newness and modernity of parties.

3   J G Blumler and D McQuail, *Television in Politics* (London: Faber, 1968), p194; *cf* Trenaman and McQuail, pp52–3 and 158.

4   Blumler and McQuail, *Television*, pp265 *et seq*; Butler and Stokes, *Political Change*, pp249–54; Cannon, in *Sociology* (1967), i, p169; E J Cleary and H Pollins, 'Liberal voting at the General Election of 1951,' *Sociol. Rev.* (1953), i, pp27–41.

5   The question about voting record was employed only in the first sample; a comparison of 1966 and 1970 votes for the second sample revealed a similar pattern.

6   Butler and Stokes, *Political Change*, pp37–8.

7   P G J Pulzer, *Political Representation and Elections in Britain* (London: Allen & Unwin, 1967), p98.

8   In the first sample, for example, 44 per cent of working-class inegalitarians intended to vote Labour compared with 56 per cent of egalitarians; for the middle class these percentages were 12 and 63, respectively; uncertainty about vote intention was greatest among egalitarians in both classes. For the second sample, 17 per cent of the inegalitarian middle-class bipartisan vote went to the Labour Party compared with 64 per cent of the egalitarian vote; figures for the working class were 48 and 86 per cent, respectively.

9   Whereas traditionalism accounts for 23 per cent of the variation, egalitarianism accounts for 18 per cent of the vote. For a discussion of this measure of 'accountability' see Galtung, *Methods*, pp427–37.

10   From Table 8.5 we can see that the manual–non-manual distinction contributes 27 per cent of the variation; traditionalism accounts for 34 per cent; and egalitarianism for 23 per cent of the two-party vote; together, the three variables account for 88 per cent of the variation.

11   See H M Blalock, 'Correlated independent variables: the problem of multicollinearity,' *Soc. Forces* (1963), 42, pp233–7. Sampling error and measurement error are particularly problematic whenever the correlation between two independent variables is high and, in this particular case, the two variables also have one item in common, that concerning private enterprise.

12   Disaggregation of the techno-economism scale shows that, for the middle class, there is a range in Conservative voting from 81 to 10 per cent; for manual workers the range is 40 to nil per cent; on traditionalism, see text.

13   Parkin, in *BJS* (1967), p285; *cf* Lockwood, in *SR* (1966), *passim*; A Piepe *et al*, 'The location of the proletarian and deferential worker,' *Sociology* (1969), iii, pp239–44; Butler and Stokes, *Political Change*, pp 144–50; and, for some American data, R D Putnam, 'Political attitudes and the local community,' *Am. Pol. Soc. Rev.* (1966), lx, pp650–4, and I S Foladore, 'The effect of neighbourhood on voting,' *Pol. Sc. Q.* (1968), 83, pp51–29.

14   K Kavanagh, in *GO* (1961), pp349–50.

15 Butler and Stokes, *Political Change*, pp470 and 52.

16 For example, see M Abrams, 'Social class and British politics,' *Public Opinion Qtly* (1961), xxv, pp342–50; Martin, in *Br. J. Sociol.* (1951); Nordlinger, *Tories*, p164; McKenzie and Silver, *Angels*, p94; Butler and Stokes, *Political Change*, pp76–80.

17 W G Runciman, *Relative Deprivation and Social Justice* (London: Routledge, 1966), pp179–87.

18 Butler and Stokes, *Political Change*, p55; *cf* D E Stokes, *The Study of Political Generations* (London: Longmans, 1968), *passim*; and W N McPhee and J Ferguson, 'Political immunisation,' in *Public Opinion and Congressional Elections*, edited by W N McPhee and W A Glaser (New York: Wiley, 1962), pp155–79.

19 See Rose, in *Sociology* (1968), *passim*; and Rose, *Politics*, p69; also, 'How much education makes a Tory?,' *New Society* (1 November 1962).

20 For a general discussion of these techniques, see H M Blalock, *Causal Interferences in Non-Experimental Research* (Chapel Hill: University of North Carolina Press, 1961), *passim*; for a defence of their application to ordinal data, see p186.

21 *Ibid*, pp35–52.

22 For a more detailed discussion of these methods, as well as an examination of the problems involved, see *ibid*.

23 The second-order multiple, $R^2_{7 \cdot 56}$ is 0·21; the sixth-order multiple, $R^2_{7 \cdot 123456}$ is 0·34.

24 The largest fifth-order multiple in both classes is given by $R_{9 \cdot 15678}$. Whereas this has a value of 0·84 in the middle class, it rises only to 0·45 in the working class.

25 Whereas less than a quarter of working-class children whose parents voted Labour were mobile into the middle class, three-fifths of those from Conservative homes were mobile into this class. Comparable data are reported in Butler and Stokes, *Political Change*, p100; McKenzie and Silver, *Angels*, suggest this may be due to differences in parental attitudes towards mobility (pp202–7 and 137–45).

26 Very few respondents in Ely or Easington were newcomers to the area: this would not be true of the first sample.

27 See, for example, Butler and Stokes, *Political Change*, pp95–101.

28 *Ibid*, pp155–60.

29 The general problems and, in particular, that of multicollinearity, make it difficult to draw firm conclusions about the relations between traditionalism, techno-economism, and egalitarianism; accordingly, this question is not discussed above.

Chapter 9

Traditionalism, Party Loyalties and Political Thought

The relation between traditionalism and political behaviour has so far been discussed only in general terms. We have shown that it does indeed exist and that, while the relation is independent of many different structural factors, traditionalism none the less interacts with them to produce considerable variation in party loyalties and electoral choice. But we have not yet established how this relation develops. What is its motivating force? Although several mechanisms have already been discussed that might lead voters to identify the Conservative Party with the dominant order, such an association must also be translated into actual electoral support for the general relation to hold. In so far as structural factors do not fully account for the link between traditionalism and voting behaviour, then other mechanisms have to be considered. We examine several possibilities in the present chapter.

Perhaps the explanation lies in a greater tendency of traditionals to accept the argument that, whether deliberately or unintentionally, a Labour government would destroy the established order. Conversely, radicals, to the extent that they do accept such arguments, might welcome such an event and thus vote Labour. Alternatively, it may be that traditionals vote disproportionately for the Conservative Party, not because they believe that another party would precipitate disaster, but simply because they believe the Conservatives more adequately represent the dominant order than does the Labour movement. Certainly, there is evidence to show not only that the Tory Party is identified more closely with dominant institutions, but also that it is more common for Tory voters to view Labour supporters in derogatory terms than it is for the latter to express disapproval of opposition supporters.[1] Closely related to this interpretation is a suggestion put forward by Parkin that voting is an extension or expression of life-style and value-commitments. Voters who adhere to deferential, aspirational, or middle-class life-styles may well look on Conservative voting as an important aspect of a total approach to life. Those who are alienated from the dominant order, on the other hand, whether adherents of a subordinate, economistic value system or of a radical, oppositional system, are likely to see Labour as an obvious party to support. Although we have offered several theoretical criticisms of this argument, it will still be worth while to examine it along with others.

A fourth possibility is that commitment to traditional institutions predisposes people to view specific issues in ways favourable to the Conservative rather than the Labour Party. For example, general support for private enterprise may lead one to appraise particular policy proposals or legislative acts in ways that indicate support for the Conservatives. Equally, it may encourage deference to the opinions of businessmen and bourgeois economists on these issues and thereby also lead to such support. Similar considerations apply to support for other dominant institutions with a continuing political relevance. Thus this explanation suggests that the link between value commitments and party loyalties is mediated through policy orientations rather than through structural factors. Finally, a causal chain running in the opposite direction could well provide an explanation for the link between traditionalism and voting behaviour. That is, support for the Conservative Party could lead to support for institutions and values with which it is closely identified. It could also lead to support for specific policies. These possibilities are neither mutually exclusive nor exhaustive—they can be combined with each other as well as with other motives. In the latter respect, we have already seen that class consciousness plays an independent role in the determination of voting behaviour. Other factors may also be significant. We now turn, however, to a consideration of the various explanations outlined above.

9.1 Defending the dominant order

In the second sample we asked people whether they felt close to one party rather than another. Such partisan self-identities, as we have already seen, were indeed related as strongly to traditionalism as was voting behaviour. They were also asked why they supported the chosen party. In addition, in the follow-up interviews, these issues were probed further. In particular, interviewees were asked about their general images of major parties, their views of party leaders, their attitudes towards party links with big business and trade unions, their impressions of party attitudes towards dominant institutions, and their desires for policy changes. The chief results of this analysis are presented below.

The first point to note is that very few of the explanations of party support were phrased in terms reminiscent of traditional Conservative Party propaganda. Attitudes towards the monarchy, Christianity, and public schools, figured not at all. Only infrequent references were made to aristocracy, empire, foreign and military policies. The only relevant theme was reference to free enterprise and nationalisation. This theme was confined to Conservative supporters and may have a more general significance. For, as Milne and MacKenzie suggest, someone who says that his reason for Tory partisanship is hostility to nationalisation is not necessarily claiming that he thinks nationalisation in itself is important. He is merely identifying himself with the Conservative Party's opposition to nationalisation, which constitutes one of the limited differences in principle between the parties. This particular difference in principle, stressed over a long period in party propaganda, has made its mark and is accepted as symbolic of the party's whole policy.[2] It could also well be symbolic of the party's general identification with the dominant order. None the less, hostility towards the unions and the Labour Party in general were just as common as references to private enterprise and nationalisation. Most frequent among Conservative supporters were references to Tory abilities in general and to their political and financial acumen in particular. Among the Labour Party supporters, on the other hand, it was the party's identification with the working class, the poor, and ordinary people that was most often cited in explanation. Abilities provided over half of Conservative justifications, justifications of Labour loyalties more often than not referred to class. This result compares closely with other studies of party images[3] and suggests that defence of the established order is hardly the critical motive of those people who vote Conservative. Instrumental reasons seem more important in both the Labour and the Conservative case—as indicated by voters' references to class and to abilities respectively.

A comparison of the replies by degree of traditionalism shows that 'traditional' Labour supporters were more likely than other Labour voters to give no reason for their allegiance and that, when they did provide a reason, they were more likely to mention family or local tradition. The other Labour supporters, especially those most disaffected from the traditional order, were more likely to offer class-related and anti-Conservative reasons. Those few radicals who identify with the Conservative Party, however, are no more likely than other Tory voters to provide tradition or no reason in justification of their party loyalty. Conservative abilities and criticisms of Labour were the reasons most frequently cited by these radical Tory supporters. A breakdown of reasons by class consciousness and traditionalism can only be indicative but it suggests that, among both Labour and Conservative supporters, those who are doubly deviant, that is, in terms of degree of class consciousness as well as of traditionalism, are more likely to give 'tradition' or else no reason for their vote. Thus, of all double deviants, half gave such reasons compared with less than a quarter of those for whom both the degree of traditionalism and the level of class consciousness pointed to support for Conservative or Labour.[4] Overall, these data suggest that voters who are deviant, not so much in terms of their basic class position but in terms of general attitudes, are less sensitive, perhaps, to the dominant order and political issues and correspondingly more open to structural and especially habitual influences on voting behaviour.

Further support for this implication may be found in the pattern of beliefs about party attitudes to the dominant order. Three main points emerged from this analysis. Firstly, most dominant institutions are not identified exclusively with one or other political party and many people find difficulty, particularly in the case of remote and symbolic institutions, in identifying which political party might be more opposed to them. Secondly, those who 'correctly' identify the party are more likely to be radical Labour or traditional Conservative voters. This reinforces the suggestion that deviant voters tend to be more insensitive, and thus less committed, to dominant values and institutions. Thirdly, few people said they would change their vote if an institution to which they were attached were abolished or reduced in significance by the party they supported. This was as true of non-deviant voters as of deviants. The only exceptions to this generalisation concerned the problem of war and peace for Conservative voters and the abolition of unions in the case of Labour voters. Most attitudes towards dominant institutions seemed lukewarm and, in many cases, were also ambivalent. Political loyalties thus seem to be stronger than those to particular dominant institutions. Certainly, defence of the traditional order does not seem to be a central factor in party loyalties and it may be that it is the latter that condition attitudes to the dominant order rather than vice versa.

The difficulties found in identifying dominant institutions and values with particular parties are well illustrated in the following statements made by respondents in the interviews:

The Communist Party is about all I can think of that would abolish the monarchy; perhaps there are a few odd Labour MPs. In my opinion we're better off with the monarchy—it holds the country together more than a president ... I think they're well liked and well loved. (*Conservative farmworker: 4T; 3E; 48 years.*)[5]

I think the parties are about equally monarchical, other than Willy Hamilton in the Labour Party, that is. This is a rank Labour area round here—they'd vote in a cardboard placard if it had Labour on it—but it's still a very Royalist place. (*Labour miner: 4T; 3E; 37 years.*)

I think they shouldn't abolish the aristocracy—they ought to have more say. If they tried to do away with them, the country would go haywire. The Liberals might try to do it, but I don't really think any party would. (*Conservative worker: 5T; 0E; 38 years.*)

None of them—perhaps the Communist Party might. I wouldn't like it at all if they did, I'd certainly vote against them. Every country needs some private businesses to balance the state industries. (*Labour worker: 3T; 4E; 27 years.*)

The sorts of statements with which radical Labour and traditional Conservative voters correctly identified particular parties with a given attitude towards dominant institutions are illustrated below:

I don't think it's likely, perhaps the Labour Party. For example, that Hamilton was against the rise: there's lots of points where I'm in agreement with Hamilton. You take Sandringham—there's acres of land wasted there, they could have good housing estates there without using good land that does grow things. (*Labour worker: 1T; 3E; 39 years.*)

Well, the Labour Party said they'd like to see them abolished last time, didn't they? My big fear about the Labour Party is this—that if they got a big enough majority, they'd turn the country communist. I think public schools are a good thing—they really teach young children properly. I'd like to send my own son to one. (*Conservative farmer: 6T; 0E; 56 years.*)

I think it's quite possible within the next generation and it would be the Labour Party that did it. It wouldn't be abolished entirely, just the cash the Royal Family gets. I think it would be a good idea. (*Middle-class Labour: 2T; 5E; 32 years.*)

I suppose the Labour Party—but if the Conservative Party is stupid enough to try to declare us neutral, I'd vote against them, too. (*Conservative mining deputy: 5T; 0E; 58 years.*)

Well, you've got to say the Conservatives to a question like that. Really, you're asking me which party is more likely to try to foment revolution in this country. I'd be dead against any attempt to do away with unions. (*Middle-class Labour: 1T; 5E; 49 years.*)

Whether or not people correctly identified which party was more likely to do so, few would actually change their votes if their own party attempted to undermine an institution of which they approved:

I don't think any of them would—perhaps the Liberal Party, I'm not sure about their policy. It wouldn't make any difference to attitudes towards the parties if one of them did abolish the monarchy. (*Labour miner: 2T; 6E; 33 years.*)

I'd like to see public schools abolished, but it wouldn't make much difference to how I voted. I suppose the Labour Party would be more likely to abolish them. (*Labour worker: 1T; 5E; 25 years.*)

If people want to go to a public school and if they're good enough, then it's all right by me; I think the master's sons went to a private school—they're real gentlemen, they are. But it wouldn't make me change my vote if the Conservative Party tried to do away with them; after all, they know best. (*Conservative farmworker: 4T; 3E; 48 years.*)

I don't know. I don't think either would—don't the Labour MPs sit on boards as well? They don't bother me much. As long as the workers are doing all right, I don't really care who runs industry—nationalisation wouldn't affect my vote one way or the other. (*Labour shop steward: 3T; 6E; 28 years.*)

Overall, then, there is little evidence to suggest that the major

M

explanation for the link between traditionalism and voting behaviour is to be found in attitudes towards the defence of the traditional order. This is not to deny that there is a correlation between support for dominant institutions and party loyalties nor to suggest that such a motive is never present. It is to argue that some other explanation or explanations must be found to account for most of the covariation between voting and traditionalism. We shall now turn to consider the view that this covariation is the product or expression of different life-styles associated with contrasting attitudes, values, and political preferences.

9.2   Life-styles and politics

It is almost redundant to argue that a farming background, or a mining background, predisposes one to think and vote in certain ways rather than others. As Runciman points out, '(t)here is nothing, in a sense, that needs to be explained about a South Wales miner voting Labour or an executive of General Motors voting Republican.'[6] While he believes that the simplest model of rational self-interest can be shown to account for this behaviour, however, it seems just as plausible to invoke the notions of life-style and political culture that prescribe or encourage particular party loyalties. Amost every aspect of his environment and experience of life reinforces the Conservative leanings of the farmer or small-holder. His children, whether they stay on the land or work in the towns, inherit these tendencies along with many other attitudes, values, and beliefs. Likewise, the superimposition of occupational and residential communities that occurs in mining areas is highly conducive to the maintenance of traditional party loyalties and corporate attitudes. Whereas commitment to the dominant order and support for the Conservative Party are encouraged in the agricultural community, in the mining community disaffection and Labour voting are the norm.

While miners occasionally vote Conservative, some farmers vote Liberal, and somewhat more farmworkers vote either Liberal or Labour, these are often temporary aberrations rather than the product of permanent party loyalties. Even in the latter case, however, these are rarely genuine deviations and usually comprise exceptions that prove the rule. On a national basis such exceptions are typically articulated with distinctive structures and cultural traditions. In agricultural cases, for example, Liberalism is traditional in the Celtic fringe areas. Likewise, farmworkers who identify with the Labour Party are more likely to work on large, mechanised, bureaucratic farms and/or those farms which are close to large urban centres.[7] Conservative miners are much less common and it seems probable that highly particular circumstances obtain in these cases. This was definitely true, for example, for those few Tory miners in the present survey. Similar considerations applied to the solitary Labour smallholder in the sample. More generally, many of the apparently deviant cases actually turned out to be spurious instances of deviance. Personal histories articulated with current life-styles usually accounted for unusual party loyalties. Rather than illustrate simple applications of the rule, therefore, we shall describe some apparent exceptions that confirm it.

During the follow-up interviews respondents were asked why they supported their chosen party. A Conservative postman from Ely replied as follows. His family split up well before the last war and he was sent into a children's home. Finding this very unpleasant, he left as soon as possible. His new home was a farm and he worked for, lived with, and enjoyed leisure activities beside, the farmer and his family. He declared that, knowing no better, he greatly enjoyed this new life and thus came to share the farmer's views on the world in general and on politics and economic affairs in particular. He also learnt to respect a gaffer's opinions and abilities in running a business. After military service, he began a new job in a diesel factory and then joined the post office. But these early years had a great impact on his whole outlook. To this day he had retained a respect for his bosses, a distrust of unions, and loyalty to the Conservative Party. He owned his own home, saved regularly, belonged to the local Conservative Association, had many Conservative friends. In addition, in other replies he made, he showed a clear understanding of the central legitimations of business enterprise, the class structure, the royal family, and religion. While his history and his politics are unusual, therefore, they are none the less well integrated. His social background provides the key to understanding not only his political attitudes and general values but also his current life-style.

Similar stories were told by two Conservative miners. When asked, they explained their partisanship in terms of family socialisation that was articulated with structural location in a clearcut manner. One had a father who was a publican, a general dealer, and a pitman at various times in his life and who believed firmly in the virtues of monarchy, free enterprise, and Conservatism. He himself was a self-employed window-cleaner and odd-jobber until bad weather and a downturn in trade forced him to enter mining. He explained his allegiance in terms of the long line of loyalists and Conservatives in his family. The second miner replied that his family had been brought up in the farming villages of Yorkshire and had always been Liberal free-traders in politics. His father had been a carpenter and moved to Durham when farming was going badly. Since the party choice in Durham was effectively between Tory and Labour, the father switched his allegiance to the Conservatives. He himself saw the way things were going, set his sights on becoming an official in the pit, achieved this, and was proud to have become middle class thereby. Conservative voting was as much a manifestation of this upward mobility and a means of showing disapproval of checkweighmen in the pit and politics, as it was a product of family socialisation. The importance of farming background in the explanation of working-class Conservatism in Easington was underlined when it was mentioned in two other interviews. For the majority of Easington residents, however, personal history and current life-style pointed in the opposite direction. Labour voting is almost built into the social structure and political culture.

In the three illustrative cases reviewed above, personal history proved to be important in explaining class deviant political loyalties. In each case, moreover, the history was articulated with significant structural factors and was associated not only with a deviant party loyalty in terms of class position, but also with class deviance in life-style and general values. All three voters, for example, scored high on traditionalism and only the postman scored high on class consciousness. In other cases, however, the political implications of structural position and life-style do not coincide with those of apparent commitments to dominant or deviant values. Our interview data suggest that, in these cases, it is life-style and structural position that are the determining factors and that, irrespective of the actual scores on traditionalism and egalitarianism, there is an insensitivity to the dominant order in particular and wider society in general. This insensitivity is manifest not only in a limited understanding of dominant values and a low level of political conceptualisation, but also in ambivalent and inconsistent attitudes to both dominant and deviant institutions. Accordingly, structural position and life-style have a more important role to play in the determination of voting behaviour. For, in contrast to those for whom general values are closely articulated with the latter factors, those who are insensitive and confused about the dominant order cannot derive clear political inferences from these values and are thus more open to the influences of life style and structural position.

The case of a Labour miner illustrates this phenomenon well. He achieved the maximum score on traditionalism and a comparatively low score on class consciousness. But, in contrast to Conservative workers with comparable scores, he displayed limited and inconsistent attitudes to the dominant order and only a low level of political consciousness. Thus any notions of competition, risk, initiative, productivity, or growth, were absent from his discussion of business and industry. In distinguishing only two classes, bosses and workers, he apparently held a traditional proletarian image of the class structure. But he also argued that, since bosses had the necessary general education and training for the job, then workers should do as ordered by them. At the same time, however, he supported the Labour Party as standing for the labouring man and declared that any worker who voted Conservative could not know that the bosses were always trying to rob workers of their hard-earned coppers. Inflation was due to the combination of workers getting too much for too little effort and bosses raising prices higher than was justified by increased costs. Unions were going too far and should not be opposing the government. Miners were right to go on strike and he himself would support any industrial action to improve the pay and conditions of railwaymen and others who backed the miners in their recent dispute. The public schools should be left alone because they were all for learning and learning is a good thing. But it is wrong for some children to get a better education than others just because their parents had more money than other parents. He was sure Britain was a democracy but could give no justification for this belief other than the king and queen. Despite these apparently conflicting and paradoxical attitudes, he was firmly committed to the Labour Party in terms of past voting. This is probably because of his integration into the local community and occupational life-world and thus his acceptance, wittingly or unwittingly, of local political norms as legitimate and valid. He saw himself as a typical Durham miner, came from a mining family, married into another, belonged to several local clubs and associations, pursued the usual local leisure activities, and so forth. In the absence of any strong ideological attachments or personal antagonisms, it would have been a difficult task for him to sustain anything but loyalty to the Labour Party.

A Conservative farmworker provided a comparable case in the Ely constituency. He, too, expressed no interest in politics. He had a couldn't-care-less attitude to most dominant institutions and voiced vehement opposition to the unions. He believed that both the unions and the high-up people, the rich, had too much influence. Politicians in all parties were concerned only with number one but the Tory Party did sometimes try to help you start up on your own. Since he wanted to become a pig farmer, he therefore supported the Conservative Party. But, in addition, everyone in his village voted that way and he was well integrated into village life. For example, he was on the committee of the local working-men's club, drank with his employer in the pub every Friday, had many friends and relatives in the local community, and had married a local girl. While this is a less clear-cut case than that previously cited, they share several features that suggest the importance of structural position and life-styles. Along with the preceding three case histories, therefore, they provide some evidence that these factors explain much voting behaviour and help to account for the covariation between traditionalism and support for one or other major political party.

In other apparently deviant cases, however, political loyalties are less clearly related to deviant values and life-styles. The explanations for party loyalties in such cases are more idiosyncratic or accidental in character and cannot usually be related to any distinctive social attributes of the person concerned. The occasional importance of such idiosyncrasies can be illustrated by two case histories. The first is that of the only Labour smallholder in our sample, the other is that of a Conservative miner. Both were asked why they supported a party not normally approved of by persons in their position. In both cases the reply was in terms of antagonisms towards a local candidate or party that cut across the usual political loyalty for his occupational group. Thus the smallholder replied as follows:

> I've voted for Churchill in the past—when he said he'd get a thing done, he'd do it. Not like now. Every man in this village was behind Churchill. I changed from Conservative to Labour because of a row with this here MP . . . I went along to a meeting to try to get some more council land for farming because I knew my contract ploughing business was coming to an end. He saw me and said, 'Aren't you that Mr Farrier—you've got a ploughing business, what do you want with more land?' I tried to explain but he gave the land to someone else. There's a lot of back-handed work on council land distribution. I've voted Labour or not at all ever since then.

A similar reason underlay the vote of the Conservative miner mentioned above. In this case it was a council house that caused the antagonism between elector and party. He replied as follows:

> I've never liked the Labour Party, it's very underhanded, especially locally. For example, after the General Strike, I left the miners' union and joined the General Workers'. The local councillors said they wouldn't give me a council house until I rejoined the miners' union, paid a fresh initiation fee, and all my back dues. Well, I wouldn't have that, would I? So I didn't get a council house until after the last war. The nationalisation of the pits meant that all the miners grouped together into one union and I joined them then. I reckon they thought that was enough. Any way, I got my house then.

While these two cases are somewhat idiosyncratic, references to local political monopolies occurred in other descriptions of political parties and justifications of party loyalties. A Labour farmworker, for example, justified his political allegiance in terms of stories told him by a local union organiser and councillor about the local farmers' control over council land, council houses, and industrial expansion as a means of keeping farm wages at a low level. Likewise, several respondents in the Easington constituency cited the rubber-stamping of local council business by the Labour members and the favouritism that occurred within the unions. Whatever the truth of such accusations for either constituency, rumours and stories along similar lines are almost bound to circulate in areas that are dominated by a single party. A certain degree of political alienation will probably stem from this and thereby provide a source of opposition to the influence of superior party organisation. Moreover, this will occur in Labour-dominated areas whether or not the local party is controlled by middle-class residents. Where this sort of domination is compounded with the first, then, as Hindess points out, working class political interest and activity will decline even further.[8] In all types of constituency, however, experiences such as those cited above and acceptance of stories about them will probably account for a certain amount of deviance from class or attitudinal norms.

Overall, therefore, our interview data suggest that at least part of the covariation between traditionalism and party loyalties can be explained in terms of the more general relation between structural position and life-style. Structural position must be understood to include one's past positions in the total social matrix as well as one's current location. Moreover, within the total matrix, the economic dimensions will be especially important in a secular and class-stratified society such as Britain. Life-style includes not only interests, attitudes, beliefs, and values, but also the patterns of interaction to which these give rise. Structural position is normally closely articulated with life-style; and inevitably so at the level of day-to-day life rather than general orientations towards the social order. At the latter level, as we have already argued, there is often considerable scope for ambiguity, inconsistency, and ambivalence. But, in so far as this arises from cross-pressures in exposure to dominant and deviant values, then structural position is still a major factor. Furthermore, even in cases of ambiguity, social location and life-style are frequently linked with the nature of political loyalties in terms of their existence, intensity, and content. This is apparent not only in the effects of structural factors, such as union membership and residential community, on voting behaviour and partisan self-identities, but also in the case histories just cited.

The most likely explanation is that the combination of structural position and routine life-style largely determines both political loyalties and orientations to the dominant order. Usually, the last two variables will reinforce each other. But, where this is not so, owing to inconsistency, ambiguity, or ambivalence in attitudes towards the dominant order, structural variables will still determine or mediate the relations between such attitudes and electoral choice. Although this might imply that attitudes to the dominant order are redundant in explaining voting behaviour, this does not actually seem to be the case. Rather, the effect is one of cumulative interaction and mutual reinforcement. This in turn is probably due to the interaction of four main factors. First, few people are so located in the social structure that they are effectively constrained to support but one political party. Secondly, it is equally rare to find voters who are totally opposed, or else totally attached, to the dominant order. Thus, while there is scope for attitudinal influences in cases of situational indeterminacy, ideological indeterminacy can often be resolved through situational constraints. Furthermore, the ambiguous attitude of the Labour Party to the dominant order serves both to aggravate this latter indeterminacy and to facilitate the influence of structural factors. Lastly, although attitudes and life-style are largely determined socially, they also help to determine subsequent social location and its interpretation. Thus decisions about residence, occupation, union membership, or leisure activities, can be influenced by pre-existing attitudes; which will also provide the framework within which such structural factors must affect future attitudes. Thus the sequence in which different situations are encountered may well be as important as the actual situations themselves. In short, there is a significant level of interaction between structural location and attitudes to the social order not only in their effects on voting behaviour but also in relation to each other. This means that electoral choice is multiply determined rather than the product of a single factor or set of factors.

9.3   Middle-class-Labour voters

We can probe these matters further by considering the determinants of Labour voting in the middle class. Although such voters are electorally deviant in terms of their basic non-manual occupational position, very few are actually deviant in terms of their general attitudes and specific structural location. Overall, for example, less than a fifth of such voters were neither radical nor class-conscious. Moreover, as we shall see in our next chapter, these attitudes were typically articulated with their position within the total societal structure. We conducted interviews with only five middle-class Labour voters and, while this number is obviously too small to draw any firm conclusions even when combined with survey data, several interesting points none the less emerged.

Firstly, as with other deviant and non-deviant voters, there is no single route to party loyalties among middle-class Labour voters. Sometimes these loyalties are inherited and reinforced by subsequent social location. In other cases they are the result of intellectual development associated with discontinuities in social location. And, in yet other cases, they follow from structural constraints emerging later in life. Thus one interviewee ascribed his political loyalties to childhood upbringing and the fact that most of his friends at work and play also supported Labour. Another, whose father was a Conservative working man, replied that he did a lot of reading in the services, engaged in a lot of discussion, and developed a growing awareness that all was not right with the world. His experience of further education reinforced this impression and he began to puzzle out ways of improving the world at large. Conversely, another middle-class Labour voter, whose father was a Labour railway worker, replied that he had set out to better himself by working in a City bank and had taken on the protective colouring of his new class—including Conservative Party loyalties. Only later, when he was made redundant, did he discover that white-collar employees were as working class as railwaymen and had a less secure job into the bargain. This led him to support socialist policies and, for want of an alternative, the Labour Party. Another such voter was brought up by apolitical but religious parents during the depression and was radicalised as a result. He identified with the Liberal Party but had always voted Labour because this promised more chance of evicting the Conservative member of parliament. Four of these voters had non-commercial occupations at the time of interview. They comprised teaching, nursing, the civil service, and local government. The remaining Labour voter was an industrial chemist. These occupations are fairly representative of middle-class Labour supporters more generally.

Secondly, those who inherited their loyalties from working-class parents without intervening political deviations were less interested in, and less articulate about, politics than the three voters who had been converted to radical sympathies. In addition, their loyalty was to the Labour movement rather than to socialism. This comes out well in the following three statements: the first is that of an industrial chemist brought up as a Labour supporter, the second that of a school teacher converted to radicalism in the army, and the third that of an operating theatre nurse radicalised in a downwardly mobile family during the depression:

> I suppose I'm more Labour than socialist—the Labour Party is more middling, the socialists are more idealistic. I can't imagine anything that would make me change my party— the parties are so similar there's not much in it anyway. Perhaps if there were a polarisation of the parties and Labour went left, then I might support the Conservatives. *(5T; 3E; 32 years.)*

> If the chances of success were more or less equal, I'd rather see a socialist type solution than a Tory solution. But I also think the Labour Party would be more successful than the Tories in handling the problems facing us today. *(1T; 5E; 49 years.)*

> The Labour Party has the right ideas, for example, equality of opportunity. But this backbone of theirs has been swamped by a preoccupation with the industrial worker—they seem to forget their basic socialism. I approve of the principle in the *Communist Manifesto*, 'from each according to his ability, to each according to his need.' But the Labour Party doesn't. *(0T; 5E; 59 years.)*

Thirdly, even among the middle-class socialists, there was some ambivalence towards the dominant order rather than outright rejection. This was apparent, for example, in attitudes towards the Tory Party, the class structure, business, the unions, and the education system. It is hardly surprising, therefore, when we find the average Labour supporter, oriented towards his party primarily in terms of an economistic outlook, is also ambivalent. Two illustrations of middle class socialist ambivalence follow:

> There's nothing I can really say that I like about the Conservative Party, nothing I can isolate. But I've got a sneaking feeling, a sort of deep-down belief, that a background of privilege, etc, is a better preparation for government. I know I should not be feeling this but familiarity with wealth, possessions, titled people, and the like, does seem to make a difference. I know that Lords can be socialists as well, there are a number of them after all, but most are Tories. (*1T; 5E; 59 years.*)

> I like the way the Conservatives have the co-operation of their own party, the way they stay united; they do have money on their side and they know how to use it—you've got to admire that even if they are directed by the purse-string holders. Having the support of big business and the City does smooth the way for Tory policies. Labour should have the same financial co-operation—or recognise that it is not there and approach things differently. I hope this doesn't seem too confused. (*0T; 5E; 39 years old.*)

Finally, in all five cases, these political loyalties are integrated with life-style and general values. In three cases, this results from the influence of attitudes on structural location as well as that of location on attitudes and life-style. The nurse and teacher, for example, chose careers in which they could help people and perhaps set the world to rights. They were also active in welfare and charitable organisations. The civil servant turned to this occupation from city banking because of redundancy and a new-found antipathy to business. The two voters with inherited Labour loyalties continued to live in predominantly working-class and Labour areas and still mixed with old friends and relatives from these areas. The survey data suggest that these patterns are not atypical and probably characterise most middle-class Labour voters.

9.4 Working-class Tories

Conservative manual workers show a similar diversity of routes
to deviant party loyalties. But in almost all cases these routes
exemplify the importance of personal histories articulated with
distinctive structural locations. Although this is an omnibus
category it is none the less valuable for that. The more an individual is exposed to conditions favourable to attachments to the
dominant order and Conservative support, the more likely is he
to abjure the Labour Party and to affirm traditional values and
institutions. This was apparent not only in Tory partisanship but
also in deference of various kinds, hostility to unions, and, in some
cases, hostility to the urban community. Idiosyncratic factors
played only a minor role in comparison with this omnibus category. Some illustrations of the latter are presented below.

Within the agricultural community proper many factors
encourage Conservative support. Close contacts with employers,
limited and relatively ineffective union organisation, integration
into the local community with its hierarchical status system and
Tory politics, and so forth, insulate workers from contacts with
Labour influences and expose them to dominant ideological
influences. Farmers and the small businessmen of the agricultural
community are particularly involved in, and committed to, traditional forms of private enterprise and they stress the risks as well
as the rewards of their chosen employment. This outlook is
frequently accepted by farmworkers themselves. Moreover,
where wage-rates are above the union-negotiated level and are
agreed on a man-to-man basis with the farmer, as was often the
case among our respondents, the farmworker has little incentive
to join a union and develops little understanding of the utility of
collective bargaining in large factories. The influences of the local
community will reinforce these impressions and opinions derived
from the work situation. The persistent effects of these factors,
even where those exposed to them have taken up other occupations, has already been noted. A number of other examples will be
noted below. But it would be misleading to imply that all of those
employed in agriculture vote Conservative. On a national basis
this is definitely untrue and, within our own sample, a third of the
farm workers voted Labour. An examination of survey and interview data suggests that the latter were not strongly committed to
Labour support in terms of party loyalties or voting record and
were also less interested in politics than Conservative farmworkers.
The usual reason for voting Labour was the nature of the times or

the belief that Labour stood for the labouring man rather more than did the Conservative Party. They also tended to be younger and more exposed to influences conducive to Labour support, such as residence on urban council estates, past employment in factories, and union membership. There are too few such voters, however, to draw any definitive conclusions about Labour voting in such occupations.

The interaction of the influences favourable to Conservative support in such circumstances can be illustrated by three case histories. A retired Conservative farm foreman explained his political allegiance in terms of upbringing and experience. He was born into a farming family, worked all his life in agriculture, had earned his position of responsibility through hard work and respect for his employers, had confronted and defeated union agitators on the farm, belonged to the local Conservative Association, had taken Lord Butler fox-hunting at Christmas along with other members of the upper class, knew the Courtauld family well, and so on. It is interesting to note that, although he had mixed with the upper classes and landed gentry, he preferred a prime minister from a working-class background. In other respects, however, he was status-conscious and opposed to the agitators found in the unions and Labour Party. Another Tory farmworker replied that, while he had been a labourer all his life, he had never supported the Labour Party. While this might seem odd to outsiders and city-dwellers, it could easily be explained by the fact that he had worked on a farm owned by the local MP. This had produced respect not only for his employer but also for all officers and gentlemen—and there were more of these in the Conservative Party. A third farmworker stated that, although his father had been a Labour-voting policeman, he himself voted Conservative. For, as a farmworker his welfare and pay depended on the welfare of farmers, and it was well-known that the Conservative Party was the farmers' party. This was often mentioned by farmworkers as a good reason for voting Conservative and demonstrates the extent to which dominant beliefs are accepted by the underprivileged.[9]

A factor common to farmworkers and several other Conservative workers in the sample was their non-union membership or involvement in weak or ineffective unions. This generated hostility to unions because of their money-grabbing militant activities and the resultant low relative wages achieved by those not in strong unions. The Conservative Party was also perceived as being more opposed to such activities than the Labour Party.

In addition, employment in small plants was also associated with limited understanding of the need for collective bargaining and, in the words of one respondent, the belief that 'a man isn't a man unless he can go and ask for a rise on his own merits instead of hiding behind the union.' This sort of belief was fairly common in Ely and was linked to the belief, as expressed by another Tory worker, that 'you've got to be a red-hot union man to vote Labour.' To the extent that such views are common to workers in a given firm or farm, then they will reinforce one another and insulate voters even more from Labour appeals. Conversely, in large factories with strong union organisation extensive intra-class communication will increase the effectiveness of these appeals.

Thirdly, in one or two cases, support for the local Conservative candidate was crucial in sustaining Conservative Party loyalties on a national level. The two most obvious cases of this pheno-menon occurred where neither the level of traditionalism nor that of class consciousness predisposed the voter in one or another political direction. The provision of help by the local MP served in both cases to mobilise loyalties to the party he represented. One Conservative worker had received help in connection with a claim to a wartime disability pension and, later, the possible closure of the business in which he was employed. Another had noted the help given to a black neighbour and was particularly impressed that this was given outside of an election campaign. In the words of one of these voters, 'Sir Harry is rather special for me—perhaps if I lived elsewhere I wouldn't vote Conservative.' Indeed, had these voters lived in a Labour-dominated area, their party loyal-ties may have been won by a Labour MP. While it would be wrong to suggest that this kind of help is a major cause of party loyalties it is none the less important to recognise that there are multiple routes to party loyalties. In particular, a wide range of factors can be relevant where general orientations and/or structural position are ambiguous in their political implications.

One final illustration of the importance of personal background articulated with structural location may be given. One Con-servative worker, who was extremely interested in foreign policy and believed that, provided foreign policy was right, then dom-estic issues could be resolved quite easily, explained his political allegiance as the result of family background and military service. His father was a Control Commissioner in postwar Germany and he himself had been an ordinary ranker in the Guards. It was this that had given him such interest in foreign policy and the great

difference in Labour and Conservative attitudes over Suez con-
vinced him that only the latter party could be trusted. This belief
was reinforced by a commitment to free enterprise and hostility
to the 'nationalise then subsidise' policies of the Labour Party.
Parental political loyalties, education in an army school, down-
ward mobility into the manual working class, and employment
in a non-union factory, must also have contributed to this loyalty
to the Conservative Party.

What is important in these case histories is not the particular
sets of circumstances cited by Tory workers in explanation of their
party loyalties but the general principles that these circumstances
illustrate. Had we interviewed other subjects or chosen different
constituencies for this research, different accounts and factors
may have emerged as important in individual cases. But the overriding impression is that party loyalties are not random but are
related to social location and orientations to the dominant order.
Within this basic context there are many different potential
combinations of institutional and orientational factors that are
compatible with, conducive towards, or overdeterminative of,
Conservative support. Many of these have been considered in the
statistical analyses of the two preceding chapters. They include
parental socio-economic standing, paternal party loyalties, type of
employment, unemployment experience, plant size, union
membership, house-ownership, religion, residential community,
and so forth. Many of the same factors emerge as significant when
individuals are asked to relate how they came to support a
particular party. Such explanations frequently referred to family
background, family and local tradition, aspects of their work
situation, and so forth. As we have argued above, and as will
become apparent in the next chapter, not only are political loyalties related to such variables but so, too, are orientations towards
the dominant order. In short, of the explanations so far considered
for the covariation between traditionalism and party loyalties,
that in terms of their codetermination by structural position and
life-style seems most plausible.

9.5 Policy orientations and party loyalties

Many studies have demonstrated a strong correlation between
approval of a particular party's stand on a range of issues and
electoral support for that party.[10] While this is often interpreted
as a demonstration of the causal significance of policy orientations, the actual direction of the causal connection, if any, is
somewhat less than unambiguous. Indeed, there are sound

theoretical and empirical reasons for questioning the importance of such orientations in the determination of electoral behaviour. Firstly, since orientations to particular policy issues are generally unstable even over short periods, it is unlikely that they are the cause of enduring partisan identities. Moreover, the correlation among such orientations is generally low so that voters typically support policies associated with several different parties. While this latter phenomenon is somewhat reduced in the case of those who 'correctly' identify the policies of the major parties and also among party activists, such persons are comparatively few in number and the phenomenon persists even here.[11] Thus, while policy orientations may partly determine transient aberrations from normal party loyalties and also play a minor role in more permanent shifts in partisanship,[12] more generally it would seem that policy orientations are neither cause nor effect of partisan identities. *A fortiori*, therefore, it is unlikely that the covariation between traditionalism and electoral behaviour is due to the mediating influence of policy orientation opinion leaders. This is not to say that traditionalism does not affect the deference given to another's opinions but it is to argue that the links between policy orientations and partisanship are too tenuous for this to have much effect. The relationship between general party images and traditionalism is likely to be more important, especially when combined with the influence of structural position on both these factors.

Less than one-tenth of respondents in the second sample referred to specific issues when justifying their support for one of the major parties. Furthermore, almost all of these references involved Conservative policy on nationalisation and private enterprise or else Labour policy on the poor and elderly. The former issue has a larger significance and is symbolic of the different images of Tory and Labour in terms of their attitudes towards the dominant institutional order. The latter issue is as much an economistic or class question as it is simply a matter of specific policies. A similar pattern was found in the follow-up interviews when respondents were asked what they liked and disliked about the main parties. The abilities of the Conservatives and Labour's image as defender of the working man were the most commonly cited positive impressions; most frequently cited as negative aspects were Labour incompetence, disunity, and nationalisation policy, and the Conservative bias towards the rich and the middle class. Moreover, when asked in these interviews which particular policies of either party they would like to see changed, the issues mentioned were either common to both major parties, such as Northern Ireland or inflation, or else symbolic of attitudes towards the dominant order, such as trade unions and disarmament. The impressions derived from survey and interview material serve simply to reinforce those of earlier research on the comparative importance of policy orientations in the determination of voting behaviour and political identities. That is to say, policy orientations appear to be unimportant in comparison with such factors as structural position and life-style.

9.6 Summary and conclusions

In this chapter we have been concerned to interpret the relationship between traditionalism and electoral choice. The available evidence suggests that most of their covariation can be interpreted in terms of an interaction between structural position, life-style, and orientations to the dominant order, such that voting is determined not by any one of these factors alone but by their dialectical relations. Structural location exercises a constraining influence over life-style and orientations towards the dominant institutional order; in turn, these factors influence subsequent social location. Support for each major party is more firmly established in certain structures than others. But orientations towards the dominant order are also associated with partisan support through their reflection in party images. The differential institutionalisation of political parties, itself the product of past interaction between societal dynamics, popular beliefs, and party political mobilisation, is probably the major cause of this covariation. Thus traditionalism is probably associated with Conservatism because both are related to social location. But traditionalism and class consciousness none the less play an important independent supporting role in the determination of electoral behaviour. For, in cross-pressured situations characterised by a structural indeterminacy of electoral choice, it is still possible for orientations to the dominant order and its class structure to have a constraining influence upon political support. Conversely, in cases of ideological indeterminacy, which, for reasons outlined in preceding chapters, are perhaps more widespread than structural indeterminacy, the effects of differential institutionalisation and mobilisation will assume greater significance. In many cases, however, structural location and orientations will reinforce or overdetermine the effects that each has on party loyalties. Other factors will be relatively unimportant.

Thus, to paraphrase and extend Parkin's analysis, people do

N

not vote Conservative because they are traditional—rather, they are traditional *and* Conservative because they are isolated from the structural conditions favourable to radicalism *and* Labour voting. At the same time, however, though to a lesser extent, their precise location in the societal matrix is determined by their social, economic and political attitudes. As we have argued above, structures of political mobilisation, such as the union and the party, play an important role in the determination of voting behaviour along with those structural factors that influence the degree of class consciousness and orientations to the dominant order. It is to a consideration of these latter factors that we now turn.

9.7 Notes and references

1 See, for example, Almond and Verba, *Civic Culture*, pp121–36; F Bealey *et al*, *Constituency Politics* (London: Faber, 1965), p212; Abrams *et al*, *Must Labour Lose?* p19; Benney *et al*, *How People Vote*, p121; McKenzie and Silver, *Angels*, pp113–20; Nordlinger, *Tories*, pp137–59; Trenaman and McQuail, *Television*, pp52–3; and D E G Plowman, 'Allegiance to political parties: a study of three parties in one area,' *Pol. Stud.* (1955), iii, pp222–34.

2 Milne and Mackenzie, *Straight Fight*, p137.

3 J Bonham, *The Middle Class Vote* (London: Faber, 1954), pp72–3; Milne and MacKenzie, *Straight Fight*, p129; *idem*, *Marginal Seat*, pp55–6; Benney *et al*, *How People Vote*, pp116–24; Trenaman and McQuail, *Television*, pp44–5; Nordlinger, *Tories*, pp157–9; Abrams *et al*, *Must Labour Lose?*, pp20–4; Butler and Stokes, *Political Change*, pp359–72.

4 There were thirty-seven 'double deviants' *in toto* who identified with a political party; eighty-eight respondents had a level of class consciousness congruent with their orientation to the dominant value system.

5 In this and subsequent quotations, nT indicates the score (n) on traditionalism and nE indicates the score (n) on egalitarianism: the higher n is, the more traditional or egalitarian the person quoted.

6 W G Runciman, *Social Science and Political Theory* (London: Cambridge University Press, 1965), p94.

7 *cf* C Bell and H Newby, 'The sources of variation in agricultural workers' images of society,' unpublished paper, University of Essex (July 1972).

8 Hindess, *Decline, passim.*

9 In fact, there is only limited correlation between agricultural wage-rates in different regions and the prosperity of the farms in those regions: see H Newby, 'The low earnings of agricultural workers: a sociological approach, *J. Agric. Econ.* (1972), xxiii, pp15–24.

10 See, for example, Benney *et al*, *How People Vote*, p146; Milne and Mackenzie, *Straight Fight*, p108; *idem*, *Marginal Seat*, p124; and Butler and Stokes, *Political Change*, pp341–58. Research in the United States has been more concerned with policy orientations: see, for example, Campbell *et al*, *American Voter*, pp33–8.

11 *cf* Milne and Mackenzie, *Marginal Seat*, p124; Butler and Stokes, *Political Change*, pp195–200.

12 On more permanent shifts, see: Benewick *et al*, in *Pol. Stud.* (1969), xvii, pp177–95.

Chapter 10

The Structural Location and Social Thought of Traditionals

In the preceding chapters we have considered the relationship between various types of deference and voting behaviour. We have shown that, while it is not greatly influenced by ascriptive socio-political deference, political choice is partly determined by attitudes towards the traditional social and moral order. Their influence is independent of many different structural factors but interacts with them to produce even greater variation in voting behaviour. The most plausible explanation for this cumulative interaction is that ideological orientations help to resolve structural indeterminacy and structural factors help to resolve ideological ambivalence in electoral choice. But this still leaves open the question of how people come to accept, reject, or hesitate about the legitimacy of the dominant order. Unless we can demonstrate some determinate causal links between social or psychological factors and traditionalism, we could be accused of showing simply that people who think like Conservatives vote like Conservatives. In this chapter, therefore, we seek to demonstrate that traditionalism is not a random ideological phenomenon but that its incidence is socially structured in determinate ways.

In our examination of ascriptive socio-political deference, we found some evidence to support the hypothesis that structural centrality and exposure to dominant institutions and values were significantly related to such deferential orientations. Parkin suggests that the same factors influence the level of commitment to the whole dominant order. He points out that the dominant value system is not institutionalised to the same extent in every stratum; rather, the lower any given stratum is in the hierarchy of power, wealth, and prestige, the less complete is this affirmation likely to be. For obvious reasons, moreover, this latter tendency is enhanced to the extent that the lower strata comprise distinct social communities rather than scattered individuals and small isolated groups. In particular, Parkin stresses the effects of both residential and occupational communities in transmitting subordinate and countercultural values. The same two factors are emphasised by Lockwood in his discussion of sources of variation in working-class images of society. In contrast with the deferential worker, the proletarian worker is held to interact and identify with his workmates rather than his employer and also to reside in a local community characterised by occupational homogeneity rather than an heterogeneous and hierarchical stratification system.[1] More generally, these are the same factors that we associated with the development of class consciousness in a preceding chapter. It is with these and other factors that we shall be concerned in the following pages.

The characteristic emphasis will be on social structure rather than individual attributes. Income, age, religion, occupational prestige, and similar attributes are not considered as important as the location of the individual within the social matrix. Thus, in so far as survey data, such as the opinion polls cited in earlier chapters, show a positive correlation between socio-economic status and affirmation of the dominant order, this must be due to a general association between such status and involvement in different types of occupational and residential community and similar structural variables. In any particular survey, however, these general correlations might not obtain owing to the absence or abnormality of the key structural factors. This is probably part of the explanation for the many discrepancies between various surveys over the role of personal attributes such as income, age, occupational prestige or skill level, and so on, in the determination of working-class voting behaviour.[2] We must look at local political generations, the source of income, the type of employment, the nature of the employing organisation, etc, in order to understand these questions. Before proceeding to such an analysis, however, it is essential to underline an obvious fact about our samples, namely, that they do not include representatives of the dominant elites of British society. At best they include a number of professional, managerial, and self-employed members of the upper middle class. There is none the less sufficient variation within the two samples to permit an initial test of the hypotheses.

10.1 The structural determinants of traditionalism
We begin our analysis with a consideration of residential community effects. The arguments developed in preceding pages would suggest that persons resident in a predominantly middle-class

constituency or an agricultural area would be more traditional than one insulated from contacts with the dominant institutional order and middle-class values by residence in a predominantly industrial and working-class community or constituency. This hypothesis can be tested by comparing rates of traditionalism in different constituencies. As expected, those resident in Ely and Woodford are more committed to the traditional dominant order than those resident in Stepney and Easington. Thus, over a half of the middle-class residents of the Isle of Ely and over two-fifths of those from Wanstead and Woodford are traditional compared with one-third in Stepney and Easington. Similarly, whereas one-fifth of Easington manual workers are traditional, traditionals comprise two and a half times that proportion of manual workers in the Isle of Ely. A corresponding degree of variation is to be found in the level of radicalism (see Table 10.1). Furthermore, when age controls are introduced, the apparent deviations found among non-manual workers in Easington and manual workers in Woodford are shown to be spurious: the former being disproportionately old and hence traditional, the latter being disproportionately young and hence radical.

Whereas the three London constituencies are compact and urbanised, Ely and Easington are geographically scattered and comprise various towns and villages. The impact of residential community is shown in comparisons of those living in different types of locality within these latter two constituencies. Thus, in Easington, whereas 31 per cent of manual workers living in towns and pit villages scored low on traditionalism, radicals comprised only 15 per cent of the manual workers resident in country villages.[3] Similarly, in the Isle of Ely, those who live on farms and in country villages and/or resided therein during childhood are much less radical than those resident in industrial or market towns. Only one in twenty-five of the former scored low on traditionalism compared with a quarter of those manual workers living in a small-town environment. Furthermore, the differences between these two constituencies persist when those with mining or agricultural jobs are excluded from the comparison —ordinary workers in Easington are only half as traditional as those in Ely. This comparison is significant because it suggests that, while residential differences can be attributed in part to occupational differences, an important residual element remains that can be attributed to genuine structural effects associated with community involvement. In comparison with residential community, 'housing class' was not consistently related to the level of

Table 10.1 TRADITIONALISM BY CLASS AND CONSTITUENCY

Trad scores	Middle class, %					Working class, %				
	Ely	W/F	W/G	Sty	E'n	Ely	W/F	W/G	Sty	E'n
Rad	17	18	29	28	17	17	23	15	24	29
Med	30	41	40	36	51	38	52	50	48	50
Trad	52	41	30	36	32	45	25	34	27	21
Total, per cent	99	100	99	100	100	100	100	99	99	100
Base, N	(86)	(126)	(79)	(50)	(65)	(100)	(52)	(102)	(96)	(127)

commitment to the dominant order. Where as a greater proportion of radical than traditional manual workers owned their homes, there was no difference in house-ownership for the same groups within the middle class.[4] This contrasts with the greater propensity of home-owners to vote Conservative whatever their degree of commitment to the dominant order.

From considerations of residential community, we now turn to an examination of occupational factors. As previously noted, there are few reasons to expect a consistent relationship between occupational prestige or income and the level of traditionalism or pattern of electoral behaviour. Thus, in our own sample, while manual workers are less traditional than non-manual workers, they have more or less the same incidence of radicalism or disaffection from the dominant order and its associated values.[5] Moreover, within the middle class, occupational prestige is negatively correlated with traditionalism;[6] in the working class, on the other hand, there is no consistent relationship between skill level and traditionalism. Similarly, there is no consistent relationship between income and traditionalism within the middle class, but there is a slight negative correlation between the two variables in the working class. The latter is probably due to covariation between types of employment and wage-rates rather than to the level of income *per se*. Agricultural workers and non-unionist workers tend to have lower incomes and also to be more traditional.[7] In all these cases, however, the differences are slight in comparison with those associated with structurally relevant variables.

Important among these latter variables are such factors as type of employment, nature of the employing organisation, plant size, and union membership. On theoretical grounds one would expect agricultural occupations to be conducive to identification with the employer and mining jobs to be conducive to identification with fellow workers. In turn this will facilitate acceptance of traditional values in the former case and their rejection in the latter case. More generally, in terms of exposure and insulation relative to the traditional order, one would expect those working in large unionised firms to be least traditional and those employed in small, non-unionised firms to be least radical. While these considerations apply especially to manual workers, they are also relevant to non-manual workers. In the latter case, moreover, the nature of the employing organisation may also be important. Workers in non-commercial organisations, especially the public service sector, will be less exposed by the very nature of their employment to pressures to accept the values associated with the dominant capitalist order. While union membership was measured in both samples, the remaining three variables were included only in the second sample.

As expected, union membership is associated with disaffection from the dominant order in both major occupational groups (see Table 10.2). The effect of union membership on traditionalism is more noticeable in the working class but it is clearly present in both occupational groups. Furthermore, it persists when constituency influences are controlled. In the Isle of Ely, for example, only 37 per cent of manually employed trade unionists are traditionals compared with 55 per cent of non-members; in Stepney these figures are 16 and 36 per cent, respectively. Similarly, middle-class union members in Wanstead and Woodford included among their number only 27 per cent of traditionals in comparison with 42 per cent among non-members; in Wood Green only one-eighth of non-manual unionists were thus attached to the dominant order in contrast to almost two-fifths of non-members. Overall, in the five constituencies, union membership produced an average of sixteen points difference in the level of traditionalism for each of the two main occupational classes.[8] This underlines the suggestion that both residential community and occupational characteristics are important independent variables in the determination of orientations to the dominant order. Further support for this argument can be found in our data on plant size, type of occupation, and the nature of the employing organisation.

Table 10.2 TRADITIONALISM BY CLASS AND UNION MEMBERSHIP

Trad scores	Middle class, %		Working class, %	
	Union members	Non-members	Union members	Non-members
Rad	27	19	27	14
Med	43	38	50	45
Trad	30	43	23	41
Total, per cent	100	100	100	100
Base, N	(122)	(284)	(281)	(199)

Plant size is important because large plants encourage horizontal rather than vertical communication and thus facilitate identification with fellow-workers rather than employers. A high level of bureaucratisation, often associated with large size, further reinforces this tendency.[9] The result is to insulate workers from contacts with middle-class or traditional dominant values and to facilitate the propagation of subordinate and countercultural values. A comparison of traditionalism rates by plant or organisational size does indeed show the expected relationship within the working class. Thus, whereas three-fifths of manual workers in plants of less than 50 employees are traditional, only one-fifth of those employed in organisations with more than 250 workers are thus attached to the dominant order (see Table 10.3). Within the middle class, however, there is a curvilinear relationship between the two variables. This may be due to the paucity of the intermediate plant size group or, more plausibly, to covariation between the type of occupation and plant size and to the differential structure of responsibilities associated with the jobs of our respondents in these organisations. In both cases, however, the effects of organisational size persist when union membership is controlled. Manual workers in large unionised plants are one-third 'radical' in comparison with a fifth of non-members employed in large plants. The figures for those employed in small plants are 19 and 11 per cent, respectively. There are corresponding variations in the level of traditionalism. Similarly, within the middle class, one-quarter of union members in large organisations are radical compared with a fifth of non-members; whereas two-fifths of union members are traditionals in the smaller plants compared with two-thirds of non-members.[10] Union membership is thus shown to be independently important yet again and to reinforce the effects of plant size.

Table 10.3 TRADITIONALISM BY CLASS AND PLANT SIZE

Trad Scores	Middle class, %			Working class, %		
	−50	51–250	251+	−50	51–250	251+
Rad	9	43	23	14	38	25
Med	40	29	36	28	34	55
Trad	51	29	41	59	28	20
Total, per cent	100	101	100	101	100	100
Base, N	(82)	(14)	(44)	(58)	(32)	(131)

Type of employment can be considered in at least two ways—the nature of the job and the type of organisation for which one works. The significance of the first aspect is revealed in a comparison of agricultural with mining workers. Whereas three-quarters of agricultural workers were traditional, only one-quarter of the manually employed colliery worker scored high on traditionalism. Those manual workers employed in neither occupation are intermediate in their average level of commitment to the traditional order. Likewise, the farmers and farm foremen were more traditional in their orientations than colliery deputies and overmen.[11] The second aspect of the type of employment also appears to be important. Inferential data based on job descriptions in the first sample[12] showed that, whereas 29 per cent of non-manual workers employed in non-commercial organisations scored high on traditionalism, 38 per cent of those employed in commercial organisations attained this score. In the second sample we measured type of employment directly. The same relationship obtained. Thus, whereas one-third of those employed in non-commercial organisations were radicals, only one-tenth of self-employed and commercially employed non-manual workers were thus disaffected from the traditional order.[13] Type of employment made only a slight difference to the level of traditionalism within the working class. This suggests that, in addition to the level of exposure to dominant values, other factors may be significant in producing an association between employment and traditionalism in the non-manual occupations. Firstly, as suggested by our interview data, radicals may consciously choose public service or non-commercial organisations in preference to commercial employment. Secondly, there may be an affinity between radicalism and the occupational ideologies associated with non-commercial occupations such as nursing, teaching, or social work. And, thirdly, such occupations may require a period of higher or further education and this, as we shall see below, is associated with disaffection from the traditional order. Certainly, in the second sample, those in non-commercial occupations include a far larger proportion of persons with some further education but in itself this does not account for all the variation.[14] The other two factors are probably important as well. Further research into these matters will clearly be valuable.

Thus, overall, economic position does seem to be related to the level of commitment to the traditional social and moral order. Although there is only a limited and inconsistent relationship between traditionalism and prestige and income, there are significant relationships with union membership, plant size, type of occupation, and type of employment. There was also a slight relationship between past or present unemployment and disaffection from the dominant order.[15] Thus the structural location of the individual within the economic system is more closely related to orientations towards central values than such individual attributes as income or prestige considered apart from their articulation with the social structure. In combination with residential community factors, occupational factors such as these account for much of the variation in traditionalism.[16] They are also related in the same way to commitment to the techno-economistic value system and to the development of class consciousness. The strength of these relationships in all three cases can be seen in the correlation coefficients reported in Chapter 8. The fact that they occur in three different contexts suggests the significance of a structural or sociological approach.

From economic position we turn to background and socialisation factors such as parental class, paternal politics, schooling, length of education, religion, and age. As regards the first two variables it is reasonable to assume that individuals brought up in non-manual families will have been more exposed to the dominant values than individuals from working-class homes. Similarly, whatever the general class position of his family, someone from an agricultural home will probably have been more exposed to traditional values than those who come from a mining family. Thirdly, if the association between Tory politics and traditional values is genuine, then persons with a Conservative father will probably be more traditional than those with a Labour, Liberal, or politically indifferent or independent father. Indeed, Kavanagh suggests that a Conservative family background produces not only working-class Conservatism in the present but also accounts for working-class deference. All three of these hypotheses receive some support from our survey data.

Family background has more effect on traditionalism among manual workers than non-manual workers. Thus downwardly mobile members of the working class are one and a half times as traditional as members who have inherited their class position. In contrast, although upwardly mobile members of the middle class are less traditional than inherited members, they are also less radical (see Table 10.4). The experience of social mobility may thus be an independent variable in determining the level of commitment to the dominant order. Furthermore, those who are upwardly mobile out of the working class probably come from families less disaffected from the dominant order—we have already noted their disproportionate number of Conservative fathers and other studies suggest that deferential and Conservative workers are more oriented to mobility.[17] The type of occupation in which

Table 10.4 FAMILY BACKGROUND AND TRADITIONALISM

Class and trad scores	Father's class*, %		Father's occupation†, %			Father's Party†, %			
	M/C	W/C	Agric	Other	Mining	Con	Lab	Lib	None/DK
Middle class									
Rad	25	19	10	25	7	19	22	10	14
Med	31	45	27	37	62	17	49	30	59
Trad	44	37	63	38	31	65	29	60	27
Base, N	(163)	(188)	(41)	(81)	(29)	(48)	(45)	(20)	(37)
Working class									
Rad	19	22	8	24	32	19	32	4	19
Med	33	48	38	44	52	29	46	33	52
Trad	48	30	54	31	16	52	22	63	28
Base, N	(54)	(371)	(52)	(99)	(77)	(21)	(110)	(27)	(67)

* Based on both surveys.
† Based on second survey only.

one's father is employed is also relevant to the level of attachment to traditional values. Thus, non-manual workers raised in an agricultural home are twice as traditional as those from a colliery family; and there is a threefold difference within the working class in this respect (see Table 10.4). This difference persists when those following in father's footsteps are excluded from this comparison; controlling for constituency also fails to eliminate it when comparing those with fathers in the chief occupation in a given constituency with individuals whose father was otherwise employed. Both comparisons point up the importance of early socialisation experiences in the determination of attitudes towards the dominant order.

The same point emerges from a comparison of traditionalism by paternal party identities as recalled by their children. In both major classes those with Conservative fathers are at least twice as traditional as those with Labour fathers. Those with a Liberal father are also disproportionately committed to the dominant order: this reflects their age and the association between Liberalism and agricultural occupations in Ely. While paternal politics may provide a large part of the explanation for middle-class traditionalism, it does not do so for the working class owing to the paucity of manual workers in our sample with Liberal or Conservative fathers. The explanation that Kavanagh offers for working-class deference is thus, like so many other arguments about deference, more applicable to non-manual workers. Finally, it is worth noting that those whose fathers left no clear political or partisan impressions are also disproportionately likely to be intermediate in traditionalism—neither generally attached nor generally disaffected in relation to the dominant order.

The nature and length of education should also be related to the level of traditionalism. Public schools and grammar schools not only provide an academic training but also inculcate commitment to central values. Wilkinson writes that 'taken together the attitudes and values inculcated by the Victorian public schools very nearly comprised a definition of conservativism.'[18] Although the position may appear different today because of changes in the dominant value system, this is still the case. Moreover, grammar schools have always been modelled on the public school system; although the material with which they work and the constraints under which they operate have necessitated certain modifications.[19] In contrast, the majority of the population has received a limited and vocational training apart from the children whose birth or abilities has qualified them for sponsorship into the less disprivileged

strata. While their elementary and modern schools also inculcate dominant values the characteristic emphasis must be
upon acquiescence rather than participation in the central institutional order. As Rose points out, 'young people are usually taught
goals that are within their grasp. For the Etonian the goal may be
going into politics; for a boy at a local secondary modern school,
being an apprentice engineer in a motor-car factory.'[20] Although
expectations may thus be successfully scaled down, schooling of
this type may not always produce attachment to the economic,
social, and political structures that make such realism essential if
a complementary self-image is to be maintained.[21]

The effects of schooling must be considered in terms of the
association between schooling and length of education. Several
studies have shown a curvilinear relationship between length of
education and Conservative voting such that those with an
extended education as well as those with a limited experience of
formal education are more likely to vote Labour.[22] Further
education was linked with Labour voting among the middle class
in our own survey (see Chapter 8). These tendencies are probably
related to variations in commitment to the traditional order. For,
whereas those with little or no secondary education will have
received only a short period of exposure to dominant values, those
with extensive education could well suffer from 'overexposure'
and come to see the discrepancies between ideals and reality in
such a way that they reject both. Furthermore, higher education
is also a source of exposure to radical, liberal, or general critical
ideas and values.[23] Thus, in addition to its curvilinear relationship
with Conservatism, it also seems reasonable to expect a curvilinear relationship between length of education and attachments
to the dominant order.

The actual relationship between traditionalism and length of
education is less clearcut than that hypothesised above. It would
seem that, while those with the longest education are also the most
radical in both classes, the least radical are those with least formal
education (see Table 10.5). This discrepancy is largely due to the
covariation between length of education and age—those who left
school before the age of fourteen are disproportionately old and
the old are disproportionately traditional. Excluding those with
a minimal education from the comparison in the middle class
(where a quadrotomous division is employed) or controlling for
the effects of age in either class reveals a closer approximation to
the curvilinear relationship expected. In the middle class, for
example, only a fifth of those who left school before their sixteenth

birthday were traditionals in comparison with well over a third (36 per cent) of those leaving between sixteen and eighteen years of age; among those staying on beyond eighteen only one-sixth attained a traditional score. Radicalism was still greatest among the latter group—54 per cent of whom were thus disaffected from the traditional order. A similar pattern was found within the working class but was less clear-cut and consistent. Experience of further or higher education, which we included among the variables in the second sample, was also related to rejection of traditional values. In each major class, those without such experience were one and a half times as likely to be traditional as those with such experience.[24]

Table 10.5 TRADITIONALISM BY CLASS AND TERMINAL EDUCATION

Trad scores	Middle class, %				Working class, %			
	−14	14–15	16–18	18+	−14	14–15	16–18	18+
Rad	20	22	28	46	19	28	35	
Med	36	45	28	34	43	50	46	
Trad.	55	32	45	20	37	23	20	
Total, per cent	101	99	101	101	99	101	101	
Base, *N*	(83)	(161)	(98)	(56)	(171)	(258)	(46)	

The type of school attended was also related to the degree of commitment to the traditional order and its effects were independent of the length of formal education. Thus, among those who attended a public or private school, 70 per cent of those who left between sixteen and eighteen are traditionals; whereas, among those who finished their full-time education after eighteen years, only one-third are traditionals. Similarly, over a third of those who went to a grammar or a technical school and ceased full-time education between sixteen and eighteen are thus attached to the dominant order in contrast to less than one-eighth of those who continued beyond eighteen years of age.[25] We had insufficient cases of extended education among those who attended elementary or secondary modern school to make a similar comparison. None the less, there does seem to be a clear relationship between educational experience and attachment to, or disaffection from, central values and institutions.

From a consideration of education and schooling we turn to

examine the relationship between traditionalism and religious commitment. Christianity and the Established church are important symbolic elements in the traditional social and moral order and their relationship to Conservative voting is now well-established even if of declining importance in determining the outcome of elections.[26] Religious commitment was measured in three different ways in our first sample: by religious self-identity, by frequency of church attendance, and by a six-item scale of religious orientations.[27] In each case and in each class, those who were committed to religious institutions and values were also more committed to the traditional order. For example, half of those who said they attended church in the week before the survey were traditionals compared with less than a quarter of those who had not been to church within the last year.[28] This correlation occurred in all religious groups—including those who reported having no religious affiliation. Similarly, those who scored 'high' on religiosity were only half as likely to be radical in either class as compared with those who scored 'low.' In the middle class they were three times as likely to be traditional; and, in the working class, two and a half times as likely as 'low' scorers to be traditional.[29] Finally, in terms of religious affiliation, those who alleged membership in a Protestant denomination were less radical than those who professed to have no religion or to belong to the Catholic faith (see Table 10.6). In the middle class both Anglicans and those belonging to other denominations were disproportionately traditional; but, in the working class, Anglicans were not more likely to be traditional than Catholics or agnostics and atheists. This class difference is probably due to a difference in the level of commitment—with working-class Anglicans more likely to be nominal members than middle-class Anglicans. This factor also seems to account for the greater traditionalism of nonconformists in both classes since they are far more likely to attend church frequently than other religious categories.[30]

Table 10.6   TRADITIONALISM BY CLASS AND RELIGION

Trad scores	Middle class, %				Working class, %			
	CoE	Other	RCs	None	CoE	Other	RCs	None
Rad	22	27	52	43	25	17	34	46
Med	36	23	26	41	53	25	43	29
Trad	42	50	22	17	23	58	23	25
Total, per cent	100	100	100	100	100	100	100	100
Base, N	135	30	23	54	150	12	44	24

Finally, we consider the relationship between age and traditionalism. Although ascriptive socio-political deference was not significantly related to age, this could well be due to the difficulties associated with this measure of deference. Given the greater symbolic and actual importance in the past of many institutions and values in the traditional dominant order, it seems reasonable to expect that age will be positively associated with traditionalism. This is indeed the case. In both classes there is a positive association between old age and traditionalism and a positive association between youth and radicalism (see Table 10.7). The association is strong enough to explain most of the variation between age and voting behaviour[31] but is also independent of most other structural factors.[32] Whereas traditionalism is positively associated with age, age is not consistently related to techno-economism. The latter has been identified as the emergent dominant value system and, while it has obvious continuities with traditionalism, it also represents a partial rejection of several major components of the traditional order. It is probably because of its continuities as well as its emergent character that both young and old tend to be committed equally to the techno-economistic order: the former have been exposed to the system *ab initio*, the latter can articulate it with traditional values. Furthermore, as noted above, techno-economism and traditionalism interact to produce considerable variation in voting behaviour.

Table 10.7 TRADITIONALISM BY CLASS AND AGE

Trad scores	Middle class, %				Working class, %			
	−29	−44	−64	65+	−29	−44	−64	65+
Rad	35	26	13	10	34	22	18	10
Med	42	45	37	32	50	55	42	44
Trad	24	28	50	58	16	23	40	46
Total, per cent	101	99	100	100	100	100	100	100
Base, *N*	(84)	(106)	(160)	(50)	(104)	(133)	(171)	(52)

Overall, therefore, commitments to the traditional dominant order are related to variations in social location. While such correlations do not, strictly speaking, tell us anything about the causation of commitments, their compatibility with the specific hypotheses and general theoretical framework outlined above does provide some *prima facie* evidence in support of our approach. Although we have concentrated on traditionalism in discussing

o

the social origins of commitment to dominant values, the results obtained for commitments to the emergent techno-economistic order were little different and particularly so for the working class (see Table 8.13). Egalitarianism was also related in similar ways to structural location and personal attributes. This is apparent not only in the correlation data but also in the incidence of egalitarian beliefs among those commited to the dominant order.

We have already stressed the possibility of combining affirmation of the dominant order with corporate class consciousness in the form of 'trade union consciousness.' This should be related to social location in the same way as is radicalism. That is, the incidence of egalitarianism among traditionals should be greatest where traditionalism itself is least common. To test this hypothesis we compared the proportions of inegalitarian traditionals, egalitarian traditionals, and egalitarian radicals, in different structural positions. Whereas the first category includes those least disaffected from the traditional order and the last category comprises those who are least attached thereto, the second category is assumed to include people who approximate closely to 'trade union consciousness.' Those with intermediate scores on either variable and those few respondents alienated from the traditional order but expressing status conscious attitudes were excluded from the analysis. In this way the hypothesis can be tested in a clear-cut manner.

The incidence of 'trade union consciousness,' especially among the working class, is indeed largely as suggested by the hypothesis. In Easington, for example, where almost two-thirds of manual workers included in this particular analysis approximated to a radical oppositional ideology, workers with a 'trade union' level of consciousness outnumbered by two-to-one those fundamentally committed to the dominant order. In Stepney the disproportion was even greater. Conversely, in the Isle of Ely, where only a fifth of relevant workers were radical and egalitarian in outlook, the 'trade union conscious' outnumbered those with an hegemonic outlook only by a ratio of three-to-two. Likewise, among manual workers in the second sample, the ratio of trade-union conscious to hegemonically committed workers was seven-to-two for those with a high index of structural position, whereas it was reduced to about five-to-four among those with a low score. Basically the same pattern was found in relation to plant size, union membership, and type of employment (see Table 10.8). The incidence of working-class 'trade union consciousness' was also related in this way to several other variables—parental class and partisan support, unemployment experience, house-ownership, and agricultural versus mining occupations.[33] In short, in almost every case, structural position was not only related to variation in commitment to the traditional order in general, but also to the extent of class consciousness among those not disaffected from the traditional order.

For the middle classes, too, the incidence of 'trade union consciousness' was generally related to structural position in the same way. For example, whereas inegalitarian traditionals outnumbered the egalitarian traditionals threefold among non-manual workers with a low structural position score, the 'trade union conscious' were twice as numerous as those committed to the hegemonic order among those with a high score. Similarly, whereas about half of the traditionals who belonged to a trade union were also egalitarian, among non-members fewer than a third were thus 'trade union conscious.' Type of employment and, to some extent, constituency were also related in this fashion to the incidence of 'trade union consciousness' (see Table 10.8). Furthermore, as in the case of manual workers, the latter was also systematically linked with variations in paternal class, paternal party loyalties, house ownership, and type of occupation.[34]

In conclusion, therefore, the data presented in this section suggest that, while orientations to the dominant economic, social, and moral order do exercise an influence on voting behaviour, they do not vary entirely at random relative to these latter factors. The covariation between traditionalism and electoral choice is not just a case of those who think like Tories voting like Tories: rather, it is a case of interaction between traditionalism and structural factors and their conjoint determination of voting behaviour. Although the effects of class consciousness modify the influence of traditionalism, this is not incompatible with the hypotheses outlined above. On the contrary, the role of 'trade union consciousness' in partisan choice was particularly stressed in the theoretical discussions that introduced these survey data. Furthermore, as has just been shown, the incidence of such 'trade union consciousness' is socially structured in precisely the same ways as is the incidence of commitments to the traditional order more generally. Indeed, part of the independent influence of structural factors on voting behaviour is eliminated when we consider not traditionalism in isolation but traditionalism as it interacts with class consciousness. If the major political parties were more differentiated and there were less likelihood of situational and ideological indeterminacy, the influence of such orientations to the dominant order

Table 10.8 HEGEMONIC, TRADE UNION, AND RADICAL RADICAL CONSCIOUSNESS BY SOCIAL LOCATION

Independent variables	Middle class				Working class			
	Rad %	TU %	Heg %	N %	Rad %	TU %	Heg %	N %
Constituency								
Isle of Ely	23	27	49	(51)	19	49	32	(37)
Woodford	24	14	62	(42)	46	38	15	(13)
Wood Green	61	12	27	(26)	33	37	30	(30)
Stepney	44	30	26	(27)	44	41	14	(41)
Easington	42	21	38	(24)	64	24	12	(50)
Union member								
Member	49	23	27	(55)	64	26	10	(96)
Non-member	29	20	51	(115)	24	45	31	(84)
Plant size								
Small	8	35	57	(37)	20	45	35	(31)
Medium	67	11	22	(09)	60	27	13	(15)
Large	43	13	43	(23)	65	22	12	(49)
Employer								
Commercial	18	24	58	(50)	42	33	25	(52)
Non-commercial	48	33	19	(21)	58	28	14	(43)
Structural position								
Low	18	22	60	(45)	15	46	38	(13)
Medium	37	29	25	(24)	41	32	27	(41)
High	62	25	13	(08)	65	28	8	(40)

would be even greater. But, just as the structure of class stratified hegemonic societies determines the extent of commitments to the dominant order, so, too, it determines the limited partisan differentiation that exists today and the considerable influence of structural and ideological cross-pressures on voting behaviour. A class-oriented analysis must pay as much attention to the latter questions as to the former.

10.2 The concomitants of traditionalism

We have now demonstrated that traditionalism exercises a significant independent influence upon political behaviour but is itself partly determined by structural factors. In this section we intend merely to examine some of the concomitants of traditionalism in the light of hypotheses and concerns expressed in the literature on commitments to the dominant order. In particular we shall be concerned with the class self-identity of traditionals and radicals; with the levels of egalitarianism and civility, political interest and political efficacy; and aspects of their social and economic thought. We begin this analysis with the relation between traditionalism and attitudes towards the class structure.

Several different views have been expressed about the relation between deference and class self-identity. Some see a working-class self-identity as the mark of the deferential; others believe the deferential is likely to be subjectively middle class; yet others suggest that either identity is possible.[35] In the case of ascriptive socio-political deference we found some support for all three views. The same pattern is found with socio-cultural deference. Although traditionals are disproportionately 'middle class' in self-identity there are none the less more 'working-class' traditionals overall than those with the former identity (see Table 10.9). Runciman has shown that the interpretation placed upon one's self-identity is an important factor in the relation between subjective class and Conservative voting.[36] This is obviously sound and similar considerations may apply to the relation between traditionalism and subjective social class. Although respondents were not asked to specify what they understood by their own 'class category,' it is possible to get some indication of this by examining the relations between egalitarianism and traditionalism within each subjective class.

Egalitarianism itself should not be perfectly correlated with traditionalism if the concept of 'trade union consciousness' is at all meaningful. For the latter implies that it is possible to seek amelioration of distinctive class interests within an order accepted

Table 10.9   TRADITIONALISM BY CLASS AND SELF-CLASS

Trad scores	Middle class, %		Working class, %	
	MC	*WC*	*MC*	*WC*
Rad	19	23	21	22
Med	32	40	38	48
Trad	49	36	40	30
Total, per cent	100	99	99	100
Base, *N*	(151)	(188)	(47)	(353)

as legitimate or at least as given. It is less likely, however, that those who are alienated from the traditional order will still be status conscious or non-class conscious. This suggests that the correlation between traditionalism and egalitarianism should assume an 'L'-shaped distribution rather than a diagonal distribution when the two variables are cross-tabulated. This does indeed seem to be the case (see Table 10.10). In both middle and working classes the percentage of egalitarians among traditionals is greater than that of inegalitarians among those who score low on traditionalism. As we have emphasised several times, it is the combination of general orientations to the traditional order with attitudes towards the class structure that determines voting behaviour. Part of the apparently deviant 'traditional' Labour vote is due to the presence of 'trade union consciousness.'

Table 10.10   EGALITARIANISM BY CLASS AND TRADITIONALISM

Egal scores	Middle class, %			Working class, %		
	Rad	*Med*	*Trad*	*Rad*	*Med*	*Trad*
Inegal	14	32	46	5	8	25
Med	20	26	31	18	28	30
Egalit	61	42	23	78	64	44
Total, per cent	101	100	100	101	100	99
Base, *N*	(86)	(161)	(159)	(102)	(226)	(145)

When we examine the interrelations among class self-identity, egalitarianism, and traditionalism, we find that the most traditional persons are those who score low on class consciousness—whatever their class self-identity. Thus three-fifths of non-manual workers who were inegalitarian were also traditional: subjective class made no difference in this respect. Similarly, among manual workers, the inegalitarians were equally traditional whether they identified with the middle or the working class. Subjective class was only associated with variation in commitments to the dominant order among those who scored high on egalitarianism—with the middle-class identifiers more traditional. Thus, whereas one third of egalitarian non-manual workers who identified with the middle class were traditional, only one-fifth of those with a working-class self-image were so attached to the dominant order. Within the manual working class, the proportions were two-fifths and one-fifth, respectively.[37] In short, although traditionalism is certainly associated with differential identification with the working or middle classes, it is more strongly linked with variation in the meanings attached to these identities whatever the nominal choice. Thus inegalitarians who identify themselves as working class must have a different understanding of this concept from that held by the egalitarian 'working-class' man.

Interview data would certainly confirm this interpretation. In addition to those whose interpretation of subjective class conformed to the standard meanings attached to these terms—meanings such as manual workers, the poor, the ordinary person, those who work for a living, or non-manual workers, the well-off, those who have got on in life, and so forth—there were also more unusual interpretations that were none the less integrated with more general social and economic beliefs. Compare the following two illustrative statements:

> There'll always be classes—education hasn't levelled things out as people expected, it's not a utopian solution. If you put people in better houses, they will always be either clean or dirty people. There are people desirous of improving their culture and there are those who degrade the present culture. It's got nothing to do with your job or your money or such like—it's all to do with your outlook on life. Myself, I try to improve on everything but I'm still working class: I still have to work on the farm along with the chaps I employ. (*Conservative farmer: 5T; 0E; 58 years old.*)

> Well, I'm working class—not a man who lifts heavy loads or bends his back but still working for a living. There are two main classes—those in types of occupation where money begets money and those where it doesn't: if someone's in the second category, then he's a worker. There's a lot of hostility

under the surface: the upper classes are very conscious of their interests—more clannish than the workers. But it doesn't take a great deal to bring the hostility to the surface—wage claims encourage a tendency that exists everywhere to classify people into 'them' and 'us.' Strikes and rising prices have the same effect. Often the workers turn against each other and they all suffer as a result—you know, the railwaymen versus the Surbiton commuter. (*Middle-class Labour: 1T; 5E; 49 years.*)

Although both these men have middle-class occupations they none the less identify with the working class. But the context within which this self-image is interpreted and the implications it has for their political behaviour are clearly quite different. In both cases, however, their views on class are reasonably well integrated with other orientations and beliefs expressed in the questionnaire and interview. More generally, not only was traditionalism associated with patterned variation in the nature of class images, but also with other aspects of social and economic thought. Even so, there is quite extensive overlap in many cases between the opinions of traditionals and radicals. This reflects the existence of 'trade union consciousness' and the more general inconsistencies and ambiguities of an hegemonic order.

Some illustrations of this phenomenon can be seen in the responses of traditionals and radicals to individual items from the egalitarianism scale. For example, whereas 84 per cent of the middle-class radicals believed the government should do something to reduce social and economic inequalities, this sentiment was also affirmed by 51 per cent of middle-class traditionals. Likewise, whereas about a half of working-class radicals believed that the idea of class struggle has some relevance to contemporary problems, this same belief is shared by a third of working-class traditionals (see Table 10.11). Obviously, not all of these expressions of agreement or disagreement will reflect genuine stable attitudes: some will be unstable or 'non-attitudes'. But, even if we were to exclude such spurious responses or otherwise allow for them, there would still be some overlap in this respect. In line with the arguments developed earlier, however, and as illustrated in the analysis of variation in the social location of 'trade union consciousness,' overlap of this kind is not random but socially structured in determinate ways. It is this social structuring of inconsistency and ambivalence that rescues the thesis of hegemony from the charge of being trivial or vacuous.

Table 10.11 PER CENT EGALITARIAN ON EGALITARIANISM ITEMS BY CLASS AND TRADITIONALISM

Item	Middle class, %			Working class, %		
	Rad	Med	Trad	Rad	Med	Trad
Government should do more to reduce social and economic inequalities (agree)	84	68	51	81	80	72
Idea of class struggle has no bearing on our current problems (disagree)	69	42	32	47	48	33
Some people are superior and deserve special rewards and privileges (disagree)	59	40	25	58	46	26
There are a few rich people and the rest are poor or have trouble managing (agree)	49	41	41	74	66	63
There is little opportunity for talented people to get ahead in Britain (agree)	22	29	27	55	46	37
Profits should go to workers and not just to those who . . .* (agree)	75	46	30	80	84	58
Everyone has enough money nowadays† (disagree)	91	83	84	100	94	84
Base, N	(89)	(164)	(160)	(105)	(232)	(144)

* This item included only in second sample scale.
† This item included only in first sample scale.

Further support for this argument can be found in other social and economic attitudes. An examination of orientations to economic institutions, for example, reveals a pattern of overlap and dissensus with resulting ambiguities and inconsistencies. Thus, whereas four-fifths of middle-class traditionals agreed that trade unions do this country more harm than good, three-fifths of the radicals shared this opinion. Likewise, whereas four-fifths of working-class radicals held that big business has too much power, this same belief is affirmed by three-fifths of traditionals. At the same time, however, half these working-class radicals and two-thirds of the traditionals agreed that 'more opportunities should be given to successful businessmen to play a major role in government.' There was a similar inconsistency among middle-class radicals and traditionals.[38] Whereas populist disaffection from big business is none the less combined with majority support for business participation in politics, attitudes towards unions are somewhat more consistent and unfavourable and especially so within the middle class. Thus, the belief that unions do much harm is reflected in agreement with the need for greater legal control over them and with the desirability of unions staying out of politics and just trying to improve their members' pay and conditions. Furthermore, not only are attitudes to unions more consistent, they are also somewhat more polarised than attitudes to dominant techno-economistic institutions and values such as big business, economic growth, science and technology, and business participation in politics.[39] In all but one case, however, those most disaffected from the traditional order are also least attached to techno-economism and least hostile to unions (see Table 10.12). The one exception is a manifestation of small business and rural oppposition to big business

Not only are traditionals in both classes more attached to the dominant economic institutions, they are also more attached to dominant social institutions, elites, and values. They are more 'deferential' in several respects. For example, working-class traditionals are twice as likely to agree that political leaders should be drawn from families used to running the country; and also twice as likely as radicals to agree that those in authority can usually be trusted to know what is best. Likewise, middle-class traditionals are more than three times as likely to agree that people nowadays just don't have enough respect for their betters; and are well over twice as likely to agree that, instead of getting ideas above their station, people should try to do their own jobs a bit better (see Table 10.13). The inconsistencies created by appeal

Table 10.12   ATTITUDES TO ECONOMIC INSTITUTIONS BY CLASS AND TRADITIONALISM

Item	Middle class, %			Working class, %			
	Rad	Med	Trad	Rad	Med	Trad	
Big business has too much power today (agree)	57	54	61	82	69	62	*
All major industries should be nationalised or publicly controlled (agree)	44	23	8	50	28	21	*
Further economic growth won't really help overcome world problems (agree)	52	36	33	48	43	39	‡
Science and technology will help man to solve problems . . . (agree)	38	71	85	63	71	80	‡
More opportunities for businessmen to play active political role (agree)	48	63	78	48	59	66	‡
Way they are run now, unions do more harm than good (agree)	58	66	82	31	59	60	*
Unions should stay out of politics and just try to improve pay and conditions (agree)	64	76	87	67	85	78	‡
There should be greater legal control over trade unions (agree)	45	71	82	35	59	65	†
Only reason for class conflict is that agitators stir up trouble (agree)	21	41	80	37	53	75	‡

*   Based on both samples.
†   Based on first sample.
‡   Based on second sample.

to populist as well as dominant values are revealed in working-class attitudes to political leadership. Thus half of those traditionals who thought it was better to be led by ordinary people who have made their own way to the top also agreed that political leaders should be drawn from families used to running the country; one-fifth of the radicals also shared this inconsistent pair of attitudes.[40] In addition to their deference towards those in authority and families used to running the country, traditionals are also more likely to agree that it is best to take life as it comes rather than try to change it and to disagree that very great changes are necessary to give ordinary people a chance for a better life (see Table 10.15). Here again there is an obvious inconsistency in the attitudes of manual workers to this pair of statements—for example, two-thirds of traditionals agree that it is best to take life as it comes and three-fifths agree that great changes are necessary to improve the lot of ordinary people. This provides one more indication of a generalised discontent (*cf* attitudes towards upper class attempts to keep workers from getting their fair share) that is combined with a pragmatic acquiescence in the *status quo*. Although such acquiescence is more common among traditionals, it is not confined to them. More than a third of working-class radicals also exhibit this sort of 'fatalistic pessimism.'[41] Furthermore, as a number of studies have shown, there is typically a major shortfall between normative beliefs about participation and activism, on the one hand, and, on the other hand, actual attempts to participate or change the social world.[42] Certainly as indicated by beliefs about unions staying out of politics, such participation as does occur is limited in its scope and radicalism.

From a brief consideration of social and economic orientations we turn to an equally brief examination of political beliefs and interests. We have already seen that traditionals are more likely than radicals to identify with the Conservative Party, whereas radicals are more likely to see themselves as Labour supporters. One can also expect that there will be a positive association between traditionalism and self-placement on the right rather than the left wing of politics. This is indeed the case. Middle-class radicals, for example, are more than ten times as likely to identify with the left rather than the right; traditionals are five times as likely to identify with the centre or the right as with the left.[43] Similarly, in the working class, radicals are seven times as likely to place themselves on the left or at the centre compared with right; whereas traditionals are more than three times as likely to identify with the centre or right rather than left.[41] It would be unwise to

Table 10.13 ATTITUDES TO SOCIAL INSTITUTIONS BY CLASS AND TRADITIONALISM

Item	Middle class, %			Working class, %			
	Rad	Med	Trad	Rad	Med	Trad	
Political leaders should come from families used to running country (agree)	4	20	34	22	28	44	‡
Better to be led by ordinary people who have made own way to top than by those born into a 'good' family (agree)	61	61	54	88	79	74	‡
Those in authority can usually be trusted to know what is best for us (agree)	21	41	39	20	30	43	‡
People nowadays just don't have enough respect for their betters (agree)	20	40	68	34	44	81	*
Instead of getting ideas above station, people should do own jobs better (agree)	36	86	92	63	81	86	‡
It's best to take life as it comes rather than try to change it (agree)	7	39	42	37	48	65	*
Only very great changes in society will give ordinary people a chance for a better life (agree)	46	49	25	84	73	58	*
Upper classes always tried to keep workers getting their fair share (agree)	71	64	27	86	78	58	*

* Based on combined sample.
† Based on first sample.
‡ Based on second sample.

place too much stress on these correlations since several studies have shown that the left–right continuum is rarely understood correctly by the population at large,[45] but they are none the less in the expected direction.

Although some authors have suggested that deferentials are politically unaware or incivil, we found little evidence for this when examining ascriptive socio-political deference. The same pattern is apparent in the relations between traditionalism (or deference to the social and moral order) and political interest and civility. In the middle class, for example, radicals and traditionals both divide three to one between those expressing interest and lack of interest respectively. Similarly, within the working class, whereas 57 per cent of radicals express interest in politics, among traditionals the percentage is 58. In both classes, those who are intermediate in degree of traditionalism are also less interested in politics.[46] Whether or not lack of interest produces ambivalence, ambivalence produces lack of interest, or both, is impossible to determine with the available data. Secondly, in neither class is there any significant variation by traditionalism in the level of civility—although there are significant but contradictory variations in the incidence of incivility. These variations are more relevant to a consideration of civility itself, however, and we postpone detailed discussion to the next chapter. What is important here is that the overall level of civility is more or less the same in both ideological groups and that neither appears to be disproportionately apathetic or incivil.

10.3 Summary and conclusions

We have now completed our examination of traditionalism—its origins, impact, and concomitants. We have shown that traditionalism interacts with structural location to explain much of the variation in voting patterns of our respondents. Traditionalism in turn has been explained in terms of the social location and personal attributes of these respondents as these influence their relative exposure to, or insulation from, the dominant institutions and values. Moreover, we have shown that the political impact of traditionalism is modified by the presence of 'economism' or 'trade union consciousness' and that the latter is also related to social location. Finally, traditionalism is seen to be systematically related to other attitudes and values but in a context of dissensus, ambivalence, and inconsistency, that is, in a context characteristic of a class-stratified hegemonic society. We now turn to examine civility.

10.4 Notes and references

1 Parkin, in *Br. J. Sociol.* (1967), xviii; Lockwood, in *Sociol. Rev.* (1966), xiv; and Piepe *et al*, in *Sociol.* (1969).

2 See, for example, on income—McKenzie and Silver, *Angels*, p84; Nordlinger, *Tories*, p170; and Runciman, *Relative Deprivation*, p172.

3 Eighteen per cent of working-class residents in towns and pit villages in Easington were traditional ($N = 114$) and 46 per cent of those resident in country villages ($N = 13$); the same relationship did not obtain for middle-class residents.

4 Thus, whereas house-owners comprise 37 per cent of working-class radicals and 27 per cent of traditionals, in the middle class these figures were 77 and 74 per cent, respectively; in both classes those intermediate in commitment to traditionalism were the least likely to be house-owners.

5 Traditionals comprised 31 per cent of manual workers and 39 per cent of non-manual workers; radicals comprised 22 and 21 per cent, respectively. Thus manual workers were most ambivalent or intermediate in commitments to the dominant order. Had we sampled Hampstead rather than Ely, these ratios may have been reversed.

6 Thus, whereas only 36 per cent of professional and managerial workers were traditional (Hall-Jones 1 and 2), 40 per cent of technical and supervisory workers (Hall-Jones 3 and 4 but including most of the farmers) and 41 per cent of routine non-manual workers (Hall-Jones 5a) obtained a similar score.

7 Excluding old age pensioners from the comparison, 38 per cent of the manual workers with an income of less than £15 per week were traditionals; 26 per cent of those with an income between £16 and £25; and only 24 per cent of those earning more than £26 a week. All figures after tax.

8 For manual workers the difference was always in the expected direction and was 18 per cent for all constituencies except Easington, where it was 9 per cent; there was more variation in the middle class but only in Stepney was the relationship reversed—due probably to the paucity of middle-class union members in the Stepney sample ($N = 4$).

9 *cf* the discussion in G Ingham, *Size of Industrial Organisation and Worker Behaviour* (London: Cambridge University Press, 1969).

10 Plant size categories were selected so as to reduce contamination due to the strong association between agricultural employment and small plant size and between mining employment and large plants: none the less, in small plants, union membership did not affect the extent of working-class traditionalism—this is probably due to the relative weakness of union organisation in these plants, a point discussed in the preceding chapter.

11 Whereas 69 per cent of farmers, farm bailiffs, and farm foremen were traditionals, 55 per cent of deputies and overmen were thus attached to the dominant order; the latter percentage is far higher than that for the 'ordinary' non-manual workers—36 per cent of whom were traditionals. This can be partly explained by age differences and also by the contempt in which several deputies held the pit-face worker (see Chapter 9).

12 This was inferred from job descriptions: non-manual occupations were obviously easier to classify on this basis but in cases of doubt the job was treated as a commercial occupation. The resulting data can only be indicative.

13 Percentages of traditionals were 49 for the commercially or self-employed and 38 for those employed in nationalised industries or by the state or a charitable organisation.

14 Just over half of the non-commercially employed reported a period of further education compared with under a third of those in commercial employment. The percentage difference in amount of radicalism between the non-commercial and commercial middle-class groups was 24 points for those with further education and 17 points for the groups without further education.

15 In assessing the impact of unemployment experience one has to control for age since length of employment is obviously correlated with opportunities for past unemployment. In both classes those who have been unemployed are less traditional than those who have never been unemployed in each of three age groups: under 29 years, 30 to 44 years, and 45 to 65 years old. For example, 14 per cent of unemployed manual workers under 29 years old are traditional compared with 21 per cent of those never unemployed; among those aged 45 to 65, these figures are 46 and 55 per cent respectively.

16 To take one example, although traditionalism is trichotomous rather than dichotomous, constituency and plant size accounted for more than half the variation in working-class traditionalism for the second sample: whereas two-thirds of those employed in small organisations in Ely were traditional, only one-fifth of those employed in large plants in Easington scored high on traditionalism.

17 See, for example, McKenzie and Silver, *Angels*, pp137–45 and 202–7; Nordlinger, *Tories*, pp168–9; and, more especially, Butler and Stokes, *Political Change*, p100, and the discussion in J H Goldthorpe *et al*, *The Affluent Worker in the Class Structure* (London: Cambridge University Press, 1969), pp116–39. *cf* footnote 25 to Chapter 8.

18 R H Wilkinson, *The Prefects* (London: Oxford University Press, 1964), p110; *cf* Miliband, *State*, pp239–45, and O Banks, *The Sociology of Education* (London: Batsford, 1968), pp111–28.

19 *cf* Banks, *Education*, pp23–4; H A Davies, *Culture and The Grammar School* (London: Routledge, 1965), *passim*; and R King, *Values and Involvement in a Grammar School* (London: Routledge, 1969), *passim*. The latter documents the failure of a grammar school to inculcate middle-class values.

20 Rose, *Politics*, p123.

21 *cf* King, *Values and Involvement*; and the study on adolescent values by Ted Tapper as reported in Kavanagh, in *Government and Opposition* (1971), vi, p351.

22 See, for example, Rose, *Politics*, p69; 'How much education makes a Tory?,' *New Society* (1 November 1962); M Abrams, 'Politics and the British middle class,' *Socialist Commentary* (October 1962), pp5–9; R Rose, 'Students and society,' *New Society* (2 January 1964).

23 *cf* Parkin, *Radicalism*, pp164–74.

24 Figures for the middle class are 32 and 52 per cent traditionals among those with and without further education, respectively; in the working class the relevant figures are 23 and 33 per cent. Further education was measured only in the second survey.

25 These data relate to both classes. The numerical bases in the case of public school alumni are rather small (12 stayed on beyond 18 years, 24 left beforehand); for the grammar school pupils, N is 33 and 115, respectively.

26 See particularly, Butler and Stokes, *Political Change*, pp124–34.

27 The six items were: 'Religion is more important than politics' (agree); 'Only one or two churches really understand God's purpose and the way to salvation' (agree); 'People who claim to have had religious experiences are probably imagining things' (disagree); 'One should try to pray every day' (agree); 'The idea of sin is very important to me' (agree); and 'Religion plays an important part in my daily life' (agree). The scale clearly measures a sectarian religiosity rather than an ecclesiastical one. The cutting points were 0–2 (low), 3–4 (medium), and 5–6 (high).

28 There were corresponding differences in radicalism: 18 per cent of those who attended within the previous week were radicals compared with 34 per cent of those who had not attended for more than a year.

29 In the middle class, 58 per cent of the 'religious' and only 19 per cent of the 'irreligious' were traditionals, while 17 and 35 per cent respectively, were radicals; in the working class these figures were 40 and 16, 18 and 37 per cent, respectively.

30 Thus, whereas only 10 per cent of Anglicans reported attendance within the last week, 38 per cent of nonconformists reported such attendance; controlling for church attendance eliminates or reverses the differences in traditionalism between these two religious groups.

31 See Chapter 8.

32 When age was controlled in each major occupational class (–44 and 45 or more years), the relation between traditionalism and structural factors persisted in almost every case: the only exceptions were church attendance and inferred type of employment in the first sample.

33 Thus, in terms of paternal party loyalties, those with a Conservative father were divided in the ratio 4:3:3 between radical, trade-union conscious, and hegemonic conscious; among those with a Labour father, these ratios were 6:3:1. Likewise, those employed in agriculture divided 1:4:5 in contrast to the miners' ratio of 6:3:1, respectively. The differences in other respects were similar but less marked.

34 Thus, whereas those with a Conservative father divided in the ratio 2:2:6 between radicalism, economism, and hegemony, those with a Labour father divided 5:2:3, respectively. Likewise, whereas house-owners had a ratio of 3:2:5, council and private tenants divided 3:5:2, respectively. Similarly, those with a commercial occupation divided 2:2:6, while those in non-commercial occupations had a ratio of 5:3:2, respectively. The ratios for parental class were less distinctive—3:2:5 for those with middle-class parents, 3:3:4 for those with working-class parents.

35 For a more detailed discussion and references, see Chapter 7, pp7.18–19 and 7.31.

36 Runciman, *Relative Deprivation*, pp170–87.

37 Half of the working-class inegalitarians were traditional, whether they identified with the middle or the working class. Subjective class was positively correlated with inegalitarianism, i.e. those identifying with the middle class were disproportionately inegalitarian in both classes.

38 A similar question on business politicians was asked in the first survey: this too was related to traditionalism. Thus, in the middle class, 27 per cent of radicals and 66 per cent of traditionals supported the idea of 'government by businessmen'; likewise, within the working class, this proposal was supported by 25 per cent of radicals and 53 per cent of traditionals.

39 The average percentage difference between radicals and traditionals on the four techno-economism items in the middle class was 25; on the four items on unions and agitators, it was 38. In the working class these figures were 27 and 16 per cent, respectively.

40 Disagreement with both statements is not inconsistent because it could simply mean that the respondent rejects any ascriptive criterion for political recruitment.

41 Several authors have emphasised the importance of 'fatalistic pessimism' in the subordinate value system: see, for example, R Hoggart, *The Uses of Literacy* (Harmondsworth: Penguin, 1958), p92; Mann, in *Am. Sociol. Rev.* (1970), xxxv; L Lipsitz, 'Work life and political attitudes: a study of manual workers,' *Am. Pol. Sc. Rev.* (1958), lviii, p951–62; and Parkin, *Class Inequality*, pp88–92.

42 See particularly, Almond and Verba, *Civic Cultures*, p187.

43 Forty-two per cent of radicals did not place themselves on the left–right continuum: the same percentage identified with the left, 12 per cent with the centre, and only 4 per cent with the right. In the case of traditionals, these figures were 53, 8, 21, and 18 per cent, respectively. This item was included only in the second survey.

44 Two-thirds of working-class radicals did not place themselves; left and centre were each mentioned by 15 per cent and only 4 per cent identified with the right. For traditionals these figures were 82, 4, 10, and 4 per cent, respectively.

45 See particularly Butler and Stokes, *Political Change*, pp205–11.

46 Thus, whereas two-thirds of middle-class intermediates expressed some interest in politics, three-quarters of radicals and traditionals did so; within the working class the difference was reduced to 3 per cent and was not significant.

Chapter 11

Civic Dispositions and British Political Culture

A major difficulty with the civic culture is its problematic ontological or methodological status. Civility is simultaneously presented as an abstract model of the political orientations favourable to democratic stability and as a concrete description of British political culture. In neither guise is it very helpful. Although the abstract model does point to the important theoretical issue of the appropriate balance between elite autonomy and popular participation in government, it fails to see that such a balance is critically dependent on the institutional context and thus cannot be established *a priori* without consideration of this broader question. Nor can this difficulty be circumvented simply by treating civility as an idiographic account of British political culture rather than as a nomological model. For it neglects important structural factors in British society that affect significantly the balance that is required and also ignores important aspects of the political culture. In its exclusive focus on civic dispositions the study of 'democratic' political culture overlooks the populist and oppositional values that coexist with civility among the subordinate classes and thus understates the potentialities for instability. Conversely, in its exclusive focus on the non-elites it ignores an important source of political and social stability. It is a merit of Eckstein's 'congruency' theory that it does suggest, albeit indirectly, the importance of institutional integration for stability and thereby implies that political stability is bound up with societal stability more generally.[1] Yet the civility studies ignore the existence of that institutional integration (or elite consensus) which we found to be a leading characteristic of the dominant value system in Britain.

Not only do the civic culture studies fundamentally misrepresent the nature of peripheral values and neglect the important empirical issue of institutional integration, however, but they also neglect the role of non-political values and beliefs in the maintenance of stability. In short, they overstate the significance of civility itself. This probably derives from their normative concern in promoting democratic stability in other countries.[2] Consequently they treat civility as inherently problematic rather than as a more or less natural concomitant of specific historical social, economic, and political structures.[3] Thus isolated from its proper structural context, the civic culture overshadows the other sources of stability. For, as argued above, social order and stability result from the interaction of many structural and cultural factors. These include the productivity of different power systems, the nature of the contradictions inherent in these different systems, the sorts of contradiction—if any—that emerge due to the dynamics of these systems, the effectiveness of the ideological hegemony, the extent of institutional integration, the level of exploitation in the power systems, and so forth.[4] Civility *per se* is important only to the extent that normative or pragmatic acquiescence is lacking and dissent is articulated in the political system. This, of course, is why Nordlinger emphasises the importance of the civic values being accepted on all sides of the major structural or ideological cleavages in society.[5] In this sense, therefore, civility can be seen as something of a long stop for the maintenance of stability.

The discussion in the present chapter should thus be seen as a complement to the earlier analysis of commitment to the traditional dominant order. It concerns attitudes that are interdependent with such commitment but also have a certain importance of their own for societal stability. It is necessary to study civic dispositions in a broader context than that adopted by the civility theorists themselves but we shall also examine these dispositions in the light of concerns and issues raised within that narrower framework. We turn first to consider the question of the distribution of civic dispositions in different groups.

11.1 The distribution of civic dispositions
The main elements of the civility concept are the emphasis on the need for authority tempered with an intermittent popular participation in government. Stability is held to depend on the more or less equal distribution of deferential and activist orientations on all sides of the major cleavages in the political system. The lack of such a distribution may lead to 'a dysfunctional segmentalisation in which opposing attitudes towards governmental authority, and thus conflicting procedural norms, are superimposed on substantive, ideological, and cultural dimensions.'[6] In turn this may

lead to a disagreement about the nature of the constitution itself. The necessary distribution can be realised in two main ways. Firstly, through a combination of different attitudes within the same individual such that he oscillates between activism and acquiescence or is moderately active at most times. Or, secondly, it may be realised through a combination of different individuals for whom one or other orientation is dominant. This suggests two ways of assessing the civility model—an examination of the overall scores on civility and also an examination of responses to individual items across partisan and ideological cleavages. Given that Britain possesses a civic culture and is stable, we should expect one or other condition to be met in the general population and to be approximated in our own surveys.

We turn straightaway, therefore, to an examination of the interrelations between party, class, and civility. Whether we examine political party members, reported voting in 1966, or voting intentions in 1968, we find that civility, as measured in the first survey, is in fact more or less equally distributed either side of the major political cleavage. Thus, while the Conservative Party members are more civil than Labour Party members, the latter have a lower proportion of the incivil. Furthermore, the overall distribution of civility scores does not differ significantly across parties.[7] A similar pattern can be seen in the relation between civility and voting behaviour. Approximately equal proportions of the civil and incivil are found within the ranks of both Conservative and Labour supporters and such differences as do occur are not statistically significant (see Table 11.1).[8] It is noticeable, however, that non-voters are markedly less civil than average; and also that Liberal voters tend to be more extreme in their civic dispositions. More or less the same pattern is apparent for voting intentions.[9]

The pattern is rather different, however, if we examine civility

Table 11.1 VOTING IN 1966 BY CIVILITY

Civility scores	Con %	Lab %	Lib %	Abst %	N
Incivil	23	20	28	42	(112)
Medium	47	53	40	44	(235)
Civil	30	27	32	14	(129)
Total, per cent	100	100	100	100	
N	(163)	(245)	(25)	(43)	(476)

in terms of both class and party (see Table 11.2). It would seem that working-class Conservative voters are less civil than their fellow workers who vote Labour, whereas there are no important differences in the middle class. This may be due to the strong association between incivility and non-voting. If one assigns the non-voters to the modal class party, i.e. Labour, or considers only the proportions who are civil, then this difference ceases to be significant. However, this is irrelevant to the middle class and an examination of the incivil non-voters does not support such an interpretation. Incivil non-voters in the working class were not more likely to be Labour voters but were also disproportionately Conservative or else constant abstainers. The same pattern was apparent in the middle class.[10] As we also found a similar pattern in the relations among civility, traditionalism, and class (see below), it would be wise to see whether or not these differences result from contrasting orientations to civic values.

Few significant inter-party differences are apparent when we examine the individual civility items. The average difference between Conservative and Labour on eleven items was 6 per cent in the working class; it was only 4 per cent in the middle class. The working-class Tories were less civil on items relating to the legitimacy of government and to political deference but were more civil in other respects. These differences could well be due to confusion in the minds of Conservative voters between the system of government in general and the Labour government in particular. It would thus be a little premature to declare that working-class Tories are less civil than working-class Labour supporters. The middle-class Labour supporters were equally civil, or somewhat less civil than, Conservatives on all items except those relating to participation by their fellow citizens in the governmental process. In both classes these differences are slight but cumulative. More impressive than the variations in response by party, however, is the generally widespread commitment to these civic values. Five of the items secured a 'civil' response from at least 90 per cent of voters and over half secured such a response from three-quarters of the major party voters. In conjunction with the survey data examined in Chapter 5, therefore, this consensus seems to provide much support for the balanced disparities model. But it can also be viewed as support for the less problematic assertion that the central values of the British political system are widely affirmed and that this has contributed to the relative stability of the system.

While data on party and civility provide some *prima facie* evidence as to the relation between ideological orientations and civic dispositions, they tell us nothing about this relation directly. We must consider this issue separately. Two contrasting arguments connect civility and commitment to central values. Shils says that distrust of the dominant order is the mark of incivil ideologues rather than of civil men. Nordlinger argues that civility must be institutionalised in all ideological groups if a democratic system is to remain stable.[11] The two views can be tested by examining civic orientations among traditionals and radicals and among inegalitarians and egalitarians.

Table 11.2 VOTING IN 1966 BY CLASS AND CIVILITY

Civility scores	Middle class, %				Working class, %			
	Con	Lab	Lib	Abst	Con	Lab	Lib	Abst
Incivil	17	19	18	38	34	21	50	46
Medium	50	44	41	38	42	58	38	50
Civil	33	37	41	24	25	21	13	4
Total, per cent	100	101	100	100	101	100	100	100
N	(110)	(94)	(17)	(21)	(50)	(151)	(8)	(22)

We find that, whereas radicals in both classes tend to score disproportionately high on civility, civility is disproportionately high among inegalitarians and especially so in the working class (see Table 11.3). But, with the possible exception of working-class egalitarians, the overriding impression is that civility is more or less equally accepted by both sets of ideological groups in both classes. Certainly, there is but limited support for Shils' view. An examination of replies to specific items shows that middle-class radicals are rather more alienated from the political system and from politics and are significantly more likely than traditionals to disagree that it is sometimes necessary to put country before party. They are also less deferential politically. They are much more open in political outlook, however, being much readier to accept popular participation in elections and decision-making. Working-class radicals are also less likely than traditionals to agree that the government should do what it thinks right even if the majority of people disagree and that, rather than criticise politicians, one should try to understand their problems a bit more. And they, too, are more open in political attitudes than traditionals in their class. Finally, the incivility of manual egalitarians stems from their greater hostility to the idea of putting country before party (a reflection of their class consciousness?), a greater alienation from the political system, and a less well-developed sense of civic duty. They also tend to give a lower proportion of civil replies on other items. Middle-class egalitarians are somewhat more alienated but are much more open in political outlook. Deference to government and politicians is less common among egalitarians in both classes.[12]

Table 11.3   CIVILITY BY TRADITIONALISM AND EGALITARIANISM

	Rad %	Med %	Trad %	Egal %	Med %	Ineg %
Middle class						
Incivil	15	25	16	22	23	14
Medium	43	43	50	39	45	53
Civil	42	31	34	38	32	33
N	(60)	(106)	(94)	(94)	(78)	(88)
Working class						
Incivil	25	29	23	34	19	14
Medium	47	51	57	52	54	49
Civil	27	20	20	14	27	37
N	(51)	(127)	(75)	(135)	(83)	(35)

We have argued that civility is a dominant value and it does seem to be firmly institutionalised in the political, ideological, and occupational groups so far considered. More than half the items included in the civility scale receive 'civil' replies from three-quarters or more of the first sample. But most of these items related to citizen duty and the basic legitimacy of the political system. Items relating to political deference and participation did not obtain this amount of agreement. It could be argued that these items are dissensual because there is no indubitably 'civil' response to them. If everyone agreed that a government should get on with its job and govern, there would be no checks on misrule. Conversely, if everyone felt equally qualified to participate in government, there would be no government. This is why the civility studies emphasise a balance between deference and participation and focus on the distribution of civic values rather than individual citizen's attitudes. In this respect, therefore, it is inappropriate to measure civility on an individual or personal level. It is for this reason that civility is best disaggregated and examined in terms of its individual components and also considered within different groups. Thus, although civility is measured for each respondent, our analysis has focused on its distribution across political and ideological groups.

The pattern of responses to individual items across these groups is what one might expect from the development of civility as a central value complex in Britain. For civility has always been weighted in favour of the 'habit of authority' and against popular participation.[13] Thus, those who affirm the traditional value system and/or support the party most closely identified therewith will tend also to affirm the legitimacy of the political system, the propriety of political deference and elitist government, and the exclusion of ordinary 'subjects' from political participation. Conversely, pressures for popular participation will tend to come disproportionately from those alienated from the dominant order and/or those who support the party less closely identified therewith. Certainly this is the pattern that we find for party support, traditionalism, and egalitarianism in our first sample. It is for this reason that discussion of civility cannot be divorced from more general considerations of attachments to the dominant order and must be treated in terms of our general theoretical framework.

Further support for these views can be found in responses to other items not included in the civility scale. Radicals, for example, are more committed to popular participation in government and to the preservation of civil liberties rather than the maintenance of social order. They are less prone to support strong leadership and to think that the Communist Party should be banned. They are less likely to agree that extreme left-wingers (and, in the middle class, fascists as well) should be banned from standing for parliament. But they do express more disaffection from parliamentary methods themselves than do traditionals in either class. This is probably because they believe, as the item itself implies, that such methods do not give everyone a good chance to change society (see Table 11.4). Similar results were obtained for cross-tabulations of these items against egalitarianism and two-party voting. Overall, these data reinforce the theoretical arguments for treating civility as a dominant value complex articulated with other dominant, but non-political values, and as a value complex more favourable to elitist, authoritarian government than is implied by the abstract civic culture model. Moreover, they show that, once attention is turned from general issues such as citizen duty and the basic legitimacy of the polity, there is less support for the political system than is implied by the civility studies.

Table 11.4 CIVIC DISPOSITIONS BY CLASS AND TRADITIONALISM

Item	Middle class, %			Working class, %			
	Rad	Med	Trad	Rad	Med	Trad	
Government should do what it thinks right even if majority disagree (agree)	47	44	63	37	44	57	*
Ordinary people should have a greater say in running the government (agree)	76	49	42	81	74	71	‡
System of government is basically fair and just (agree)	70	79	95	80	68	83	**
Parliamentary methods give everyone a good chance to change society (agree)	25	53	67	22	32	54	‡
Politics is a fraud and betrayal of public trust (disagree)	60	55	21	38	38	27	**
Majority of people not qualified to vote on today's problems (disagree)	42	29	26	36	27	25	†
Few strong leaders would do more good than all the laws being discussed (disagree)	65	49	25	63	32	29	†
Communist Party should be banned (disagree)	92	74	47	77	60	52	†
Extreme leftwingers should not be allowed as candidates in elections (disagree)	95	76	66	94	61	67	†
Maintaining social order more important than guaranteeing everyone freedom (disagree)	62	40	16	61	39	35	*

* Based on both samples.
† Based on first sample.
‡ Based on second sample.

11.2 Attitudes to Democracy in Britain

Although we did not measure civility as such in the second sample, we none the less included several items from the original civility scale along with several others analysed above. Moreover, in the follow-up interviews, we asked several questions about attitudes to democracy in Britain and the appropriate role of the citizen. The replies were rather confused but several points still emerged. We began with a question about the extent to which governments pay attention to ordinary people and then moved to questions on the role of parties and elections and finally asked about the proper role of ordinary citizens in the political process.[14]

The majority of those interviewed believed that governments pay little or no attention to ordinary people except that elections lead them to improve things at least temporarily and/or to make fresh promises and also that opposing parties help keep governments on their toes. The general conclusion was that Britain was a democracy. The usual reasons cited for this being freedom of speech, communications, etc, followed by the existence of elections and the monarchy. When asked about activism, the majority of interviewees replied that ordinary people ought to let the government get on with its job of government without interference and/or attempt to influence the government by working through institutionalised channels—especially the MP for a constituency. Almost as frequent, however, were fatalistic and apathetic replies to the effect that it was not worth bothering as the government carried on regardless of public opinion. This latter reply was often coupled with general references to the need for referenda or more frequent visits by the local MP to hear his constituents' views and explain his party's policies. Only two interviewees, both middle-class Labour supporters, expressed a wish for more grass roots action outside party policies. Disaffection was common in all three sets of ideological and political group but was twice as great among Labour voters as Conservatives and one and a half times as great among radicals and egalitarians as among traditionals and inegalitarians.[15]

The following comments are representative of the replies made by different respondents. First, on the attention paid by government:

> Very little attention really. Public opinion doesn't seem to matter much, the government doesn't care, it seems to make up its own mind. It's something you learn to live with, it's

been going on for such a long time. (*Labour miner: 2T; 6E; 33 years.*)

I don't think they pay much attention because they've got their own ideas about what is best for the country and it doesn't matter what ordinary people think. (*Conservative miner: 4T; 4E; 45 years.*)

I think they take too much notice of a loud minority—not the majority view. The majority of British people sit back and accept things as they come and so the government only has to listen to a vocal minority; the majority of people are not made that way—they want peace and quiet, the others just want to dictate and see their own way. As for the government, if they think they can win by appeasement—they ought to look back at the last world war—a crunch must come sooner or later and the longer it's left, then the worse it gets. (*Conservative smallholder; 5T; 0E; 56 years.*)

I don't think governments bother much, they're too concerned with feathering their own nest. I suppose people don't care much about government either—they always rely on someone else (like the unions). But I don't let it upset me, I try to manage—there are some people who're always grumbling, but you've got to take it in your stride. (*Conservative farmworker: 4T; 3E; 48 years.*)

Not very much, it's the government's job to govern; it has to do what's right and hope the people will see that it's right in the long run; if they tried to explain things more, it would help. But if it tried to do what everyone wanted, it wouldn't be for the best. (*Conservative farmer: 6T; 2E; 51 years.*)

Second, on the role of elections:

I think you need them: it keeps the government on its toes if it thinks it's going to be turned out of office if things go wrong. As long as you have elections it doesn't matter too much whether the government listens in between times. (*Conservative farmer: 6T; 2E; 51 years.*)

I don't see how they can have much effect—they're only held once every five years. (*Conservative worker: 4T; 5E; 47 years.*)

If elections were more regular, they would do; they'd pay more attention then because they'd have to work harder for the job; they'd do better work; it's the same in politics as it is in industry. (*Conservative mining deputy: 4T; 3E; 49 years.*)

Well, it's a way to voice an opinion: but the government's got to get on with the job, whatever party's in power. (*Labour shop steward: 1T; 3E; 43 years.*)

I suppose the obvious comparison to make is with countries where elections don't take place. It's difficult to say. It probably makes the government slightly more benevolent, shall we say, than in Russia. That's the obvious comparison, of course, and rather facile—but then it's not really a socialist country. (*Middle-class Labour: 1T; 5E; 49 years.*)

I think certain issues are more important in elections, perhaps more prominence is given to particular issues in one area, in another area, other issues will be emphasised. But I imagine most people just vote for the leaders. Possibly, parties might change some policies to stay in office. (*Middle-class Labour: 0T; 5E; 25 years.*)

I think governments would worry if they thought they would be forced into an election by what they're doing; but at the moment they worry more about the inner circle at Westminster than about public opinion—they get worried if the whips can't control the MPs, not if public opinion is dissatisfied with the government. They know they can keep the masses quiet very easily—elections don't occur too often, they know when they're going to occur. (*Middle-class Labour: 0T; 5E; 39 years.*)

Of course they make a difference—with the majority of people backing them, governments can do more. (*Labour miner: 7T; 2E; 58 years.*)

All you get is promises and more promises: the Labour Party does not intend to keep them, sometimes the Tories do. (*Conservative worker: 4T; 4E; 45 years.*)

Third, on the role of parties:

Well, a coalition would be better in every sense of the word: it is healthy to have more parties—it keeps politicians alive;

the Conservative Party knows it's got to fight hard to keep its policies going, or else it will lose status and the Labour Party will get in next time; it's exactly the same for the Labour Party—it has to work hard to maintain its policy. It works for both. Oppposition keeps the government on its toes. (*Conservative farmer: 5T; 0E; 58 years.*)

Sometimes a change is a good thing. (*Labour worker: 1T; 3E; 39 years.*)

There's got to be parties, otherwise we'd have a Russian-type system, but there's not much difference between them. The Labour Party is too secure round here to have to worry what we think and the Conservative Party doesn't seem to care. (*Labour miner: 0T; 6E; 31 years.*)

I wouldn't like to see a one-party system if that's what you mean; having two or more parties does provide a brake on the other party. (*Middle-class Labour: 5T; 3E; 32 years.*)

It's a good thing to have different parties because they're each fighting for their particular beliefs—so they take more interest in ordinary people. (*Conservative farm worker: 4T; 3E; 48 years.*)

It's exactly the same as with elections—competition is very important in politics as everywhere else; without competition, everything is a little bit worse. (*Conservative worker: 5T; 0E; 36 years.*)

I think there ought to be one complete government without Labour or Conservative; they ought to put it to the people to pick the best men from all parties. That would be best. (*Conservative worker: 5T; 0E; 38 years.*)

Well, you've got the Labour Party to look after the workers, the Conservative Party to look after the rich and the better off; nothing to grumble about there. We can all vote if we want to. (*Labour shop steward: 1T; 3E; 43 years.*)

We can quote the old lady there, 'it doesn't seem to matter much which party gets into power, it always seems to be the government that wins.' There's not really much difference between the parties—they help each other to stay in power. (*Middle-class Labour: 0T; 5E; 39 years.*)

The replies to the question on democracy tended to combine

dominant stereotypes with references to the disaffection expressed earlier in the interview. Typical replies were as follows:

We're half-democratic; I feel tempted to say 'sham-democratic'—but that would be going too far. For example, we do have elections at guaranteed intervals, it's possible to have them at shorter intervals, we're allowed to vote for which ever party we wish in comparative secrecy. So we're democratic to that extent but how much effect does one vote really have? I'm beginning to think the normal methods of going about things—democracy and all that—are a good thing—from the point of view of the government rather than the elector. (*Middle-class Labour: 0T; 5E; 39 years.*)

It's a good system but there's not much choice between parties. I suppose, if I had to say why it's good, I'd point to Hyde Park Corner—if someone said things like that in Russia they'd be shot. (*Labour miner: 1T; 6E; 31 years.*)

We're a democracy all right—I mean, take for example the royalty—there's a lot of people don't want to see them done away with like what's happened in other countries—it just leads to trouble; it helps keep us together, the country I mean. More than that—there must be master and man, you've got to have someone who tells you how to row the boat. (*Labour worker: 5T; 4E; 59 years.*)

Yes, we are because we've got freedom of speech (not like China or Russia); we can voice our opinions, they can't. (*Conservative farm worker: 4T; 3E; 48 years.*)

Yes, we're definitely a democracy; we've got freedom of speech and freedom of choice—you can say what you like within limits, set by the slander and libel laws, and they apply to all and sundry; you can say what you like as long as you put up with the consequences. You've got freedom of choice in government, where you live, where you work, and you've got freedom of movement. That sounds like democracy to me. (*Conservative post foreman: 5T; 5E; 54 years.*)

That's a bloody stupid question, isn't it? You tell me, what sort of say does an ordinary worker have—bloody none. (*Conservative farm overseer: 3T; 4E; 33 years.*)

Oh, quite democratic—we have the royal family, the right to

> speak, freedom of speech, and so on. (*Conservative miner: 4T; 4E; 45 years.*)

> Well, democracy means where the people have a large say in running a country, so I'd say we're only half democratic. There must be countries more democratic than Britain—perhaps on the Continent, such as France, with its referenda. (*Conservative worker: 5T; 0E; 38 years.*)

Finally, on the appropriate role of the ordinary citizen, typical replies were as follows:

> You take the MP for this constituency—the electors in Easington should take their ideas to him, he'll channel them in the right direction and make sure they're acted upon. That's all that's necessary. (*Conservative miner: 5T; 3E; 76 years.*)

> I think you should vote the right men in, then leave it to them to decide what's best; some things they ought to consult the citizens on, but really we do put them there to govern and let us get on with the job of living from day to day. (*Conservative worker: 2T; 2E; 42 years.*)

> Once you've voted, it's in the hands of your MP—you've got to trust him, if you don't you shouldn't vote for him. It's up to the MPs to decide what is best for the country. (*Labour miner: 7T; 2E; 58 years.*)

> I don't know what to say to that one, it's a job to say; I don't think I can answer, let's say they shouldn't play a very big role. (*Conservative farm worker: 4T; 4E; 26 years.*)

> I think the government ought to be left to govern, it can't work if ordinary people keep demanding a say in what's done. They're listening to public opinion now, through their MPs, and they get their views through attending meetings, and so on. There's just a big chain of meetings and exchanges of view, and finally it gets back to the government and then they decide. Anyway much of it is too baffling for people to understand—especially all that economics. (*Labour electrician: 2T; 4E; 31 years.*)

> They ought to do more than vote—there ought to be a meeting every two months with your MP so that you can discuss issues with him and the next month there ought to be

a meeting with the other candidate so you can hear his side. (*Labour worker: 5T; 4E; 59 years.*)

Well, I don't do anything like that myself but I do see it would be beneficial to us if we did study, like, for example, attending a briefing at school in the evenings. (*Conservative farm worker: 4T; 3E; 48 years.*)

Well, do they answer your questions—some MPs answer, some just ignore you; it's not worth bothering in most cases. (*Conservative farm foreman: 6T; 2E; 70 years.*)

Everyone should take their responsibilities more seriously— but most people just sit back and let others do it. They ought to form groups I suppose but the government wouldn't listen, so perhaps that's why they don't even try. (*Conservative worker: 4T; 5E; 47 years.*)

Really, you're asking how much activity we should all go in for beyond voting—well, we're all too docile really and I don't exclude myself here. I suppose they should become members of the local party, play an active part, go canvassing. They could join small local groups—claimants' unions, tenants' associations, consumer associations, and this sort of thing. These are bound to have a cumulative effect. (*Middle-class Labour: 1T; 5E; 49 years.*)

I think referendums are a good idea, to find out how people are thinking; if too many people write to their MP, then he couldn't reply to them all and wouldn't be able to take part in politics himself. Referendums would get round this. You should write to your representative over individual grievances, yes, but not on more general issues. For this there ought to be fairly regular consultation. (*Conservative mining deputy: 4T; 3E; 49 years.*)

These views illustrate the combination of attachment to, and disaffection from, the political system that is characteristic of subordinate or mass political culture in Britain. Other studies reveal the same pattern.[16] Of particular interest is the fact that those who are disaffected from the dominant order or class conscious are none the less committed more often than not to the dominant political order. One of the main reasons for this may be that, whereas unions and political movements exist to voice and organise disaffection from the social and economic order, there are no comparable groups that oppose the political system. The unions and the Labour Party are as attached to civil politics as is the Conservative Party. Populist disaffection is thus able to co-exist quite easily with acceptance of the narrowly delimited political role accorded to the ordinary person. Furthermore, even where a more active role is seen as appropriate or necessary, an oft-noted shortfall between theory and practice combines with the general inaccessibility of government to render the system stable.[17] As long as institutional integration is assured, popular acquiescence (facilitated by government efforts at symbolic reassurance[18]) is completely compatible with political stability. In turn, popular acquiescence can be maintained by continued expansion of output from the economic, political, and social systems. This is the situation in Britain.

11.3   Sources of civic culture

There are several different competing theories of the origins of civility. Of particular interest are mass theory, personality theory, and hegemonic theory. We consider some of the evidence for each. We will begin with a brief look at mass theory. This posits the need for a well-developed secondary group structure to mediate between the elite and the non-elite and to inhibit the mobilisation of subordinate classes in extreme, mass movements. It is essential for all, or most, citizens to be involved in these groups and it is also essential that their memberships be overlapping and pluralist rather than monolithic and cumulative in their impact so that loyalties are divided and pressures towards extreme views moderated. In short, membership of voluntary organisations facilitates acceptance of the civic culture as well as other dominant values.[19] If so, there should be apositive correlation between associational involvement and civility in our sample.

There is some evidence to support mass theory. Thus Almond and Verba report that membership in any organisation—even if the member does not feel that this is politically relevant and it involves little activity on his part—is related to greater subjective political efficacy. Nordlinger found that organisation members in the English working class are significantly more likely to be potential activitist. An increase in civility towards supporters of other parties is also found by Verba with the shift from simple organisational involvement to multiple membership of committees. And Berry's study of two Liverpool constituencies shows that the politically active have more organisational memberships and are more involved in such organisations than the general public.

Several other studies also demonstrate a correlation between organisational involvement and political competence and participation.[20]

In our own survey, we do find the expected association between affirmation of civil values and organisational involvement. Thus, among non-manual workers, 22 per cent of association members and 32 per cent of non-members are incivil; likewise, in the working class, 21 per cent of members and 34 per cent of non-members were incivil. The association is especially marked within the working class in terms of frequency of organisational memberships. Manual workers who belong to three or more organisations are almost twice as civil as those who belong to none. There is a less marked but similar relationship for the middle class. Finally, we also find a positive correlation between committee membership and civility in both classes. Thus 20 per cent of officials and 29 per cent of those not officials are incivil in the middle class; in the working class, these figures are 18 and 32 per cent, respectively. There are corresponding differences in the degree of civility.[21] On three different measures of organisational involvement, therefore, we find some support for mass theory. However, as we implied above, the same data can be interpreted in support of hegemony theory in so far as organisation involvement exposes one to dominant values.

The essential idea underlying the various personality theories of commitment to democratic values is that only those with certain personality traits (whether they be tenderminded, non-authoritarian, philanthropic, empathic, intraceptive, inner-directed, open-minded, or whatever) are capable of meeting the functional requirements of a system of democratic politics.[22] In this research we are able to examine the relations between three personality variables and civility: anomy, misanthropy, and authoritarianism.[23] Since civility involves a philanthropic attitude to fellow citizens and a moderate (but not excessive) deference to leadership, we would expect to find negative correlations between both misanthropy and authoritarianism and civility. This is indeed the case. In both classes, philanthropy and non-authoritarianism are positively associated with civility (see Table 11.5). Anomia is a different type of personality variable. It measures a generalised sense of personal despair rather than a specific personality trait; and it has a high factor loading on 'feelings of uncertainty and pessimism, distrust bordering on suspicion, extreme pessimism about the future, cynicism about the motives of others, and a general perception of society as rapidly changing with most people lonely, distrustful, and unrelated to each other.'[24] It would thus seem that anomia is closely linked to 'idiocy' or privatisation—a lack of integration into the community—and to apathy and alienation. We may reasonably expect, therefore, a negative correlation between anomia and civility. This, too, is the case (see Table 11.5).

Table 11.5   PERSONALITY, CLASS, AND CIVILITY

Personality variables	Middle class, %			Working class, %		
	Inciv	Med	Civil	Inciv	Med	Civil
Philanthropy						
Low	36	20	14	48	23	22
Medium	36	49	36	27	34	31
High	28	31	50	25	34	47
F-Scale						
High	17	27	13	38	29	15
Medium	46	27	24	43	33	29
Low	36	46	64	19	39	56
Eunomia						
Low	48	20	5	57	32	14
Medium	33	48	29	35	43	22
High	19	32	65	8	26	63
Base, *N*	51	119	90	67	132	54

Thus we find considerable support for the personality theory of democratic stability. However, personality is not unrelated to social experience and structural location[25] and these results, too, may also support an hegemonic interpretation of stability. It is interesting to note, for example, that misanthropes, authoritarians, and anomics all appear disproportionately alienated politically and reject the rights of fellow citizens to participate in the political process. Moreover, anomics have a much less well-developed sense of citizen duty than do eunomics—especially in the working class.[26] All three variables are quite strongly associated with a sense of political inefficacy and the high scorers are disproportionately concentrated among non-members of associations, residents of Stepney, the working class, those with limited formal education, and so forth.[27] In short, it is those persons with least contact with dominant institutions and values who are most misanthropic, authoritarian, and anomic, as well as least committed, perhaps, to civic values.

Finally, we turn to the hegemonic theory of stability. Any

examination of civility is complicated by the fact that, whereas both unions and the Labour Party mediate and organise disaffection from dominant economic and social values, no comparable structures exist to perform these functions *vis-à-vis* political institutions. None the less, it is still reasonable to hypothesise that civility will be disproportionately high among those most exposed to middle-class values through their structural location and personal attributes. Thus, those resident in middle-class constituencies, with non-manual ocupations, with non-manual parents, with many association memberships (most associations having an authority structure congruent with the governmental or political system), with grammar school educations, and so forth, ought to score disproportionately high on civility. Those without such personal attributes or social location, on the other hand, should be disproportionately incivil.

It should already be apparent that non-manual workers are disproportionately civil compared with manual workers. Only 21 per cent of the latter score high on civility in contrast to 35 per cent of the former. Furthermore, there is also a positive correlation between civility and status within each major occupational class. Thus, whereas 40 per cent of managerial and professional workers are civil, this figure drops to 23 per cent among the routine non-manual workers. Likewise, whereas 29 per cent of skilled manuals are civil, only 22 per cent of the semi-skilled and unskilled attain this level of civility.[28] Similarly, we have already established that persons in both classes who belong to associations, who belong to several associations, and who are association officials or committee members, are more civil than those who are not. In terms of constituency, there is a positive correlation between civility and residence in a middle-class constituency—but only for manual workers. A third of the manual employees in Woodford are civil compared with less than a fifth in both Wood Green and Stepney.[29] In the middle class, however, there is a slight negative correlation between civility and residence in a middle-class constituency. Although there are no differences in the level of incivility, two-fifths of Stepney non-manuals compared with a third of those from Woodford and Wood Green are civil. Underlying this anomaly is the lesser respect for the rights of participation of fellow citizens characteristic of middle-class residents of the latter two constituencies. The reverse pattern is found for paternal class but the explanation is similar. Thus, while 42 per cent of non-manual workers who are from non-manual families of origin are civil, only 29 per cent of those from a working-class background attained this score. Conversely, in the working class, 25 per cent of those with working-class fathers are civil compared with only 15 per cent of those who have been downwardly mobile. Not only are the latter more restrictive in their views of political participation, they are also more alienated from the (Labour?) government.

Schooling and education are also related to civility. Thus 67 per cent of grammar and technical school alumni in the middle class are civil, while only 27 per cent of those from elementary or modern schools attained the same score. Likewise, within the working class, 30 per cent of grammar-school alumni were civil compared with 21 per cent of elementary and modern school students. Secondly, none of those with an education beyond 18 years in the working class and only a seventh of those in the middle class were incivil compared with 30 per cent and 37 per cent, respectively of those whose education ended before fourteen years. There were similar but less marked differences within both classes for the degree of civility. The length of formal education is obviously bound up with the type of school attended. An examination of their covariation with civility shows that the latter is less important than the former. Length of education accounts for one and a half times as much variation as schooling; together they account for a fifth of the variation. Such education as the type of school has may be due to the variations in the type of civic education given therein;[30] or to the type of home background associated with recruitment to one or other school.

Overall, therefore, we also find much evidence for the 'hegemony' theory of stability. Since the other two theories can be subsumed under the hegemony theory but the latter cannot be subsumed under either mass or personality theory, it seems reasonable to conclude that hegemony theory is more useful. Moreover, as we have already seen, civility is correlated with commitment to other dominant values and institutions; and such commitments are also related to structural location and personal attributes in the way suggested by that theory. Moreover, we found some evidence for separate variation in the subcomponents of civility according to attitudes to other dominant institutions. This also suggests that hegemony theory is appropriate. Likewise, we found several suggestive correlations between structural position scores and civic dispositions in the second sample. For example, while 44 per cent of middle-class respondents with a low structural score believed that the government should do what it thinks right even if the majority of people disagree, only 26 per cent of those with a high score shared this belief. In the working class, these figures were 59 per cent and 32 per cent, respectively. Conversely, those with a low structural position were less likely to agree (especially in the middle class) that ordinary people should have more say in the running of government (see Table 11.6). In other respects, too, those with a high structural position score are disaffected from the political and legal systems more than those scoring low on exposure to conditions and experiences favourable to the rejection of dominant values and institutions (see Table 11.6). Thus data from both samples suggest that civility is as much the product of structural position and personal attributes as is traditionalism—and that both are usefully interpreted in terms of a model of popular beliefs in a class-stratified hegemonic society.

11.4   Summary and conclusions

In this chapter we have examined the nature, distribution, and sources of commitment to the civic culture. We have found that there is widespread commitment to the primacy of the non-political, to the civic duty of voting, to the essential legitimacy of the political system, and to the obligation to take a moderate interest in political affairs. Furthermore, such commitment is more or less equally distributed on either side of the major political and ideological cleavages in the English political system. Half or more of all political and ideological groups examined also affirmed the ideas of independent government action in the face of popular disapproval and of a universal franchise not dependent on intellectual attainments. Most respondents, however, agreed that the majority were unqualified to vote on contemporary problems: but this can be taken to indicate either distrust of fellow citizens' political wisdom and/or political deference to those who do understand such problems.[31] Overall, therefore, we found some support for the argument that stable democracy depends on a wide-spread commitment to civic values on either side of the main cleavages in the political system so as to ensure the necessary balance between deferential and participatory attitudes occurs in all the major conflict groups.

But, whereas the *overall* scores on civility were similar for the different political and ideological groups examined above, the pattern of civic dispositions differed in several respects. Radicals, egalitarians, and Labour supporters were less deferential and more alienated politically; attachment to civil liberties and popular political participation were less common among Conservatives,

Table 11.6 STRUCTURAL POSITION AND CIVIC DISPOSITIONS

Item	Middle class, %			Working class, %		
	Low	Med	High	Low	Med	High
Government should do what it thinks right even if majority disagree (agree)	44	42	26	59	33	32
Ordinary people should have a greater say in the running of government (agree)	44	46	61	70	72	76
Whole of politics is a fraud and betrayal of public trust (disagree)	83	82	78	81	67	54
Parliamentary methods give everyone a good chance to change society (agree)	53	46	52	47	42	28
There is one law for the rich and another for the poor in this country (disagree)	83	68	61	75	43	38
There is not enough difference between the major parties to provide a real choice in elections (disagree)	60	44	30	53	29	30
Base, N	(81)	(50)	(23)	(32)	(84)	(112)

Low = 0, 1, and 2; Medium = 3 and 4; High = 5, 6, and 7 on Index of Structural Position.

inegalitarians, and traditionals. These attitudes also varied according to the structural position of respondents. Furthermore, responses to several items that expressed populist criticisms of the political system rather than dominant justifications or values suggest there is more disaffection from the political system than is implied by the civility studies. In combination with the opinion poll data cited in Chapter 5, therefore, these results suggest that any support for the civility studies has to be seriously qualified.

We also examined the sources of civility in terms of three competing theories of commitment to civic politics. There was some evidence to support the mass thesis that involvement in voluntary associations encourages the formation of civic attachments and also the personality approach that certain types of personality are better able to meet the demands imposed by a democratic political system. Thirdly, there was also some evidence in favour of the view that rejection of civic values is associated with isolation from conditions and experiences favourable to the acceptance of dominant values more generally. In so far as associational involvement is one such condition and personality structure is determined by social location and experiences, the other approaches can be subsumed under the hegemonic approach. Since the latter was also found to account for much of the variation in traditionalism, deference, and techno-economism, egalitarianism, this suggests that the hegemony approach is particularly fruitful and parsimonious in the study of political culture. Much more work is required to establish its value unequivocally but we have already provided much evidence in its favour.

We were unable to examine the extent to which these civic dispositions were actualised in political conduct. For example, although we found that the incivil were more likely to abstain in elections and to intend abstaining at the next election, it is difficult to establish whether this is due to a greater reluctance of the civil to admit to non-voting (non-voters were under-represented in the sample) or to a genuine causal link between civility and turnout. However, there was a positive correlation between civility and reported attempts to influence local or national government in the middle class: 23 per cent of the civil and 9 per cent of the incivil reported such an attempt.[32] And there was also a positive correlation between civility and political interest in both classes. Whereas 84 per cent of non-manual 'civil' subjects expressed an interest in politics, only 51 per cent of the incivil did so. Likewise, 65 per cent of the working-class respondents who scored high on civility expressed some interest in politics compared with 54 per cent of the low-scorers. Yet there are no real behavioural indices of the relative impact of civility and we are unable to assess the extent to which the civil are actually more disposed to vote, to defend civil liberties, to support the need for decisive government action in times of crisis, and so on.

This chapter has thus made less of a contribution to our understanding of English political culture than those on deference and traditionalism. This derives at least in part from the difficulties involved in measuring civility and in relating emergent cultural properties to social structure and stabiliy. Within the more general context of this monograph, however, this chapter has provided further evidence in support of the theoretical approach to political culture that we advocated in the introductory chapters. In our final chapter we turn to examine this approach once more and to suggest further lines of theoretical and empirical inquiry.

11.5   Notes and references

1   Eckstein, in *Division and Cohesion*, pp232–69.
2   It may also be related to a professional bias among political scientists such that they exaggerate the importance of political factors.
3   *cf* A Hacker, 'Liberal democracy and social control,' *Am. Pol. Sc. Rev.* (1957), li, pp1,009–26; C B McPherson, *The Real World of Democracy* (London: Oxford University Press, 1966), pp1–11 and *passim*.
4   See Chapter 3 and Jessop, *Social Order*, *passim*.
5   Nordlinger, *Tories*, p214; similarly, Lipset stresses the importance of political legitimacy where economic and political effectiveness is poor—see Lipset, *Political Man*, pp77–96.
6   Nordlinger, *Tories*, p215.
7   Half the Conservative Party members were civil, one-third intermediate on civility, and one-sixth incivil; for the Labour Party these proportions were two-fifths, half, and one-tenth, respectively. Numerical bases were obviously small in both cases; 38 Conservatives, 15 Labour members.
8   Although the χ^2 for the two-party vote was not statistically significant at the 0·10 level, that for the full table (including Liberals and non-voters) is significant at 0·01 level.
9   About two-fifths of both Labour and Conservative intentions were from the civil; this compares with half the Liberal intentions and a sixth of intending abstainers; the D Ks had a civility profile similar to the main party voters.
10   Of ten working-class incivil non-voters, three were regular abstainers and five former Conservative voters; in the parallel group of eleven middle-class subjects, five were regular non-voters and four were Tories.
11   *cf* Shils, *Torment*, pp231–7, and *idem*, in *Sewanee Rev.* (1958), lxvi, *passim*. Nordlinger, *Tories*, p215.
12   Data on civility and other items for traditionalism are given in Table 11.4; similar results obtained for party and egalitarianism.
13   *cf* Almond and Verba, *Civic Culture*, pp222–3; Rose, in *Political Culture and Political Development*, edited by Pye and Verba, pp83–128;

and A P Thornton, *The Habit of Authority* (London: Allen & Unwin, 1966), *passim*.

14 *cf* the questions asked by Butler and Stokes, *Political Change*, pp27–34.

15 *Ibid*: only 13 per cent of their national sample held a 'well-developed understanding of popular control through a competitive party and election system, to which they felt British politics conformed' (34) and 40 per cent had no clear view of such control. Thus, our own data are similar to these.

16 *cf* Butler and Stokes, *Political Change*, pp27–34; Almond and Verba, *Civic Culture*, Chapters 4, 6, 7, and 8; Mann, *Am. Sociol. Rev.* (1970); Nordlinger, *Tories*, pp113–18; Rose and Mossawir, *Pol. Stud.* (1967); and the poll data cited in Chapter 5 above.

17 On the shortfall, Almond and Verba, *Civic Culture*, pp479–87.

18 *cf* M Edelman, *The Symbolic Uses of Politics*, *passim*.

19 The mass society literature is quite extensive: the best introduction is W A Kornhauser, *The Politics of Mass Society* (London: Routledge, 1959). See also: J R Gusfield, 'Mass society and extremist politics,' *Am. Sociol. Rev.* (1962), xxvii, pp19–30; P Selznick, *The Organisational Weapon* (New York: McGraw-Hill, 1952); E Allardt, 'Institutionalised *v* diffuse support for Radical Political Movements,' *Trans. Fifth World Congress of Sociol.*, 1962, pp369–80; Newton, *Sociology of British Communism*, pp100–11; and D Berry, *The Sociology of Grass Roots Politics* (London: Macmillan, 1970).

20 Almond and Verba, *Civic Culture*, pp307–22; Nordlinger, *Tories*, pp120–3: S Verba, 'Organisational membership and democratic consensus,' *J. Pol.* (1965), xxvii, pp467–97 (there were no consistent results for partisanship in the comparison between members and non-members); Barry, *Grass Roots Politics*, pp80–112.

21 The civility profiles in the tests of mass and personality theory differ from those in other tables owing to differences in the treatment of D Ks in the original computation of scores on which these tables are based: the basic correlations are unaffected by this.

22 For an overview of different personality theories in politics, see F Greenstein, *Personality and Politics* (Chicago: Markham, 1969); R E Lane, *Political Ideology* (New York: Free Press, 1967) pp400–12; and C Bay, *The Structure of Freedom* (Stanford: Stanford UP, 1958), *passim*.

23 The anomia scale was designed by Srole, the misanthropy scale by Rosenberg, and the *F*-scale by Lane: see—L Srole, 'Social integration and certain corollaries,' *Am. Sociol. Rev.* (1956), xxi, pp709–16; M Rosenberg, 'Misanthropy and political ideology,' *Am. Sociol. Rev.* (1956), xx , pp690–95; and R E Lane, 'Political personality and political choice,' *Am. Pol. Sc. Rev.* (1955), xlix, pp173–90.

24 *cf* D L Mieser and W Bell, 'Anomia and differential access to the achievement of life goals,' *Am. Sociol. Rev.* (1959), xxiv, pp189–202; and E L Struening and A H Richardson, 'A factor analytic exploration of the alienation, anomia, and authoritarianism domain,' *Am. Sociol. Rev.* (1965), xxx, pp768–75 (quote from pp769–70).

25 See, e.g. D Stewart and T Hoult, 'A social psychological theory of the authoritarian personality,' *Am. J. Sociol.* (1959–60), lxv, pp274–9; the authors argue that authoritarianism is linked to social isolation and limited role playing.

26 For example, 20 per cent of the anomic working class but only 2 per cent of the eunomic agreed is that it was important to vote even when your own party stood no chance of winning.

252 Traditionalism, Conservatism and British Political Culture

27 The τc correlation between anomia and a four-item scale of efficacy was −0·40 in the working class and −0·48 in the middle class; associational membership correlated −0·31 and −0·29, respectively.

28 Technical and supervisory non-manual workers were 39 per cent civil.

29 Similarly, 22 per cent of Woodford manuals, 30 per cent of Wood Green manuals and 26 per cent of Stepney manuals were incivil.

30 *cf* E Litt, 'Civic education, community norms, and political indoctrination,' *Am. Sociol. Rev.* (1963), xxviii, pp69–75; D McQuail, *et al*, 'Elite education and political values,' *Pol. Stud.* (1968), xvi, pp 257–66.

31 In the latter sense, it could thus be a dominant value.

32 *cf* 6 and 3 per cent, respectively, in the working class.

Chapter 12

Concluding Remarks

Two themes have been emphasised in recent studies of British politics. One theme traces the stability of the political system to consensus on such civic virtues as deference to authority, intermittent participation in decision-making, and respect for civil liberties. The other theme explains the electoral success of the Conservative Party in terms of deference to its leaders and a respect for its general economic and social policies. It is with these themes that we have been concerned in the present analysis. First we related them to the more general concerns of the political culture approach in order to demonstrate the different levels of explanation and conceptual problems involved. Then the themes themselves were subjected to a critical reappraisal and an effort was made to synthesise and reformulate them. This involved us in theoretical argument as well as empirical evaluation and required original research as well as a survey of available data. Much of this study has been taken up with a presentation of fresh evidence in order to evaluate the validity of the two themes and the alternatives we have formulated. In this last chapter, therefore, we intend to review the arguments and data and to elucidate their general implications. We begin with a brief recapitulation of the two themes.

12.1 A recapitulation

The deference theme focuses upon working-class conservatism and attempts to explain it in terms of two kinds of political support for the Conservative Party. Deferential supporters are characterised by a preference for an ascribed, socially superior leadership, whereas secular or pragmatic supporters are oriented in an instrumental manner to the economic and welfare capabilities manifested by different political parties. A number of specific criticisms were offered. Firstly, the deference theorists did not analyse the nature of deference in sufficient detail and so were led to include several distinct types within their explanatory schema. Since these distinct types have different political implications, however, it is by no means certain that the proffered explanation is adequate. This problem is related to another. Not only do the deference theorists have a confused notion of deference, they also ignore the possible mechanisms (apart from electoral propaganda or scare-mongering) that relate deference to actual electoral choice. The significance of this problem is shown by the fact that about a half of 'deferentials' in the deference studies actually vote Labour. In this context there is no discussion of such key issues as the extent to which deference and secularism can be combined, the extent to which 'trade union consciousness' undermines the influence of deference, the extent to which the Labour Party can realistically be held to reject the dominant values and institutions, and so forth. Thirdly, the deference theorists ignore almost completely the structural bases of deference and secularism. This is unfortunate because it vitiates their implicit criticisms of class theories of voting. The latter remain plausible until it is shown that deferential voting is incompatible with class theory and some alternative account of Labour voting is provided. Neither task is attempted, let alone accomplished, by the deference theorists. In addition, they give no consideration to middle-class Labour voting or the applicability of the deference thesis to middle-class Conservatism. A fifth, and related, problem concerns the applicability of this thesis to working-class Conservatism in other Western liberal bourgeois democracies. Lastly, deference theory neglects the possibility of changes in the dominant values and thus in the recipients of deference. The emergence of techno-economism is simply ignored along with its possible consequences for voting behaviour.

Almost all these problems stem from a failure to relate cultural phenomena to structural dynamics. Political culture research should be as concerned with the social bases of meaning systems as with the influence of these systems on political behaviour. It is for this reason that we treat deference to social and political elites as one aspect of commitment to the dominant values and institutions of a class-stratified hegemonic society. Not only does this point to possible connections between structural position and individual consciousness of society, it also facilitates international research through its employment of a culturally non-specific theoretical framework. In both cases we should think in terms of dominant and subordinate value systems, institutional integration, consensus, insulation from and exposure to different values, situational and ideological indeterminacies, and so forth, rather than particular orientations and personal attributes. Only in this way can the problems of the deference thesis be transcended and fruitful cross-national research be conducted.

The civility theme is concerned with a delineation of a political culture that 'best fits' stable democracy. The civic culture is an allegiant participant political culture. It is characterised by the combination of normative acquiescence in the central political order with intermittent participation tempered by parochial and subject orientations. Although it has a certain plausiblity or common-sensical appeal, the civic culture approach can be criticised on several fundamental grounds. Firstly, notwithstanding its claims to realism, civility theory does not recognise the implications of inequalities in the distribution of power for the relevance of consensus in producing stability. It overstates its importance in this respect relative to that of institutional integration. At the same time, moreover, it neglects the existence of oppositional or subordinate values and thus overstates the level of consensus on civic values. Thirdly, it isolates the civic culture from its historically specific institutional context and simply develops it as an abstract model of 'balanced disparities' favourable to democratic stability in all countries. It is thus unable to explain stability in different institutional contexts and also involves circularity when civility is invoked to explain stability within the institutional context whence it was abstracted. Lastly, the civility theorists pay insufficient attention to the manner and extent of the institutionalisation of civic values. In short, in the same way as deference theory, this theme is characterised by a lack of concern for the relations between cultural orientations and social dynamics. The resulting problems can be overcome only by a reformulation of the postulated relationship between civility and democratic stability in terms of a more general theory of socio-cultural dynamics.

Our own approach to both themes relies on their reformulation in terms of a theory of social order in class-stratified hegemonic societies.[1] Deference is seen as an expression of commitment to a dominant order; civility is seen as a dominant value subsystem concerned specifically with the political order. Deference can take a number of forms which are more or less conducive to support for the Conservative Party. Civility ensures the moderation of political demands and participation whatever party is supported. But commitment to the dominant values is not equally distributed through society. Certain structures are conducive to the emergence of subordinate or oppositional values; others are more conducive to acquiescence in the traditional dominant order. Furthermore, since subordinate classes can never be fully incorporated into the centre nor fully insulated from it, there will always be a measure of ambiguity and inconsistency in attitudes towards both dominant and deviant values. This pattern is also encouraged by the difficulties inherent in the transmission of complex belief systems with the consequent concretisation, fragmentation, and constriction of dominant and oppositional meaning systems. Although the resulting dissensus and confusion are conducive to stability, they also ensure that persons with pure 'proletarian' or 'deferential,' and 'civil' or 'incivil,' orientations are unlikely to be found. It is therefore essential to consider the role of structural factors in the mediation of voting behaviour and in the maintenance of societal stability. It is for this reason that we have been concerned with the interaction of structural and cultural factors in this reformulation and review of deference and civility.

12.2   The survey data

We began by considering the data available from opinion polls and sociological surveys. This revealed several important features of mass political culture. Firstly, it showed that there was consensus on the validity or legitimacy of general and symbolic institutions and values, such as monarchy, established religion, private enterprise, and management, that was none the less combined with disaffection from specific aspects or manifestations of these dominant institutions. Secondly, in addition to these specific criticisms, there was agreement with more general populist indictments of the dominant order. Thirdly, within this basic pattern of general consensus and specific or populist disaffection, it was found that those least committed to the dominant order were manual workers and Labour supporters. Fourthly, notwithstanding the disproportionate disaffection of Labour supporters, the extent of consensus and overlap of opinions were such as to suggest the inadequacy of deference, traditionalism, or status consciousness as an explanation of Conservative voting. Fifthly, there was some slight evidence for the existence of consistent covariation in attitudes to different dominant institutions and also, sixthly, for an emergent techno-economist dominant value system. Lastly, the pattern, content, and incidence of mass orientations lent considerable support to the arguments for a reformulation of deference and civility along the lines outlined earlier.

Although these data certainly reinforced the theoretical arguments, especially those concerning the inadequacy of the deferential voting theme, they did not provide enough information to permit a definitive test of the original or reformulated theories. Survey data from a fresh study was obviously required so that more rigorous tests could be conducted. For example, it still remained to be seen how the incidence of ambivalence and disaffection varies with changing structural contexts. Likewise, we had no information concerning the mediation of electoral choices in ambivalent situations. Similarly, data were lacking about the inter-relations between commitment to the dominant order and voting behaviour within classes; and about those between civility and traditionalism. We therefore conducted a new inquiry into these and similar questions employing slightly more sophisticated indicators of commitment and structural position'. The basic information was gathered through postal questionnaires followed in the second survey, by a number of interviews.

In our own surveys, only one-eighth of respondents chose as the Prime Minister a politician with an elite background; and almost one-half chose a politician who had been upwardly mobile from the manual working class. Furthermore, over a third were either indifferent in the matter or stated alternative criteria of selection. And, in the second survey, almost three-quarters of respondents disagreed with a more general statement that political leaders should be drawn from families used to running the country. The electoral impact of these deferential orientations was limited and especially so in the manual working class. Moreover, when we compared the efficacy of ascriptive socio-political deference and traditionalism in explaining Conservative support, we found that it was the latter that was particularly important. This confirmed our suggestion that the deference theorists underestimated the complexities of deference and suggests that they were also too ready to discount its future influence in a different form. None the less, the structural incidence of such ascriptive socio-political deference was more or less the same as that implied by our theoretical arguments.

Turning to traditionalism, we found that it accounted for much of both working-class and middle-class Conservative support whether assessed in terms of past voting behaviour or partisan self-images. It was also more strongly related to voting behaviour than was egalitarianism. The combined effects of traditionalism and egalitarianism were greater than those of either variable alone. They explained four-fifths of the variation in the two-party vote

R

for middle-class subjects; and about half of the variation in the case of manual workers. Techno-economism was also significantly related to electoral support for the Conservatives. None the less, neither this nor traditionalism (nor, indeed, the two conjointly or in combination with egalitarianism) fully accounted for the observed variation in voting behaviour. Furthermore, although orientations to traditional or emergent dominant values might explain electoral choice at the extremes, there remains the problem of explaining this choice in the case of those who are ambivalent or intermediate in their orientations. The role of structural factors is particularly crucial for such persons but is also significant in other cases. Thus structural factors have most impact among those middle-class voters who are intermediate in degree of commitment to the traditional order rather than among those more or less fully committed to, or alienated from, that order. They were about equally important among both those committed to the traditional order and those ambivalent about it in the working class; this was probably due to the greater cross-pressures on working-class traditionals to vote Labour. Indeed, whereas traditionalism and structural position are equally important factors for the middle class, our index of structural position explains a greater part of the variation in the working-class two-party vote.[2] Thus it would seem that a theory of voting behaviour originally developed to explain deviant partisan support in the working class is actually more applicable to the middle class; while the class theory that the deference theorists wished to replace would seem to provide a better explanation of working-class voting after all. However, this would be to misinterpret our reformulation of deference and class theories and to misrepresent the implications of our data. These both emphasise the importance of interaction between structural and ideological factors in the determination of voting behaviour. Where there is situational indeterminacy, orientational factors assume a particular importance; conversely, where there is ideological indeterminacy, a crucial role is played by situational factors. In addition, social location influences a person's ideological outlook; and this in its turn affects his subsequent social location. Thus voting behaviour is the outcome of a complex interactive process rather than the result of objective class position or specific orientations.

In an effort to understand the rationale of the covariation of traditionalism and Conservative support, we conducted several open-ended interviews with selected respondents from the second surveys. These showed quite clearly that this covariation was not due to any felt need to defend the dominant order but was actually the product of interaction between structural position, attitudes, and availability for party mobilisation. Although various dominant institutions were not generally identified exclusively with one or other of the main parties, partisan support was generally seen as an expression of a life-style closely articulated with orientations to dominant institutions and/or structural position. It was also apparent that at least some of the political support that was seemingly deviant in terms of orientations to the dominant order could be understood as the product of insensitivity to that order and/or idiosyncratic factors difficult to incorporate into a general model of electoral behaviour. There was little evidence that policy orientations played anything but a minor role in explaining the covariation between traditionalism and Conservative support.

We then examined the relations between traditionalism and social location in order to test our model of the structural causes of differential commitment to the traditional order. As hypothesised, those most committed to the traditional order were those people who were most exposed to contact with dominant institutions and values; those who were most insulated from such contact and who were exposed to deviant values were also least committed to that order. Thus the ideal-typical traditional worker lived in an agricultural rural area and worked on the land or in a small factory with a weak union or no union at all; his father was employed in agriculture and supported the Tory or Liberal Party; he himself earned a low wage which limited his opportunities to travel and also belonged to local voluntary organisations and clubs; he was old, with a limited elementary school education, and was religious. Conversely, the ideal-typical radical worker lived in a traditional proletarian community and worked in a large, unionised factory; his father was a miner or other manual worker and had supported the Labour Party; he himself belonged to local clubs and associations, had experienced a period of unemployment, had received some further education, was young and irreligious. While some of these factors were also relevant in the middle class, their weighting was different and they interacted with other factors. Self-employment and employment in non-commercial occupations were important; and experience of further education also differentiated radicals from traditionals. The structural incidence of 'trade union consciousness' was also explicable in these terms. Those committed to the traditional order were more likely to be class conscious in situations where traditionalism was limited in extent. This, together with the fact that there is a systematic covariation between traditionalism and attitudes towards other dominant institutions in their general and specific manifestations, suggests that the theoretical approach employed in this work throws fresh light on some old questions.

Lastly, we examined the nature of civility. Our data supported the thesis that, in a stable democratic political system, there will be widespread commitment to the central political values; and that such commitment will be distributed more or less equally on all sides of the main cleavages in that system so as to ensure a balance between deferential and participatory attitudes within each conflict group. At the same time, however, there was disaffection from specific aspects of the political system and a disjunction between affirmation of general democratic principles and their application in specific cases. Furthermore, there were also significant differences in the balances struck by various political and ideological categories. These latter results necessarily qualify any assessment of the civility theme and point to the need for an approach such as we advocated above. This approach also receives some support from an examination of the incidence of different orientations—these are related not only to personality variables and associational involvement but also to structural location more generally. Commitment to civic values and attachment to specific aspects of the political system appear to be structured in the same way as commitment to the dominant traditional order.

We now turn to consider the implications of our reformulation of the deference and civility theories and of the evidence that we presented above. In addition to the areas in need of further research in British politics we shall also consider the implications for comparative political research.

12.3 Comparative political research

A frequently voiced criticism of the deference thesis is that similar proportions of the working class support conservative parties in countries that do not have a traditional ruling class such as we find in Britain. It is therefore concluded that some other, more general factor must be found to explain working-class Conservatism. This argument is plausible but misleading. Comparative data certainly point to the need for a more general approach; they do not imply that deference is necessarily unimportant in Britain. The deference theorists themselves allow for pragmatic support for the Conservative Party based on its actual achievements rather than the ascribed qualities of its elite. Moreover, notwithstanding the implications of their operational definitions, these theorists have extended the meaning of deference to include commitment to dominant institutions and values in general. It is certainly true that other countries do not have precisely the same educational, religious, imperial, and educational traditions as Britain. But it is equally certain that they do not have exactly the same sort of conservative party. General explanations of party support that choose to ignore important differences between parties ought not to scorn generalisations about dominant value systems. Instead of an emphasis on deference to upper-middle-class public school and/or Oxbridge alumni, comparative analyses of electoral behaviour should examine the relations between orientations to the dominant order, whatever it comprises, and support for different parties. The same approach adopted in this research can be employed in other countries once allowance has been made for variation in the content of dominant values, the extent of institutional integration, the different relevance of specific institutional structures for exposure and insulation, variation in the appeals made by parties and the interests they represent, and so forth. In this way new light may be thrown on traditional concerns of political science.

The available data from other European countries would seem to support this approach. Whereas class is usually regarded as constituting the only important basis of support for parties in Britain, two such bases are usually identified for Continental Europe. They are class and religion.[3] But in those societies where religious or anti-clerical parties are important it is usually the case that religion is an important element in the dominant value system or else a major focus of institutional malintegration. The Christian Democrats in Germany illustrate the former case, the latter is illustrated by the various religious and anti-clerical parties in France.[4] In both sorts of case it is necessary to distinguish between political appeals to religious values, political representation of religious interests, religious motives for party support, and differential political loyalties between religious groups.[5] These four are not necessarily inter-related. Thus differential political loyalties may reflect the articulation of religious outlook with class or other structural characteristics rather than religious motives *per se*. Similarly, the appeals of party leaders to religious or anti-clerical values may simply reflect their desire to maximise support or counter class or other appeals rather than a desire to implement religious policies. In short, the same circumspection must be employed in the interpretation of 'religious politics' as is so often recommended in the treatment of 'class politics.' It is therefore particularly important to examine the articulation between dominant values, structural position, party characteristics, and voting behaviour. One or two examples must suffice.

The CDU is supported by almost all the dominant elites in Germany: businessmen, bureaucrats, editors, military leaders, Catholic and Protestant leaders, white-collar union officials, and so forth. The appeal to religious values is but one strand in its attempts to mobilise electoral support by appealing to the dominant values of a new Germany. It is not strongly reflected in governmental policies nor in religious motives for electoral support. Indeed, Linz argues that an interpretation similar to that of McKenzie and Silver is required to explain working-class conservatism in Germany as well as Britain.[6] Several analyses show that CDU support is concentrated among non-union members, those employed in small plants, persons integrated into the dominant order through voluntary organisations, unskilled workers, those resident in small towns and rural agricultural areas, those who attend church regularly, those with middle-class origins, the self-employed, women, the elderly, and so forth. There is a complementary pattern of support for the SPD.[7] In many cases religious attachments are related to structural position in a similar way so that religiosity and conservatism can be viewed as the conjoint products of structural position.[8] Other surveys point to considerable overlap between supporters of different parties in their attitudes towards various questions; while Almond and Verba's research on German civility shows that voters accept the traditionally quiescent and deferential role ascribed them in their political culture.[9] Furthermore, as in Britain, there is also some disaffection from the political system that is reflected in the popular belief that 'those on top will do with us as they please anyway.'[10] Thus, although all the requisite sets of data are not available to connect structural position, orientations to dominant values, voting behaviour, and political stability, it would seem that Germany is not dissimilar to Britain in the applicability of our theory to voting and political order.

Religion has been more divisive in France with both religious and anti-clerical parties being important. The Third Republic was particularly beset by religious conflict. More attention to religious factors is therefore necessary in examining exposure to, and insulation from, competing dominant values. In addition to educational networks and ecclesiastical institutions, for example, involvement in masonic or religious associations or membership of an anti-clerical (Communist or Socialist) union rather than a Catholic union can become politically relevant.[11] Ecological and survey data suggest that communism is particularly strong in traditional urban working-class areas, in large unionised factories, among the labourers on big farms in north-eastern France, among lower civil servants and public employees, among small farmers in impoverished and dechristianised areas, and so forth. Socialist support derives from similar groups but is less strong among industrial workers in most areas; centre-right and right-wing parties gain their support from quite different structural bases. Non-left voting is particularly strong, for example, among white-collar workers in private organisations, among the petty bourgeoisie, among farm labourers on medium-sized farms who are socially integrated into their employer's family, among farmers in prosperous and traditionally religious regions, among members of Catholic trade unions, among the urban bourgeoisie, and so forth.[12] Although support for right-wing parties does seem strongly related to religious commitment, the latter is not exactly randomly distributed throughout the social structure. Rather, anti-clericalism and irreligiosity are related to class consciousness and all three occur disproportionately among those most isolated from contact with dominant values and institutions. French society is so malintegrated, the social structure so complex, the party system so fragmented, that religion appears to be the sole electoral base of most French parties. If a more detailed analysis were made, however, it could well emerge that our own approach provides a better explanation.[13]

Similar analyses can be applied to other countries. This requires that we first analyse the distribution of power in that society and determine the content and integration of the dominant values and institutions. Then we must examine the extent to which various social structures expose citizens to dominant, subordinate, and oppositional values. Political parties must also be considered in terms of their orientations to the dominant values and the extent of derogation or approbation they receive from dominant elites. Fourthly, we must consider the structure of electoral mobilisation in so far as it is independent of these other factors. It will then be possible to examine the interaction between these four factors to explain the voting pattern in any given country. Thus, while the explanation is bound to differ from country to country, it will be couched in similar terms. In the Netherlands, for example, special attention would be paid to the *verzuiling*, or pillarisation, of Dutch society.[14] In Belgium, on the other hand, the political, economic, and social inequalities that overdetermine the language problem will require special attention.[15] The temporal power of the Catholic Church must not be ignored in the explanation of Italian voting behaviour.[16] Other factors will be important elsewhere in this respect.

Comparative analysis of this kind helps determine the critical factors that explain Conservative success in Britain and the importance of religion for electoral mobilisation in other countries. Most significant are the institutional integration among elites and the broad consensus on dominant values in Britain. These result from a specific historical development that also encouraged the dominance of a single conservative party identified with the dominant order and also inhibited the emergence of a radical oppositional party. The strength of the Conservative Party is thus based on a successful claim to a monopoly of the dominant order together with a successful appeal to 'trade union consciousness.' Specific religious appeals are unnecessary because it is identified with all the central institutions and because the dominance of Anglicanism has inhibited religious conflict and anticlericalism. In these circumstances, only those workers insulated from dominant institutions and also available for mobilisation by Labour are able to maintain deviant political loyalties. Most European countries lack this degree of institutional integration and consensus and so have a plurality of conservative parties and/or one or more radical oppositional parties.[17] Furthermore, several have a dominant Catholic Church or are about equally divided between Catholic and Protestant faiths. In this context, therefore, religion could be important as a means of countering radical opposition, reinforcing dominant values, and as a focus of conflict as such. In combination with 'trade union conscious' appeals it enables conservative parties to amass sufficient working class and peasant votes to ensure a share in governmental power. The actual extent and incidence of such support depends on the factors and principles outlined above.[18]

Our approach is not only applicable to electoral behaviour but also to political stability. However, we would stress that political stability is bound up with societal stability overall and that many structural factors must be considered as well as 'civility.' The distribution of power, the extent of institutional integration, the productivity of the different power systems in relation to the nature of 'trade union conscious' expectations, and similar questions must be considered in order to specify the balance between participatory and deferential orientations that is necessary for political stability. As Lijphart has shown in his comparison of Scandinavian and Anglo-American systems, on the one hand, with the 'consociational democracies' of Austria, Switzerland, and the Benelux nations, on the other hand, this balance varies greatly from one country to another. It is fundamentally wrong to present a single pattern as universally appropriate regardless of particular social structure configurations or historical developments. This is not to say, on the other hand, that no general theory of stability is possible or worth while. It is simply to state that such a theory must consider the question of stability in terms of a framework and assumptions that allow for extensive cross-national differences without a corresponding loss in rigour.

12.4 Further research

It should be obvious from the preceding remarks on comparative political research that there is still much work to be done on comparative electoral behaviour and political stability. Equally obviously, it will be necessary to conduct such research within an analytical framework similar to that adopted above. We shall now turn to consider the areas where further research would be valuable. These involve not only survey research but also more detailed historical and structural studies relating to the twin themes with which we have been concerned in this work.

Firstly, more detailed consideration must clearly be given to the structure of power and exchange relations that exists in Britain. Only then will it be possible to provide an adequate account of the dominant value system. Whereas we simply postulated a model of the power structure, it would be valuable to assess its validity before conducting further research into electoral behaviour. Moreover, if the dominant values are changing as a result of changes in the power structure, such research will clearly have to examine somewhat different orientations from traditionalism or ascriptive socio-political deference. In this connection British entry into the Common Market could play a significant role if it were to be identified more or less exclusively with the Conservatives—although the net beneficiary of changes in party support is difficult to determine. It is more likely, however, that the EEC will be accepted by all parties, albeit with differing enthusiasm as in the case of capitalism, as a necessary constraint on their actions in office and one to be justified in terms of techno-economism and other emergent values. The past history of both parties certainly suggests that they sooner or later embrace those values and institutions necessary to their electoral survival.

Secondly, much more research needs to be conducted into those processes whereby people come to accept or reject the dominant institutions and values. Various studies have shown that schools and the mass media, for example, have only a limited impact in efforts to inculcate dominant values.[19] This suggests that affirmation of dominant values is less important than the absence of concepts and values for structural criticism. In this respect such agencies of socialisation may still be significant because they structure discussion in particular ways rather than others through the presentation of selected information in particular contexts. However, it is also apparent that symbolic and general institutions and values are widely accepted. If schools and the mass media are not critical agencies in this respect, it must be considered what other institutions or processes are important. More generally, it is still necessary to develop a more explicit theory of exposure to and insulation from dominant values and institutions. As indicated earlier, the relevant structures and experiences will vary from society to society; they will also vary from dominant value to dominant value within a given society. Again, the effects of changing structures of power must be considered along with other changes in social structure. Changing residential patterns, the growth of an important white-collar union movement, increasing geographical mobility, and many other factors must be considered in this context.

Thirdly, more research is necessary into the structural mediation of electoral mobilisation. For reasons already indicated, there are many voters subject to ideological indeterminacies in party support and who are thus available for mobilisation by several parties. The role of specific social structures in reducing these indeterminacies and limiting availability to a particular party merits further attention. Whether it is simply a question of 'who gets there first' or there are determinate mechanisms that articulate the relationship between structural location and party support has not been satisfactorily established.[20] While there is undoubtedly an irreducible and important historical dimension to this problem, other factors should be more significant if the sociological approach is valid. The role of structural mediation in the middle-class vote is still problematic although our own research throws some light on the question. New research into this question will be particularly welcome.[21]

Fourthly, much more research is required into the nature of the consensus necessary for societal stability in relation to the structural dynamics of society. Here we are concerned less with the relation between consensus and institutional integration than with that between both phenomena and contradictions in the social structure.[22] In many respects the extent of consensus is irrelevant to stability as long as there is institutional integration and the different power systems are producing the necessary output to satisfy the demands made upon them. It is when the output falls short of expectations that difficulties begin for the dominant elites and for the subordinate classes. Problems of leadership and participation in solving these difficulties become acute and are aggravated by the contradictions inherent in, and emergent from, the different systems. Popular participation is often necessary but must also be channelled along acceptable lines so that the elites maintain their overall control of society. The necessary balance between participation and deference must now be maintained despite the probable drop in pragmatic acquiescence resulting from the ineffectiveness of the power systems and its 'dereifying' consequences. Although it is precisely at such moments that 'civility' or its equivalents in other societies is most necessary and least likely. And it is in these conditions that least research has been conducted into civic dispositions. This must obviously be remedied.

There are other respects too in which the theoretical schema employed in this research demands further investigation and clarification. But if these four problems could be satisfactorily resolved by further research, then much progress would have been made in our understanding of electoral behaviour and political stability. As it is we can none the less claim to have thrown some traditional questions—reflected in the two themes with which we have been concerned throughout this study—into a new light. Not only has our theoretical framework proved useful in its allotted role, it also permits a more general study of voting and stability in a cross-national perspective. It is to be hoped that our framework and assumptions can be tested in this context as well.

12.5 Notes and references

1 The theory is developed at length in Jessop, *Social Order*, pp112–43 and *passim*.

2 This remains true when one compares the effects of structural position and ideal types of consciousness (radical, trade union, and hegemonic): conjointly the two variables account for 95 per cent of the variation with structural position somewhat stronger.

3 *cf* R Rose and D Urwin, 'Social Cohesion, Political Parties and Strains in Regimes,' *Comp. Pol. Stud.* (1969), ii, pp7–67. In ten Continental European countries considered in this study, twenty-nine parties were based solely or jointly on religion and twenty-seven on class; seven parties had a heterogeneous base and linguistic differences and regional differences contributed four and six parties, respectively.

4 For general introductions to both countries, see: Edinger, *Politics in Germany, passim*; and H W Ehrmann, *Politics in France* (Boston: Little-Brown, 1968), *passim*.

5 *cf* Sartori's discussion of class politics, in *Politics and the Social Sciences*, edited by Lipset, pp65–100.

6 *cf* J Linz, 'Cleavage and Consensus in West German Politics; the early fifties,' in *Party Systems and Voter Alignments*, edited by Lipset and Rokkan, pp283–321, at p292. On CDU and the dominant elites, see Edinger *Politics in Germany*, p244.

7 On social bases of voting, see Linz, in *Party Systems and Voter Alignments, passim*; K Liepelt, 'The infra-structure of party support in Germany and Austria,' in *European Politics: a Reader*, edited by M Dogan and R Rose (London: Macmillan, 1971), pp183–202; Edinger, *Politics in Germany*, pp246–8.

8 *cf* Linz, in *Party Systems and Voter Alignments*, edited by Lipset and Rokkan, p293.

9 *Ibid*, pp305–15; Edinger, *Politics in Germany*, pp81–122; Verba, in *Political Culture and Political Development*. pp131–54; Almond and Verba, *Civic Culture, passim*.

10 *cf* Edinger, *Politics in Germany*, p108.

11 *cf* Ehrmann, *Politics in France*, pp48–9; R F Hamilton, *Affluence and the French Worker in the Fourth Republic* (Princeton: Princeton University Press, 1967), p234.

12 On social bases of voting, see M Dogan, 'Political cleavage and social stratification in France and Italy', in *Party Systems and Voter Alignments*, edited by Lipset and Rokkan, pp129–96; Hamilton, *Affluence and the French Worker, passim*; Ehrmann, *Politics in France*, pp210–44.

13 See, for example, C Y Glock and R Stark, *Religion and Society in Tension* (New York: Random House, 1965), pp203–12; G Adam and M Maurice, 'L'eglise catholique et le monde ouvrier,' in Société Française de Sociologie, *Tendances et Volontés de la Société Française* (Paris: SEDEIS, 1966), pp285–321.

14 *cf* H Daalder, 'The Netherlands: opposition in a segmented society,' in *Political Oppositions*, edited by Dahl, pp188–236; and A Lijphart, *The Politics of Accommodation: Pluralism and Democracy in the Netherlands* (Berkeley: University of California Press, 1968).

15 V L Lorwin, 'Belgium: religion, class, and language in national politics,' in *Political Opposition*, edited by Dahl, pp147–87.

16 *cf* Dogan, in *Party Systems and Voter Alignments*, edited by Lipset and Rokkan, pp129–96; S H Barnes, 'Italy: oppositions on left, right, and center,' in *Political Oppositions*, edited by Dahl, pp303–31; G Galli and A Prandi, 'The Catholic hierarchy and Christian democracy in Italy,' in *European Politics*, edited by Dogan and Rose, pp353–9.

17 *cf* G Smith, *Politics in Western Europe* (London: Heinemann, 1972), pp38–40; for a discussion of the specific historical factors involved, see Lipset and Rokkan, 'Cleavage structures, party systems, and voter alignments: an introduction,' in *Party Systems and Voter Alignments*, edited by *idem*, pp1–63.

18 See particularly Chapter 2.

19 On the media, see D McQuail, *Towards a Sociology of Mass Communications* (London: Collier-Macmillan, 1969), pp44–54; on schools, see, e.g. King, *Values and Involvement in a Grammar School, passim.*

20 Hamilton, *Affluence and the French Worker*, notes the significance of 'who gets there first' in explaining support for different parties; *cf* Lipset on socialism and communism in *Political Man.*

21 See particularly the forthcoming study by I M Crewe on middle-class politics in Britain.

22 *cf* Jessop, *Social Order, passim.*

Bibliography

Abrams, M, 'Social class and British politics,' *Public Opin.Q.* (1960), xxv, pp342–50.

——, 'Politics and the British middle class,' *Socialist Commentary* (October 1962), pp5–9.

——, 'Social class and politics,' in *Class*, edited by R Mabey (London: Blond, 1966), pp19–32.

——, 'Some measurements of social stratification in Britain,' in *Social Stratification*, edited by J A Jackson (London: Cambridge University Press, 1968), pp133–44.

Abrams, M, *et al*, *Must Labour Lose?* (Harmondsworth: Penguin, 1960).

Abrams, P, 'Well-bred law,' *Sunday Times* (18 August 1963).

Acton Society Trust, *Management Succession* (London: Acton Society Trust, 1958).

Allen, V L, 'The ethics of trade union leaders,' *Br.J.Sociol.* (1956), vii, pp314–36.

——, *Trade unions and the Government* (London: Longmans, 1960).

Almond, G, and Verba, S, *The Civic Culture* (Princeton: Princeton University Press, 1963).

Almond, G, and Powell, B, *Comparative Politics* (Boston: Little-Brown, 1966).

Amery, L S, *Thoughts on the English Constitution* (London: Oxford University Press, 1964).

Anderson, P, 'Origins of the present crisis,' in *Towards Socialism*, edited by *idem* and R Blackburn (London: Fontana, 1965), pp 11–52.

——, 'Problems of socialist strategy,' in *Towards Socialism*, edited by *idem* and R Blackburn (London: Fontana, 1965), pp221–90.

Apter, D E, 'The role of traditionalism in the political modernisation of Ghana and Uganda,' *World Pol.* (1960), xiii, pp45–68.

Apter, D E, and Joll, J, Editors, *Anarchism Today* (London: Macmillan, 1971).

Arnold, T, *Symbols of Government* (New Haven: Yale University Press, 1935).

Ayer, A J, 'Man as a subject for science,' in *Politics, Philosophy, and Society*, edited by P Laslett and W G Runciman (Oxford: Blackwell, 1967), pp6–24.

Bachrach, P, *The theory of democratic elitism* (London: University of London Press, 1969).

Bagehot, W, *The English Constitution*, Fontana edition, edited by R H S Crossman (London: Fontana, 1965).

Banks, O, *The Sociology of Education* (London: Batsford, 1968).

Barratt-Brown, M, 'The controllers of British industry,' in *Can The Workers Run Industry?*, edited by K Coates (London: Sphere, 1968), pp36–74.

Barry, B, *Sociologists, Economists, and Democracy* (London: Collier-Macmillan, 1970).

Bay, C, *The Structure of Freedom* (Stanford: Stanford University Press, 1958).

Bealey, F, *et al*, *Constituency Politics* (London: Faber, 1965).

Beattie, A, Editor, *English Party Politics*, 2 volumes (London: Weidenfeld and Nicolson, 1970).

Beer, S H, *Modern British Politics* (London: Faber, 1965).

Bell, C, and Newby, H, 'Sources of variation in agricultural workers' images of society,' unpublished paper (University of Essex, 1972).

Benewick, R, *et al*, 'The floating voter and the liberal view of representation,' *Pol. Stud.* (1969), xvii, pp177–95.

Benney, M, and Geiss P, 'Social class and politics in Greenwich,' *Br. J. Sociol.* (1950), i, pp310–27.

Benney, M, *et al*, *How People Vote* (London: Routledge, 1956).

Berelson, B R, *et al*, *Voting* (Chicago: University of Chicago Press, 1954).

Berry, D, 'Party membership and social participation,' *Pol. Stud.* (1969), xvii, pp196–207.

——, *The sociology of grass-roots politics* (London: Macmillan, 1970).

Birch, A H, *Representative and responsible government* (London: Allen & Unwin, 1964).

Birnbaum, N, 'Great Britain: the reactive revolt,' in *Revolution in World Politics* (New York: Wiley, 1962), pp31–68.

Bishop, T J H, with Wilkinson, R, *Winchester and the Public School Elite* (London: Faber, 1968).

Blackburn, R, and Cockburn, A, Editors, *The Incompatibles: Trade Union Militancy and Consensus Politics* (Harmondsworth: Penguin, 1967).

Blalock, H M, 'Correlated independent variables: the problem of multicollinearity,' *Soc. Forces* (1963), 42, pp233–7.

Blumler, J G, and Ewbank, A, 'Trade unions, the mass media, and unofficial strikes,' *Br. J. Ind. Rel.* (1970), viii, pp32–54.

Blumler, J G, and McQuail, D, *Television and Politics: its uses and influence* (London: Faber and Faber, 1968).

Blumler, J G, *et al*, 'Attitudes to the Monarchy: their structure and development during a ceremonial occasion,' *Pol. Stud.* (1971), xix, pp149–71.

Bochel, J M, and Denver, D T, 'Religion and voting: a critical review and a new analysis,' *ibid*, (1970), xvii, pp205–19.

Brittan, S, *Steering the Economy* (Harmondsworth: Penguin, 1971).

Bukharin, N I, *Historical Materialism* (Ann Arbor: University of Michigan Press, 1969).

Burke, E, *Reflections on the Revolution in France* (Harmondsworth: Penguin, 1968).

Butler, D E, and Pinto-Duschinsky, R, *The British General Election of 1970* (London: Macmillan, 1970).

Butler, D E, and Stokes, D E, *Political Change in Britain* (London: Macmillan, 1969).

Butt, R, *The Power of Parliament* (London: Constable, 1968).

Campbell, A, *et al*, *The American Voter* (New York: Wiley, 1964).

Cannon, I C, 'Ideology and occupational community; a study of compositors,' *Sociol.* (1967), i, pp165–85.

Chapman, R A, *The Higher Civil Service in Britain* (London: Constable, 1970).

Cleary, E J, and Pollins, H, 'Liberal voting at the General Election of 1951,' *Sociol. Rev.* (1953), i, pp27–41.

Clements, R V, *Managers* (London: Allen & Unwin, 1958).

Collison, P, and Millen, J, 'University Chancellors, Vice-Chancellors, and College Principals: a social profile,' *Sociol.* (1969), iii, pp 6–109.

Converse, P E, 'The nature of belief systems in mass publics,' in *Ideology and Discontent*, edited by D E Apter (New York: Free Press, 1964), pp206–61.

——, 'Attitudes and non-attitudes; continuation of a dialogue,' in *Quantitative Analysis of Social Problems*, edited by E R Tufte (London: Addison-Wesley, 1970), pp168–89.

Copeman, G H, *Leaders of British Industry* (London: Gee, 1955).

Coxon, A P M, 'An elite in the making,' *New Society* (26 October 1964).

Crick, B, *In Defense of Politics* (Harmondsworth: Penguin, 1964).

——, *The Reform of Parliament* (London: Weidenfeld and Nicolson, 1964).

Czudnowski, M M, 'A salience dimension of politics for the study of political culture,' *Am. Pol. Sc. Rev.* (1968), pp878–88.

Dahl, R A, *Who Governs?* (New Haven: Yale University Press, 1961).

——, Editor, *Political Oppositions in Western Democracies* (New Haven: Yale University Press, 1968).

Davidson, D, 'Actions, causes, and reasons,' *J. Phil.* (1963), lx, pp685–700.

Davies, H A, *Culture and the Grammar School* (London: Routledge, 1965).

Dogan, M, 'Le vote ouvrier en Europe occidentale,' *Rev. Fr. Sociol.* (1960), i, pp25–44.

——, 'Political cleavages and social stratification in France and Italy,' in *Party Systems and Voter Alignments*, edited by S M Lipset and S Rokkan (New York: Free Press, 1967), pp129–96.

Eckstein, H H, *A Theory of Stable Democracy* (Princeton: Center of International Studies, 1961).

——, 'The British political system,' in *Patterns of Government*, edited by S H Beer and A Ulam (New York: Random, 1962), pp70–269.

——, *Division and cohesion in democracy: a study of Norway* (Princeton: Princeton University Press, 1966).

Edelman, M, *The Symbolic Uses of Politics* (Urbana: University of Illinois Press, 1967).

Edinger, L, *Politics in Germany* (Boston: Little-Brown, 1968).

Edinger, L, and Searing, D, 'Social background in elite analysis,' *Am. Pol. Sc. Rev.* (1967), lxi, pp428–45.

Ehrmann, W H, *Politics in France* (Boston: Little-Brown, 1968).

Erbe, W, 'Social involvement and political activity,' *Am. Sociol. Rev.* (1964), xxix, pp198–215.

Foladore, I S, 'The effect of neighbourhood on voting,' *Pol. Sc. Q.* (1968), 83, pp518–29.

Foot, P W, *The Politics of Harold Wilson* (Harmondsworth: Penguin, 1968).

Galli, G, and Prandi, A, 'The Catholic hierarchy and Christian democracy in Italy,' in *European politics*, edited by M Dogan and R Rose (London: Macmillan, 1971).

Galtung, J A, *Theory and Methods of Social Research* (London: Allen & Unwin, 1967).

Gamson, W A, *Power and Discontent* (Homewood: Dorsey Press, 1968).

Garside, W R, *The Durham Miners* (London: Allen & Unwin, 1971).

Gilmour, I, *The Body Politic* (London: Hutchinson, 1969).

Glasser, R, *The New High Priesthood* (London: Macmillan, 1967).

Glock, C Y, and Stark, R, *Religion and Society in Tension* (New York: Random House, 1965).

Goldstein-Jackson, K, 'The judicial elite,' *New Society* (14 May 1970).

Goldthorpe, J H, *et al*, *The Affluent Worker*, 3 volumes (London: Cambridge University Press, 1968–9).

Grainger, J H, *Character and Style in English Politics* (London: Cambridge University Press, 1969).

Greenstein, F I, *Personality and Politics* (Chicago: Markham, 1969).

s

Gusfield, J R, 'Mass society and extremist politics,' *Am. Sociol. Rev.* (1962), xxvii, pp19–30.

Guttsman, W L, *The British Political Elite* (London: MacGibbon and Kee, 1963).

Gyford, J, and Haseler, S, *Social Democracy: Beyond Revisionism* (London: Fabian Society, 1971).

Habermas, J, *Toward a Rational Society* (London: Heinemann, 1971).

Hacker, A, 'Liberal democracy and social control,' *Am. Pol. Sc. Rev.* (1957), li, pp1009–26.

Halsey, A H, and Trow, M A, *The British Academics* (London: Faber, 1971).

Hamilton, R F, *Affluence and the French Worker in the Fourth Republic* (Princeton: Princeton University Press, 1967.)

Harris, L M, *Long to Reign Over Us?* (London: Kimber, 1966).

Harris, N, *Competition and the Corporate Society* (London: Methuen, 1972).

Heller, R, 'Britain's top directors,' *Management Today* (March 1967).

Hill, S, 'Dockers and their Work,' *New Society* (17 August 1972).

Hindess, B, *Decline of Working Class Politics* (London: MacGibbon and Kee, 1970).

Hoggart, R, *The Uses of Literacy* (Harmondsworth: Penguin, 1958).

Hughes, D D, and Pinney, E L, 'Political culture and the idioms of political development,' in *Comparative Politics and Political Theory*, edited by E L Pinney (Chapel Hill: University of N. Carolina Press, 1966), pp67–96.

Ingham, G K, 'Plant size: political attitudes and behaviour,' *Sociol. Rev.* (1969), xvii, pp235–49.

——, *Size of Industrial Organisation and Worker Behaviour* (London: Cambridge University Press, 1969).

ITA, *Religion in Britain and Northern Ireland* (London: ITA, 1970).

Jackson, R J, *Rebels and Whips* (London: Macmillan, 1968).

Jessop, R D, 'Civility and traditionalism in English political culture,' *Br. J. Pol. Sc.* (1971), i, pp1–24.

——, *Social Order, Reform, and Revolution* (London: Macmillan, 1972).

Kahan, M, *et al*, 'On the analytical dimensions of social class,' *Br. J. Sociol.* (1966), xvii, pp122–32.

Kaufmann, G, Editor, *The Left* (London: Blond, 1966).

Kavanagh, D, 'The deferential English: a comparative critique,' *Government and Opposition* (1971), vi, pp333–60.

——, *Political Culture* (London: Macmillan, 1972).

Kelsall, R K, *Higher Civil Servants in Britain* (London: Routeldge, 1955).

Kim, Y C, 'The concept of political culture in comparative politics,' *J. Pol.* (1964), xxvi, pp313–35.

King, R, *Values and Involvement in a Grammar School* (London: Routledge, 1969).

Kornhauser, W, *The Politics of Mass Society* (London: Routledge, 1959).

Lane, R E, 'Political personality and electoral choice,' *Am. Pol. Sc. Rev.* (1955), il, pp173–90.

——, *Political Ideology* (New York: Free Press, 1962).

Lenin, V I, *What Is To Be Done?* (London: Panther, 1970).

Levin, M B, *The Alienated Voter* (New York: Holt, Reinhart, Winston, 1960).

Levi-Strauss, C, 'Social structure,' in *Anthropology Today*, edited by A L Kroeber (New York: 1965), pp524–53.

Liepelt, K, 'The infra-structure of party support in Germany and Austria,' in *European Politics*, edited by M Dogan and R Rose (London: Macmillan, 1971), pp183–202.

Lijphart, A, 'Typologies of democratic systems,' *Comp. Pol. Stud.* (1968), i, pp3–44.

——, *The Politics of Accommodation: Pluralism and Democracy in the Netherlands* (Berkeley: University of California Press, 1968).

——, 'Consociational democracy,' *World Pol.* (1969), xxi, pp207–26.

Linz, J, 'Cleavage and consensus in West German politics: the early 'fifties,' in *Party Systems and Voter Alignments*, edited by S M Lipset and S Rokkan (New York: Free Press, 1967), pp283–321.

Lipset, S M, *Political Man* (London: Heinemann, 1959).

——, 'Must Tories always triumph?,' *Socialist Commentary* (November 1960), pp10–14.

——, *The First New Nation* (London: Heinemann, 1964).

——, *Revolution and Counter-revolution* (London: Heinemann, 1969).

Lipsitz, L, 'Work life and political attitudes,' *Am. Pol. Sc. Rev.* (1964), lviii, pp951–62.

Litt, E, 'Civic education, community norms, and political indoctrination,' *Am. Sociol. Rev.* (1963), xxviii, pp69–75.

Lockwood, D, 'Sources of variation in working class images of society,' *Sociol. Rev.* (1966), xix, pp249–67.

Lupton, T, and Wilson, S, 'The social background and connections of top decision-makers,' *Manchester School* (1959), xvii, pp30–51.

McCloskey, H, 'Consensus and ideology in American politics,' *Am. Pol. Sc. Rev.* (1964), lviii, pp361–82.

McCloskey, H, and Schaar, J H, 'Psychological dimensions of anomy,' *Am. Sociol. Rev.* (1965), xxx, pp14–40.

MacIntosh, J P, *The British Cabinet* (London: Methuen, 1968).

MacIntyre, A C, 'The idea of a social science,' *Proc. Aristotelian Society* (1967), pp95–114.

——, 'A mistake about causality in social science,' in *Politics, Philosophy, and Society*, edited by P Laslett and W G Runciman (Oxford: Blackwell, 1962), pp48–70.

McKenzie, R T, *British Political Parties* (London: Heinemann, 1963).

McKenzie, R T, and Silver, A, *Angels in Marble* (London: Heinemann, 1968).

McPhee, W N, and Ferguson, J, 'Political immunisation,' in *Public Opinion and Congressional Elections*, edited by W N McPhee and W A Glaser (New York: Wiley, 1962), pp155–79.

McPherson, C B, *The Real World of Democracy* (London: Oxford University Press, 1966).

McQuail, D, *Towards a Sociology of Mass Communications* (London: Collier-Macmillan, 1969).

Mann, M, 'The social cohesion of liberal democracy,' *Am. Sociol. Rev.* (1970), xxxv, pp423–39.

Marcuse, H, *One-Dimensional Man* (London: Sphere, 1968).

Marcuse, H, *et al, A Critique of Pure Tolerance* (London: Cape, 1969).

Martin, D, *A Sociology of English Religion* (London: Heinemann, 1967).

Martin, F M, 'Social status and electoral choice in two constituencies,' *Br. J. Sociol.* (1952), iii, pp231–41.

Meier, D L, and Bell, W, 'Anomia and differential access to the achievement of life goals,' *Am. Sociol. Rev.* (1959), xxiv, pp189–202.

Miliband, R, *The State in Capitalist Society* (London: Weidenfeld and Nicolson, 1969).

——, 'The Capitalist State—Reply to Nicos Poulantzas,' *New Left Review* (1970), 59, pp53–60.

——, *Parliamentary Socialism* (London: Merlin, 1964).

Milne, R S, and MacKenzie, H C, *Straight Fight* (London: Hansard, 1954).

——, ——, *Marginal Seat* (London: Hansard, 1958).

Morgan, D J H, 'The social and educational background of Anglican bishops—continuities and changes,' *Br. J. Sociol.* (1969), xx.

Moser, C A, *Survey Methods of Social Investigation* (London: Heinemann, 1969).

Moser, C A, and Scott, W, *British Towns* (Edinburgh: Oliver and Boyd, 1961).

Nairn, T, 'The British political elite,' *New Left Review* (1964), 23, pp26–53.

Nairn, T, 'The fateful meridian,' *ibid.* (1970), 60, pp3–35.

Nettl, J P, *Political Mobilisation* (London: Faber, 1967).

——, 'Consensus and elite domination: the case of business,' *Pol. Stud.* (1965), xiii, pp22–44.

Newby, H, 'The low earnings of agricultural workers,' *J. Agric. Econ.* (1972), xxiii, pp15–24.

Newton, K, *The Sociology of British Communism* (London: Allen Lane, 1967).

Nordlinger, E A, *The Working Class Tories* (London: MacGibbon and Kee, 1967).

Ostergaard, G N, and Halsey, A H, *Power in Cooperatives* (Oxford: Blackwell, 1965).

Parkin, F, 'Working class Conservatives: a theory of political deviance', *Br. J. Sociol.* (1967), xviii, pp278–90.

——, *Middle Class Radicalism* (Manchester: Manchester University Press, 1968).

——, *Class Inequality and Political Order* (London: MacGibbon and Kee, 1971).

Parsons, T, '"Voting" and the equilibrium of the American political system,' in *American Political Behaviour*, edited by E Burdick and M Brodbeck (New York: Free Press, 1959).

Pateman, C, *Participation and Democratic Theory* (London: Cambridge University Press, 1970).

——, 'Political culture, political structure, and political change,' *Br. J. Pol. Sc.* (1971), i, pp297–311.

Pelling, H M, *A History of British Trade Unionism* (Harmondsworth: Penguin, 1963).

——, *Social Geography of British Elections, 1885–1910* (London: Macmillan, 1967).

Piepe, A, *et al*, 'The location of the proletarian and deferential worker,' *Sociol.* (1969), iii, pp239–44.

Plowman, D E G, 'Allegiance to political parties,' *Pol. Stud.* (1955) iii, pp222–34.

Public Schools Commission, *First Report: Volume 2* (London: HMSO, 1968).

Pulzer, P G J, *Political Representation and Elections in Britain* (London: Allen & Unwin, 1967).

Putnam, R D, 'Political attitudes and the local community,' *Am. Pol. Sc. Rev.* (1966), lx, pp650–4.

Pye, L W, and Verba, S, *Political Culture and Political Development* (Princeton: Princeton University Press, 1965).

Pye, L W, 'Political culture,' *Int. Encycl. Soc. Sc.*, xii, pp218–25.

Ranney, A, *Pathways to Parliament* (London: Macmillan, 1965).

Research Services Limited, *Savings and Attitudes to Share Ownership* (London: Research Services Limited, 1962).

Robb, J H, *Working Class Anti-Semites* (London: Tavistock, 1954).

Rogow, A A, with Shore, P, *The Labour Government and British Industry* (Oxford: Blackwell, 1955).

Rose, R, 'Political ideas of English party activists,' *Am. Pol. Sc. Rev.* (1962), lvi, pp360–71.

——, 'Students and society,' *New Society* (2 January 1964).

——, 'England: the traditionally modern political culture,' in *Political Culture and Political Development*, edited by L. W. Pye and S Verba (Princeton: Princeton University Press, 1965), pp83–129.

——, *Politics in England* (London: Faber, 1965).

——, *Influencing Voters* (London: Faber, 1967).

'Class and party divisions: Britain as a test case,' *Sociol.* (1968), ii, pp129–62.

——, *People in Politics* (London: Faber, 1970).

——, 'Materialism which moves the voter,' *The Times* (5 June 1970).

Rose, R, and Mossawir, H, 'Voting and elections: a functional analysis,' *Pol. Stud.* (1967), xv, pp174–201.

Rose, R, and Urwin, D, 'Social cohesion, political parties, and strains in regimes,' *Comp. Pol. Stud.* (1969), ii, pp7–67.

Rosenberg, M, 'Misanthropy and political ideology,' *Am. Sociol. Rev.* (1966), xxi, pp690–95.

Roth, A, *The Business Background of MPs* (London: Parliamentary Profiles, 1972).

Runciman, W G, 'Some recent contributions to the theory of democracy,' *European J. Sociol.* (1965), vi, pp173–85.

——, *Social Science and Political Theory* (London: Cambridge University Press, 1965).

——, *Relative Deprivation and Social Justice* (London: Routledge, 1966).

——, *A Critique of Max Weber's Philosophy of Social Science* (London: Cambridge University Press, 1972).

Rush, M, *The Selection of Parliamentary Candidates* (London: Nelson, 1969).

Samuel, R, 'The deference voter,' *New Left Rev.* (1960), i, pp9–13.

Sartori, G, 'From the sociology of politics to political sociology,' in *Politics and the Social Sciences* (London: Oxford University Press, 1969), pp65–100.

Schumpeter, J A, *Capitalism, Socialism, and Democracy* (London: Allen & Unwin, 1950).

Seeman, M, 'Alienation, membership, and political knowledge,' *Public Opin. Q.* (1966), xxx, pp353–67.

Selznick, P, *The Organisational Weapon* (New York: McGraw-Hill, 1952).

Shils, E A, 'Ideology and civility,' *Sewanee Rev.* (1958), lxvi, 450–80.

——, *The Torment of Secrecy* (London: Heinemann, 1956).

——, 'Tradition and Liberty: Antinomy and Interdependence,' *Ethics* (1958), lxviii, pp153–65.

——, *Political Development in the New States* (Hague: Mouton, 1965).

——, 'The prospects for Lebanese civility,' in *Politics in Lebanon*, edited by L Binder (New York: Wiley, 1966), pp1–13.

——, 'Deference,' in *Social Stratification*, edited by J A Jackson (London: Cambridge University Press, 1968), pp104–32.

Skidelsky, R, *Politicians and the Slump* (Harmondsworth: Penguin, 1970).

Skinner, B F, *Beyond Freedom and Dignity* (London: Methuen, 1972).

Sklair, L, 'Techno-economism: ideology of our times,' paper presented to the British Sociological Association Conference, York (1972).

Smelser, N J, *Theory of Collective Behaviour* (London: Routledge, 1962).

Srole, L, 'Social integration and certain corollaries,' *Am. Sociol. Rev.* (1956), xxi, pp709–16.

Stacey, B G, and Green, R T, 'Psychological bases of political allegiance among white-collar males,' *Br. J. Clin. Soc. Ps.* (1968), vii, pp45–60.

Stacey, M, *Tradition and Change* (London: Oxford University Press, 1960).

Stewart, D, and Hoult, T, 'A social psychological theory of the authoritarian personality,' *Am. J. Sociol.* (1959–60), lxv, pp274–9.

Stewart, M, *The British Approach to Politics* (London: Allen & Unwin, 1965).

Stinchcombe, A S, *Constructing Social Theory* (New York: Harcourt, Brace and World, 1966).

Stokes, D E, *The Study of Political Generations* (London: Longmans, 1968).

Struening, A L, and Richardson, A H, 'A factor analytic exploration of the alienation, anomia, and authoritarianism domain,' *Am. Sociol. Rev.* (1965), xxx, pp768–75.

Thayer, G, *The British Political Fringe* (London: Blond, 1965).

Thompson, D, *The Democratic Citizen* (London: Cambridge University Press, 1970).

Thompson, E P, 'The peculiarities of the English,' *Socialist Register 1965*, edited by R Millband and J. Saville (London: 1965) pp311–62.

Thornton, A P, *The Habit of Authority* (London: Allen & Unwin, 1966).

Townsend, P, and Bosanquet, N, Editors, *Labour and Inequality* (London: Fabian Society, 1972).

Trenaman, J, and McQuail, D, *Television and the Political Image* (London: Methuen, 1961).

Verba, S, 'Organisational membership and democratic consensus,' *J. Pol.* (1965), xxvii, pp467–97.

——, 'Germany: the remaking of a political culture,' in *Political Culture and Political Development*, edited by L W Pye and S Verba (Princeton: Princeton University Press, 1965), pp131–54.

Walker, J, 'A reply to "Further reflections on the elitist theory of democracy",' *Am. Pol. Sc. Rev.* (1966), lx, pp391–2.

Watkins, A, 'The death of deference,' *New Statesman* (9 January 1970).

Weekend Telegraph, 'Is Britain still really democratic?,' *Weekend Telegraph* (26 October 1969).

Weinberg, I, *The English Public Schools* (New York: Atherton Press, 1967).

Wertheimer, E, *Portrait of the Labour Party* (London: Putnam's, 1929).

Westergaard, J, 'The rediscovery of the cash nexus,' in *Socialist Register 1970*, edited by J Saville and R Miliband (Londn: Merlin Press, 1970), pp111–38.

Wider Share Ownership Council, *Sharing the Profits* (London: Garnstone Press, 1968).

Wilkinson, R, *The Prefects* (London: Oxford University Press, 1964).

Williams, R, Editor, *New Left May-Day Manifesto 1968* (Harmondsworth: Penguin, 1968).

Willmott, P, and Young, M, *Family and Class in a London Suburb* (London: New English Library, 1967).

Winch, P, *The Idea of a Social Science* (London: Routledge, 1958).

Worsley, P, 'The distribution of power in industrial society,' *Sociol. Rev. Monogr.* (1964), 8, 1964, pp15–34.

Worsthorne, P, *The Myth of Socialism* (London: Cassell, 1971).

Yinger, J M, 'Contraculture and subculture,' *Am. Sociol. Rev.* (1960), xxv, pp625–35.

Young, M, and Willmott, P, 'Social grading by manual workers,' *Br. J. Sociol.* (1956), vii, pp337–45.

——, *Family and Kinship in East London* (Harmondsworth: Penguin, 1962).

Young, N, 'Prometheans or troglodytes,' *Berkeley J. Sociol.* (1967), xii, pp1–27.

Index